DOCTOR
WHO

DOCTOR WHO

A HISTORY

Alan Kistler

LYONS PRESS
Guilford, Connecticut
An imprint of Globe Pequot Press

Lyons Press is an imprint of Globe Pequot Press.

Doctor Who and the TARDIS are registered trademarks of the British
Broadcasting Corporation, Broadcasting House, Portland Place, London,
W1A 1AA, United Kingdom.

Photos on pp. 44, 77, 186, 241, and 256 courtesy of Alan Kistler.

Project editor: Lynn Zelem
Layout: Joanna Beyer

Library of Congress Cataloging-in-Publication Data
Kistler, Alan.
 Doctor Who : a history / Alan Kistler.
    pages cm
 Includes index.
 ISBN 978-0-7627-9188-0
 1. Doctor Who (Television program : 1963-1989) 2. Doctor Who
 (Television program : 2005-) I. Title.
 PN1992.77.D6273K58 2013
 791.45'72—dc23
                                            2013027420

Printed in the United States of America
10 9 8 7 6 5 4 3 2 1

To my grandparents Alan and Marie, who always encouraged me to look behind the scenes of stories I enjoyed. To the Doctor Who Restoration Team. To all those strange and creative minds, crew-members, and artists who have contributed over the years to this paradoxical hero and made it possible for all of us to join in fantastic journeys across the multiverse and imagination. To my friends who asked why I didn't write this years ago, you're all too kind.

CONTENTS

THE DOCTORS

"I've come to help. I'm the Doctor."

—NINTH DOCTOR, FROM "DALEK" (2005)

Even if you're new to *Doctor Who,* you likely know that the titular character isn't just recast from time to time but changes within the story itself through a process called regeneration. This transformation alters the brain cells to some degree, giving each version of the Doctor his own traits, mannerisms, and preferences. Many people (including some characters within the show) refer to the different incarnations as "First Doctor," "Second Doctor," and so on. All of the Doctors are actually the same person, thanks to the hero's memory remaining (mostly) intact despite the outward changes. The Nurture part of the equation remains constant, while Nature shifts.

Unlike other franchises that recast the hero, characters in the story realize a change has happened. The Doctor sometimes jokes about being a "different man" in his past, but refers to the memories and actions of previous incarnations as his own, saying at times that what really changes is not who he is but his point of view. For instance, the Tenth Doctor said he fought in the Last Great Time War rather than saying "another version of me fought in the war."

Throughout this book, we will be referring to the various Doctors and the actors who've played the role. To make things easy, here's a quick rundown of the people who've played the part officially. We'll discuss unofficial Doctors portrayed by Peter Cushing, Richard E. Grant, and others later. Feel free to check back as you read through; no one has to know.

CLASSIC *DOCTOR WHO* (1963–1989)

William Hartnell, First Doctor
> b. January 8, 1908, d. April 23, 1975
> first appearance: November 23, 1963, age fifty-five
> final regular episode: October 29, 1966, age fifty-eight

Patrick Troughton, Second Doctor

    b. March 25, 1920, d. March 28, 1987

    first appearance: October 29, 1966, age forty-six

    final regular episode: June 21, 1969, age forty-nine

Jon Pertwee, Third Doctor

    b. July 7, 1919, d. May 20, 1996

    first appearance: January 3, 1970, age fifty

    final regular episode: June 8, 1974, age fifty-five

Tom Baker, Fourth Doctor

    b. January 20, 1934

    first appearance: June 8, 1974, age forty

    final regular episode: March 21, 1981, age forty-seven

Peter Davison, Fifth Doctor

    b. April 13, 1951

    first appearance: March 21, 1981, age twenty-nine

    final regular episode: March 16, 1984, age thirty-two

Colin Baker, Sixth Doctor

    b. June 8, 1943

    first appearance: March 16, 1984, age forty

    final regular episode: December 6, 1986, age forty-three

Sylvester McCoy, Seventh Doctor

    b. August 20, 1943

    first appearance: September 7, 1987, age forty-four

    final regular episode: December 6, 1989, age forty-six

Paul McGann, Eighth Doctor

    b. November 14, 1959

    on-screen appearance as the Doctor: May 14, 1996, age thirty-six

MODERN *DOCTOR WHO* (2005–PRESENT)

Christopher Eccleston, Ninth Doctor
> b. February 16, 1964
> first appearance: March 26, 2005, age forty-one
> final regular episode: June 18, 2005, age forty-one

David Tennant, Tenth Doctor
> b. April 18, 1971
> first appearance: June 18, 2005, age thirty-four
> final regular episode: January 1, 2010, age thirty-eight

Matt Smith, Eleventh Doctor
> b. October 28, 1982
> first appearance: January 1, 2010, age twenty-seven
> final regular episode: December 25, 2013, age thirty-one

????, Twelfth Doctor
> b. ????
> first appearance: December 25, 2013, age ????

Some fans have wondered if there might be other incarnations not seen on screen. Was there a Doctor before William Hartnell? The transformations from Second to Third and from Eighth to Ninth weren't shown, so might there have been extra incarnations in between? The program itself has dismissed these ideas. In the TV story "The Three Doctors" in 1973, the Time Lords refer to Hartnell's incarnation as the original. In the TV special "The Five Doctors" in 1983, the Fifth Doctor says he's regenerated four times. David Tennant's adventures "Human Nature" and "The Next Doctor" have him look over images of only nine previous incarnations. And in Matt Smith's episodes "The Lodger" and "The Name of the Doctor," he is called the Eleventh Doctor.

INTRODUCTION

"There's a blue box. It's bigger on the inside than it is on the outside. It can go anywhere in time and space, sometimes even where it's meant to go. When it turns up, there's this bloke in it called the Doctor. And there will be stuff wrong and he will do his best to sort it out. And he will probably succeed because he's awesome."

—NEIL GAIMAN, WONDERCON 2011

Musings on the possibility of time travel and visiting other worlds litter the annals of human culture. Many ancient mythologies have stories about a person catapulted into the future, often as a result of long sleep or visiting a strange realm where time passes more quickly than on Earth. But for centuries, no stories depicted a future era or any people or artifacts that might come from the future into the present. Cultures took it for granted that they couldn't know what lay ahead, while some societies even considered predicting the future to be taboo since only God could know such things (though some did speculate about the politics and social realities ahead).

But attitudes change. In 1733, seven years after Jonathan Swift wrote *Gulliver's Travels,* Samuel Madden penned "Memoirs of the Twentieth Century," a fictional letter supposedly written in 1997 and given to him by his time-traveling guardian angel. In 1843, one of the most famous time-travel stories appeared: *A Christmas Carol* by Charles Dickens. The main character Scrooge not only could move forward and backward through time, but he also changed his own future after learning where it led. Other tales of interest include:

1848: Edgar Allen Poe publishes the essay "Eureka: A Prose Poem," adapted from a lecture he gave on his own beliefs concerning the nature of the universe. Though it receives poor reception, the piece muses on the possible formation of new and parallel universes, which becomes a focus for scientists and writers to come. It also includes ideas that presage the structure of the atom, the Theory of Relativity, and the Big Bang Theory, which would not be accepted by the scientific community until eighty-three years later in 1931.

1871: Lewis Carroll's *Through the Looking-Glass,* in which Alice discovers that everyday objects can possess secret doorways to other worlds, an idea echoed by C. S. Lewis in his 1950 novel about four siblings and a special piece of furniture.

1888: H. G. Wells publishes "The Chronic Argonauts," in which a scientist time travels thanks to technology rather than spirits, hoping to find a new era to call home. Seven years later, Wells develops this idea further in the novel *The Time Machine.*

1941: Robert Heinlein's short story ""—And He Built a Crooked House—"" in the magazine *Astounding Science Fiction,* in which an architect builds a tesseract house, containing an internal space several times larger than what its outside dimensions should hold.

1942: Henry Kuttner's short story "Time Locker," featuring a container that seems bigger inside and acts as a doorway into the future, altering the dimensions of whatever enters it.

1953: BBC's *The Quartermass Experiment* is the first original science fiction television series written for an adult audience. The hero Bernard Quartermass is an idealistic and highly moral scientific pioneer who defends Earth from alien threats. Some consider him to be the first original hero of British television.

1955: Poul Anderson's story "Time Patrol," depicting a group of trained professionals who safeguard history from being altered by conquerors and time terrorists. Sequel short stories followed that year, all of them collected in the 1960 book *Guardians of Time.*

Then, in 1963, Sydney Newman, Verity Lambert, and others brought forth a television program featuring a strange alien and his seemingly ordinary wooden box that could take you to any world you could imagine at any point in history or the future.

Doctor Who premiered on November 23, 1963, the day after the death of C. S. Lewis and the assassination of President Kennedy. It was designed as a science fiction adventure series that also had some educational value for children. The original plan was to broadcast it for a full year. Instead, the show lasted for twenty-six years, ending in 1989 after transmitting 159 television stories divided among 695 episodes and one television special. The program spawned numerous tie-in materials, such as: novels published by Target, Telos, and Virgin; comics published by Marvel and IDW; magazines, including *Doctor Who Magazine*; BBC radio shows; toys and games; spin-off series, plural; and two theatrical films.

Who is the Doctor? He is a somewhat reckless scientist from the planet Gallifrey in the constellation of Kasterborous, a member of the Time Lords, who act as custodians over reality. One day, he turned his back on his people and left in an old time-travel capsule (a "TARDIS") that he stole from a repair shop, leading to many adventures with many traveling companions. Several times during the classic program, the Doctor clashed with the Time Lords, who saw him as a barely tolerable renegade, despite his heroics.

After the classic program's cancellation, a TV movie was made in 1996 for the Fox network here in America, in hopes of igniting a new television series. It didn't, but the movie demonstrated that there was still great interest in the franchise, leading to new novels from BBC Books as well as original audio plays from Big Finish Productions that continue to this day, with actors from the classic program reprising their old roles in brand new adventures.

Doctor Who finally returned to BBC One in 2005, thanks to the efforts of BBC One Controller Lorraine Heggessey, BBC Wales Head of Drama Julie Gardner, and new show runner Russell T. Davies. Unlike *Battlestar Galactica* in 2003, *Batman Begins* in 2005, or *Casino Royale* in 2006, this wasn't a reboot of the franchise but a continuation. In the new program, the Ninth Doctor reveals he is now the last Time Lord, as his people were wiped out during the Last Great Time War. Despite the tragedies and losses he's suffered, he continues to travel through reality with various companions, acting as our teacher, hero, judge, and friend.

Since its return, *Doctor Who* has become a major institution in British television and a notable success in other countries, including America in particular. It has launched multiple spin-off series, video games, interactive episodes, animated specials, and even major orchestra concerts celebrating the music of the program. *Doctor Who* has won five consecutive awards at the National Television Awards from 2005 to 2010 and received the 2006 British Academy of Film and Television Arts (BAFTA) award for best drama series.

What were the initial ideas for who the Doctor is? How did each incarnation of the Doctor develop his personality? What ideas were thrown out? How much was planned, and how much was improvised? This book explains not only how the franchise came to be but also why it matters so much to so many people.

So here's to another fifty years of the mysterious Doctor, a benevolent madman in a blue box who believes in the strength of intellect and romance over brute force and cynicism.

DOCTOR WHO

Building the Show

"It wasn't just a children's show, even though it started as a children's show. It always had another dimension to it."
—BARRY LETTS, *DOCTOR WHO* PRODUCER 1967–1974

In 2007, the modern *Doctor Who* broadcast an episode called "Human Nature," written by Paul Cornell and adapted from his Seventh Doctor novel of the same title, published in 1995. In it, our alien hero, played at the time by David Tennant, decides to hide from certain enemies by taking on a new identity. Using technology called a chameleon arch, he biologically shifts his DNA and brain from that of a Gallifreyan to an Earth-born human, his memories replaced with a fictional life of growing up in Europe. In this new incarnation, when asked about his childhood, he says that his parents were named Sydney and Verity. Certain fans smiled at the mention of these names, referencing the two people who brought what became the *Doctor Who* franchise to life.

The initial creative force behind *The Avengers* and *Doctor Who*, described as "quintessentially British," Sydney Newman was not in fact from the UK. He was born in Toronto, Canada. In 1938, when nineteen years old, Newman almost took a position with Walt Disney, but couldn't secure a work permit. Instead he took a job at the National Film Board of Canada as a film editor, going on to a career as a film and television producer, eventually becoming supervisor of drama productions for the Canadian Broadcasting Corporation in 1954. Journalist Paul Rutherford once said that Newman's work at the CBC marked him as a "great champion of both realistic and Canadian drama."

By 1958, Newman's work caught the attention of the Associated British Corporation, franchise holder of ITV, a new network and the BBC's rival. ABC offered Newman a position as producer, and he moved to England. Quickly disillusioned, he found much of the network's programming took an unfair view of the working middle class and focused on stories that appealed to the upper class. Nevertheless, he headed the successful new program *The Avengers* and produced the anthology programs *Armchair Theatre* and *The Wednesday Play,* work that many considered groundbreaking. During this time, Newman met Verity Lambert.

Initially hired as a shorthand typist at ABC, Lambert had moved her way up to production secretary before working under Newman in *Armchair Theatre.* She proved just how capable she could be on November 30, 1958, when an actor died during the live broadcast of the drama *Underground.* Director Ted Kotcheff went to the studio floor to deal with the situation, leaving Lambert to direct the cameras of *Armchair Theatre.* Newman later said of Lambert: "She had never directed, produced, acted, or written drama—but, by God, she was a bright, highly intelligent, outspoken production secretary who took no nonsense and never gave any—but all with winning charm."

Lambert left ABC in 1961 to work as personal assistant to producer David Susskind in New York. She later rejoined ABC but as a production assistant, despite her experience. She decided to leave the industry altogether if she didn't see signs of advancement in a year.

Meanwhile, after some negotiation, the BBC offered Newman the position of head of drama. He began in December 1962 and hoped to shake things up. In a 1984 interview, he said, "The BBC drama was still catering to a highly educated, cultured class rather than the mass audience which was not aware of 'culture' as such and had no real background. But above all, I felt that the dramas weren't really speaking about common everyday things." Newman's new approach to drama at the BBC ensured that he and Lambert would cross paths again soon.

A NEW FAMILY PROGRAM

Soon after joining the BBC, Newman absorbed the duties of the Children's Department into the greater Drama Department, then divided the work of Drama into Plays, Series, and Serials departments. In early 1963, he attended a meeting concerning the Saturday evening schedule. *Grand National Grandstand,* a popular sports program, usually ended by 5:15

p.m., followed by half-hour classic literary adaptations for children, then *Juke Box Jury* at 5:45, a music panel program popular with teens. Ratings showed that viewership dropped dramatically after *Grandstand* and didn't pick up again until *Juke Box Jury,* so the BBC sought a new "Saturday tea-time program" to keep people watching during the half hour in between.

By his own admission to colleagues, Newman cared little for classic literature anyway, preferring science fiction books, so he decided on a science fiction program featuring heroic figures. He once famously stated: "I love them [science fiction stories] because they're a marvelous way—and a safe way, I might add—of saying nasty things about our own society." Newman envisioned a show with a broad premise adaptable to practically any kind of story. As many later remarked, he wanted to follow the old BBC adage that broadcast programming was meant "to inform, educate, and entertain."

Newman told Donald Wilson, head of serials and a respected filmmaker, to put together an outline for this program, lasting fifty-two weeks and divided into several multi-episode stories with cliffhanger endings. To develop the idea, Wilson brought in John Braybon and Alice Frick, both of whom had done a report the previous year regarding possible new BBC science fiction programming. They had concluded that original stories would fare better than adaptations of existing literature and that stories involving time travel and telepaths could prove popular. Rounding out the story meeting, Wilson also brought in C. E. Webber, who had written many successful BBC adaptations.

Ten years earlier, the BBC had premiered *The Quartermass Experiment*, featuring Bernard Quartermass of the British Experimental Rocker Group, portrayed by actor Reginald Tate. The year 1955 saw the broadcast of a sequel series, *Quartermass II,* followed by a third TV series entitled *Quartermass and the Pit* in 1959. There were also two film adaptations during the 1950s. The success was something that Wilson's group wanted to emulate. Following the Quartermass serials, the BBC had broadcast *A for Andromeda* in 1961, in which a group of scientists receive alien instructions to build an intelligent computer, which then in turn creates a life form named Andromeda. The show spawned a sequel series in 1962 entitled *The Andromeda Breakthrough*.

While the Quartermass and Andromeda serials relied heavily on contact with aliens, Wilson suggested this new program revolve around a time machine, discussing Poul Anderson's recent *Guardians of Time* collection. He also preemptively prohibited the inclusion of another all-knowing computer. Alice Frick argued that it might be "more modern" to have the heroes travel in a flying saucer rather than a time machine. Braybon thought the program should be set in Earth's future and that the cast be "scientific troubleshooters, established to keep scientific experiments under control for political or humanistic reasons."

Webber put together the basic pitch. He dismissed children as main characters, believing that kids didn't care for protagonists younger than themselves. He proposed a cast of three:

THE HANDSOME YOUNG MAN HERO
(First character)
A young heroine does not command the full interest of older women; our young hero has already got the boys and girls; therefore we can consider the older woman by providing:—

THE HANDSOME WELL-DRESSED HEROINE AGED ABOUT 30
(Second character)
Men are believed to form an important part of the 5 o'clock Saturday (post-*Grandstand*) audience. They will be interested in the young hero; and to catch them firmly we should add:—

THE MATURE MAN, 35–40, WITH SOME "CHARACTER" TWIST
(Third character)
Nowadays, to satisfy grown women, Father-Figures are introduced into loyalty programmes at such a rate that TV begins to look like an Old People's Home; let us introduce them ad hoc, as our stories call for them.

Webber then detailed a base for the troubleshooters, consisting of a small lab and a comfortable office/living area that "would not have been out of place in Holmes' Baker Street." Each of the three would be a specialist in a different field, and "if the two men sometimes become pure scientist and forget, the woman always reminds them that, finally, they are dealing with human beings."

Webber evidently didn't think much of the dramatic impact of science fiction ("S.F.") stories in general, as evidenced by his final notes in the document:

a. S.F. deliberately avoids character-in-depth. In S.F. the characters are almost interchangeable. We must use fully conceived characters.

b. S.F. is deliberately unsexual; women are not really necessary to it. We must add feminine interest as a consequence of creating real characters.

c. Because of the above conditions, S.F. does not consider moral conflict. It has one clear overall meaning: that human beings in general are incapable of controlling the forces they set free.

In April 1963, Sydney Newman looked over Webber's pitch and opposed all three main characters being experts, believing dialogue between them wouldn't naturally explain science fiction plot elements in a way that children would easily understand. Newman also wanted a teenage girl in the show, someone to get into trouble in ways the adults didn't.

Newman then focused on developing the mature man character, making him a "senile old man" of 720 to 760 years of age, an alien scientist who had escaped from a distant planet in a spaceship that he wasn't sure how to operate. This (possibly stolen) spaceship was also a time machine and would serve as headquarters for the main characters. Newman later suggested that this time ship be bigger on the inside. As Donald Wilson included these notes into what was still called the "Saturday evening serial," Newman settled on the title of *Dr. Who,* intending that the opening story would feature the old man wandering in a foggy street, amnesiac and only calling himself "the Doctor." The other characters would ask "Doctor Who?" and it would become the old man's alias, as he didn't recall his real name.

DR. WHO

C. E. Webber wrote a new pitch for the newly titled *Dr. Who* program. Here is how he described the new, slightly larger cast of characters:

BRIDGET (BIDDY)
A with-it girl of 15, reaching the end of her Secondary School career, eager for life, lower-than-middle class. Avoid dialect, use neutral accent laced with latest teenage slang.

MISS McGOVERN (LOLA)
24. Mistress at Biddy's school. Timid but capable of sudden rabbit courage. Modest, with plenty of normal desires. Although she tends to be the one who gets into trouble, she is not to be guyed: she also is a loyalty character.

CLIFF
27 or 28. Master at the same school. Might be classed as ancient by teenagers except that he is physically perfect, strong and courageous, a gorgeous dish. Oddly, when brains are required, he can even be brainy, in a diffident sort of way.

To justify Cliff performing impressive feats in the stories, a handwritten note from Sydney Newman here reads: "Top of his class in the parallel bars." Webber's pitch continues:

These are the characters we know and sympathise with, the ordinary people to whom extraordinary things happen. The fourth basic character remains always something of a mystery, and is seen by us rather through the eyes of the other three. . . .

DR. WHO
A frail old man lost in space and time. They give him this name because they don't know who he is. He seems not to remember where he has come from; he is suspicious and capable of sudden

malignance; he seems to have some undefined enemy; he is searching for something as well as fleeing from something. He has a "machine" which enables them to travel together through time, through space, and through matter.

The pitch document suggests that Dr. Who, an experienced time traveler, already has influenced many myths and fairy tales on Earth. One section reads: "Was it by means of Dr. Who's machine that Aladdin's palace sailed through the air? Was Merlin Dr. Who? Was Cinderella's Godmother Dr. Who's wife chasing him through time? Jacob Marley was Dr. Who slightly tipsy, but what other tricks did he get up to that Yuletide?" Later on, the pitch describes how this traveler is the crux of the show.

He remains a mystery. From time to time the other three discover things about him, which turn out to be false or inconclusive (i.e. any writer inventing an interesting explanation must undercut it within his own serial-time, so that others can have a go at the mystery). They think he may be a criminal fleeing from his own time; he evidently fears pursuit through time. Sometimes they doubt his loss of memory, particularly as he does have flashes of memory. But also, he is searching for something which he desires heart-and-soul, but which he can't define. If, for instance, they were to go back to King Arthur's time, Dr. Who would be immensely moved by the idea of the quest for the Grail. This is, as regards him, a Quest Story, a Mystery Story, and a Mysterious Stranger Story, overall.

While his mystery may never be solved, or may perhaps be revealed slowly over a very long run of stories, writers will probably like to know an answer. Shall we say:—

The Secret of Dr. Who: In his own day, somewhere in our future, he decided to search for a time or for a society or for a physical condition which is ideal, and having found it, to stay there. He stole the machine and set forth on his quest. He is thus an extension of the scientist who has opted out, but he has opted farther than ours can do, at the moment. And having opted out, he is disintegrating.

One symptom of this is his hatred of scientist, inventors, improvers. He can get into a rare paddy when faced with a cave man trying to invent a wheel. He malignantly tries to stop progress (the future) wherever he finds it, while searching for his ideal (the past).

Adjacent to the description of this secret background information, a handwritten note from Sydney Newman reads: "Don't like this at all. Dr. Who will become a kind of father figure—I don't want him to be a reactionary."

Webber's pitch also brings in another revelation of the Doctor's background:

Wherever he goes he tends to make ad hoc enemies; but also there is a mysterious enemy pursuing him implacably every when: someone from his own original time, probably. So, even if the secret is out by the 52nd episode, it is not the whole truth. Shall we say:—

The Second Secret of Dr. Who: The authorities of his own (or some other future) time are not concerned merely with the theft of an obsolete machine; they are seriously concerned to prevent his monkeying with time, because his secret intention, when he finds his ideal past, is to destroy or nullify the future.

Newman strongly disagreed with this as the Doctor's goal, writing a single dismissive word: "Nuts."

Webber proposed an introduction story entitled "Nothing at the End of the Lane." Biddy would be walking through the fog with her teachers Lola and Cliff, discovering the mysterious and amnesiac Doctor wandering in a daze. He would lead them into his time machine, sending it into flight before they understood what was happening.

At the bottom of Webber's pitch, Newman's overall judgment was: "I don't like this much—it reads silly and condescending. It doesn't get across the basis of teaching of educational experience—drama based upon and stemming from factual material and scientific phenomena and actual social history of past and future." Newman also insisted that the mysterious Doctor should be a character who would "take science, applied and theoretical, as being as natural as eating," in other words: a figure who embraced progress rather than disrupted it.

The program's pitch altered again. Lola McGovern became Barbara Wright, a history teacher. Cliff became Ian Chesterton, a science teacher and Barbara's trusted friend. Biddy became Susan, a teenage student already traveling with the Doctor. Rather than implying any criminality, Newman's newly generated character description suggested another explanation for why the Doctor left his world:

> A man who is 764 years old—who is senile but with extraordinary flashes of intellectual brilliance. A crotchety old bugger— any kid's grandfather—who had, in a state of terror, escaped in his machine from an advanced civilisation on a distant planet which had been taken over by some unknown enemy. He didn't know who he was any more, and neither did the Earthlings, hence his name, Dr. Who. He didn't know precisely where his home was. He did not fully know how to operate the time-space machine. In short, he never intended to come to our Earth. In trying to go home he simply pressed the wrong buttons—and kept on pressing the wrong buttons, taking his human passengers backwards and forwards, and in and out of time and space.

Meanwhile, Newman was assembling the team that would directly head *Dr. Who*. Rex Tucker acted as interim "caretaker" producer until an official one was hired. David Whitaker joined as script editor and Anthony Coburn joined as a staff writer. Whitaker would maintain character consistency and Coburn worked closely with him on further developing the main characters. He was also set to write the show's second story, involving an adventure with cavemen. Written by Webber, the opening story "The Giants" would be a multi-episode tale conceived by Newman in which the Doctor's ship temporarily shrinks its travelers.

Finally, Newman contacted Verity Lambert about leaving ABC and becoming his full-time producer. In the documentary *Doctor Who Origins*, Lambert explained, "He phoned me and said, 'Verity, what do you know about children?' And I said, 'Nothing, absolutely nothing at all.' He said, 'Well, there's a new children's series that we're going to make, and we're looking for a producer, and you're one of the people who I have suggested be seen for the job.'"

Along with now being the BBC's only female producer at the time, Verity Lambert was also the youngest (just twenty-seven years old). Though Lambert may not have been Newman's first choice, he later said—and said often—that she had been the right choice. In 1993, he told *Doctor Who Magazine*, "I think the best thing I ever did on that was to find Verity Lambert. I remembered Verity as being bright and, to use the phrase, full of piss and vinegar! She was gutsy, and she used to fight and argue with me."

Newman wanted true universal viewing rather than a children's show that parents and older siblings had to endure. Lambert agreed and advocated morality lessons at the center of the stories. She also insisted time and time again to actors, writers, and directors that stories not be dumbed down. In the commentary for "The Time Meddler," Lambert said, "I was absolutely adamant that the actors played it for real. . . . Children know when they're being patronized. I mean, more than adults actually."

Along with finding the heart of the program that Newman had conceived, it was also Lambert herself who cast the first actor to play our strange, paradoxical hero.

The Music of Who

*"Everyone remembers the music . . . and the way the music would
sort of cook through the walls. You could hear it down the street."*
—PAUL MCGANN, EIGHTH DOCTOR

The theme music of *Doctor Who* remains one of the most famous tunes
in science fiction programming. The television show has had many
versions, various bands have covered it, and there have been remixes
and parodies.

Verity Lambert wanted the theme music to immediately establish a
mysterious atmosphere. She went to the Radiophonic Workshop, since
they worked at lower prices than other studios, and showed the *Doctor
Who* title sequence to Ron Grainer, who had composed a memorable
theme for the documentary *Giants of Steam* (and later composed music
for *The Prisoner*).

Grainer noted the timing of the title sequence's distorted images and
the flying words "Doctor Who." He quickly wrote down an outline, with
notes marking how sounds would evoke wind and bubbles, and handed it
to staffer Delia Derbyshire to realize it. Later nicknamed a "sculptress of
sound," Derbyshire, a counterculture woman known for creating horror
soundtracks, orchestrated "hymns for robots" and arranged the sound of
the world's first electronic music fashion show. Working before the age of
synthesizers, midi, and modern sequencing equipment, she individually
hand-cut the notes with tape and brought Grainer's composition to life
using feedback, filtered white noise, manually operated swoops, and
high harmonics.

When she played it for Grainer, he reportedly was so impressed that
he asked, "Did I write that?" To which Derbyshire responded, "Well, most
of it." She took pride that people couldn't quite figure out how she
had produced the piece and heavily disapproved of how often producers
later altered the theme for different Doctors. Eighteen years later, John
Nathan-Turner had the theme redone with a synthesizer, an instrument
that Derbyshire discouraged since she believed electronic music should

be handmade. Hearing the *Doctor Who* themes of the 1980s, she told her friends that she had disowned the music.

Although Ron Grainer received credit as composer in the television credits, he tried to split the royalties with Derbyshire, but BBC rules didn't allow it. It wasn't until 1973, when the music of *Doctor Who* was released for purchase, that Delia Derbyshire finally received credit for her work, gaining her many Whovian fans.

The music of *Doctor Who* was celebrated in a whole new way in 2006, when a charity concert for Children in Need was held at the Millennium Center in Cardiff, Wales. David Tennant hosted *Doctor Who: A Celebration,* featuring the BBC National Orchestra of Wales performing incidental music of the modern program's first two years, composed by Murray Gold, as well as the theme. Cybermen, Ood, and other strange beings walked among the audience, looming over children before disappearing into the shadows.

In 2008 and 2010, the Royal Albert Hall held *Doctor Who* concerts as part of the annual Proms series. David Tennant couldn't appear for the first in person due to prior commitments, but he did make an appearance via a mini-episode broadcast in the Hall. Matt Smith, Arthur Darvill, and Karen Gillan hosted the 2010 *Doctor Who* Prom.

To this day, the end credits of *Doctor Who* mention Ron Grainer but not Delia Derbyshire.

2

Who Is the Doctor

*"I don't make threats. But I do keep promises. And I promise you,
I shall cause you more trouble than you bargained for."*

—FIRST DOCTOR, FROM "THE SENSORITES" (1964)

The core of the Doctor's character was still being formed. While Sydney Newman did not like the Doctor seeming dangerous, Lambert believed it was an excellent quality. But instead of having him act with deliberate malice, she suggested that the Doctor have obvious character flaws that invited or created danger: insensitivity, overconfidence, a short temper, and an occasionally narrow-minded focus on his goals. She also wanted the character to have a childlike spirit to counter these flaws, believing the paradox of his personality would interest older viewers.

"I rather liked the cantankerous bit," Lambert told *Dreamwatch* in 2004. "Getting [people] into terrible scrapes because he wouldn't listen, and always thinking he knew best. But when he was being sweet, he was quite touching and vulnerable."

But who was this actor behind the alien? Though he said at times that his father was a farmer, William Hartnell was born out of wedlock in 1908, the son of Lucy Hartnell and a father he never found. Raised by his mother and his aunt Bessie, Hartnell later found a father figure in art collector Hugh Blaker. A great lover of horses, Hartnell trained as a jockey before entering the theater in 1925. During World War II, he served for eighteen months in the Tank Corps, leaving due to mental distress and saying later that military life was too much for his nerves.

Many of Hartnell's subsequent roles were militaristic or authoritarian characters and he gained great recognition as Sergeant Major Percy Bullimore in *The Army Game*. When Lambert approached him about *Doctor Who,* he initially resisted, frustrated by type-casting as gruff authority figures. But Lambert, with director Waris Hussein, convinced him that this was a very different role that would appeal to kids, a character his own grand-children could enjoy.

Lambert wanted Hartnell for the role because she believed he would deliver the element of danger that she wanted in the Doctor.

> There was a malevolent side to Bill, which I had thought was important in the Doctor. . . . He was terribly sweet and terribly kind when he wanted to be, but you always had that thing that he could get everyone into trouble by . . . not being quite the way he should. . . . That combination of he's a rather gentle and kindly person who could then turn into a bit of a rogue.

At age fifty-five, William Hartnell became the first and, thus far, oldest actor to portray the program's hero. Around this time, the show was retitled *Doctor Who* and the main character was now simply called the Doctor rather than use the program's full title as his alias (we'll discuss the hero's name in more detail in the sidebar "The Hero with No Name").

AN ELEMENT OF MAGIC

"Then what are you like?"
"I don't know—Gandalf. A space Gandalf."
—AMY POND AND THE ELEVENTH DOCTOR IN A SCENE CUT FROM
"THE VAMPIRES OF VENICE" (2011)

Webber's script for the initial *Doctor Who* story "The Giants" did not impress interim producer Rex Tucker, and he finally rejected it on the grounds that it would be too difficult and costly to film. After Tucker left, the script went back into the production schedule, partly due to a lack of completed stories. Lambert and Whitaker, howwever, thought it was "thin on inci-dent and character," so it was rejected again (though its concept became the basis of a later adventure, "Planet of the Giants," scripted by Louis Marks). Coburn's cavemen story would now immediately follow the pro-gram's first episode, already written by Webber and entitled "An Unearthly Child." Coburn adapted this script to work as the opener to his cavemen tale and made some changes, such as making the character Susan the Doctor's granddaughter.

After reading the new script, Whitaker added a note that read: "Regarding Doctor Who, I feel that he should be more like the old Professor that Frank Morgan played in *The Wizard of Oz,* only a little more authentic. Then we can strike some of the charm and humour as well as the mystery, the suspicion, and the cunning." Hartnell agreed, thinking Coburn's script made the character too "bad tempered." Wishing to appeal to children rather than frighten them, he asked for more pathos and humor in the role, later suggesting that the Doctor combine "the Wizard of Oz and Father Christmas." In an interview with *Radio Times* in December 1972, Hartnell said, "The original Doctor was pig-headed and irascible, certainly, but there was also an element of magic in him—and that was what I wanted to bring out."

Although the Doctor was no longer going to have amnesia, the production team kept the idea that he didn't quite know how to pilot his old and unreliable ship. This was partially due to the fact that he had stolen the ship, although this fact wasn't actually revealed to audiences until the end of the sixth year. Why the Doctor had stolen a time ship and run from his people was never decided, though, and as far as Verity Lambert was concerned it wasn't important. For her, the mystery surrounding his past helped foster his air of danger and she enjoyed Webber's suggestion that the Doctor was a criminal who left his planet to flee punishment.

Hartnell and Newman both wanted the stories to describe science and science fiction elements in basic concepts and ideas rather than technical jargon that might confuse children. As Hartnell told *Reveille* in 1965, "It's an adventure story, not a scientific documentary. And Doctor Who isn't a scientist. He's a wizard. . . . I see Doctor Who as a kind of lama. No, not a camel. I mean one of those long-lived old boys out in Tibet who might be anything up to 800 years old, but look only 75."

"AN UNEARTHLY CHILD"

The first episode of *Doctor Who* was almost as far as the program got. Initial footage of "An Unearthly Child" didn't impress Sydney Newman. He criticized technical difficulties, direction choices, and cast performances. In particular, Susan seemed too alien, and the Doctor still felt too sinister. But rather than scrub the project, Newman had the episode redone from scratch, even though this would delay the intended November 16 airdate. A new version of "An Unearthly Child" produced much better results and became the official first episode, with the original unaired version later nicknamed the "pilot," even though the BBC was not in the practice of filming pilots then. Some believe that this extra effort on the first episode ensured that the show still holds up today as an engaging and entertaining story.

A few overt changes were made for the final version of "An Unearthly Child." A remark that the Doctor and Susan were from the forty-ninth century was removed, with Susan now vaguely remarking that they were from another time, another world. Susan was given a new outfit so that she seemed younger. While the Doctor had worn a modern jacket and tie in the pilot, he was now to be a visual paradox, someone who lived in a spaceship but looked as if he belonged in the nineteenth century. He was given a high-wing collar, cravat, and checkered trousers. Many years later, Fourth Doctor Tom Baker remarked during interviews that this facet of the show established the Doctor as "anti-fashion," a trait that carried on into different incarnations.

With the premiere episode reshot and ready to go, filming continued and marketing began. Sadly, some publications decided not to pay much attention to the show, thinking it odd and with little potential for a real audience. In the autumn of 1963, BBC Radio broadcast an audio trailer featuring William Hartnell explaining the premise:

> The Doctor is an extraordinary old man who owns a time and space machine. He and his granddaughter, Susan (played by Carole Ann Ford), have landed in England and are enjoying their stay until Susan arouses the curiosity of two of her schoolteachers (played by William Russell and Jacqueline Hill). They follow Susan and get inside the ship, and Doctor Who decides to leave Earth, starting a series of adventures which I know will thrill and excite you every week.

And so, on Saturday afternoon, November 23, 1963, several viewers watched as wispy images shifted across the screen, accompanied by a haunting tune and the flying title: "Doctor Who." The theme music plays on as we approach the large wooden gate of I. M. Foreman's scrap yard at 76 Totter's Lane in Shoreditch, London. The gate opens, and we move forward to see a strange object surrounded by junk: a police public call box humming with power.

Many years later, Sixth Doctor Colin Baker recalled the program's strange music and opening scene in the documentary *The Story of Doctor Who*: "I was a law student. . . . I'd been out, and I came back and my four or five flatmates had just turned the television on . . . and I can remember very clearly, a kind of, almost an eidetic image of coming into the door, leaning on the banister, which is inside the door, and I was actually still there twenty-five minutes later. I hadn't moved." When I brought up the initial adventure to Fifth Doctor Peter Davison in an interview, he remarked how effective this episode had been for children like himself. "You're at school, and you think of all the adventures you want to have, especially when you feel that others may not understand you. . . . So you have this girl who's clever and interesting, but people wonder about her and laugh. So you connect to that, and then she goes off, and you find out her home is this police call box that can go off to space. . . . And on top of all that, it's piloted by this mysterious and funny man. Fantastic."

The Doctor is presented as a mercurial personality, either easily distracted or pretending to be because it annoys the inquisitive schoolteachers who have unwittingly discovered his time ship, and whose questions he dismisses as childish and ignorant. After gentle mockery, the Doctor explains that he and his granddaughter Susan are exiles, unable to return to their home planet, now traveling through space and time "without friends or protection." That is all the detail he gives. He doesn't say his people are called Time Lords (which would be revealed six years later), nor that his planet is named Gallifrey (as established more than ten years later).

The Doctor grows concerned about the teachers, believing that they'll lead others to learn about him and the TARDIS (evidently, he fears an enemy beyond the simple Earth authorities he can easily evade). Susan argues that they're kind people and should be released. What's more, she wants to stay in England rather than continue wandering through time and space. The Doctor pretends to concede but then activates the ship's controls. Susan grabs him, and he either throws the wrong switch or doesn't finish inputting the data. In either case, it's too late. The ship takes flight. Moments later, the TARDIS lands somewhere, the Doctor looks alarmed, and someone's shadow looms outside. An intertitle then announces: "Next Episode: The Cave of Skulls."

Although many families enjoyed the show and positive reviews were forthcoming, the ratings didn't stack up as hoped. The assassination of President John F. Kennedy overshadowed much of television over the following days.

With this in mind, the BBC decided to rebroadcast "An Unearthly Child" the following week, with the second episode of the series following. As a result, more people came to enjoy the strange Doctor, his odd grandchild, and their two unwilling traveling companions. "An Unearthly Child" brought 4.4 million viewers. The next episodes of the initial story arc were "The Cave of Skulls," "The Forest of Fear," and "The Firemaker," bringing in 5.9 million viewers, 6.9 million viewers, and 6.4 million viewers respectively.

"SENILE OLD MAN"

Sydney Newman's initial proposal envisioned the Doctor as scatterbrained and forgetful. Hartnell's episodes have some line flubs, which have been attributed to the actor being forgetful himself, but several who worked with him have pointed out that flubs are an inevitable consequence of limited rehearsal time and episodes that were mostly taped "live," as the budget could only afford one or two takes for most scenes. According to Carole Ann Ford, who played Susan, "I think a lot of it was mischievousness as well. . . . He did actually delight in changing a few words here and there. . . . Little word things [made him laugh]."

In several episodes, the Doctor refers to companion Ian Chesterton by the wrong name, calling him "Chatterton," "Chesterfield," or some other approximation. William Russell, who played Chesterton, often said that Hartnell deliberately did this to add humor to the role, which the audience could interpret as the Doctor being addlebrained or intentionally teasing.

While many spoke lovingly of William Hartnell and his fatherliness, he was occasionally difficult. Carole Ann Ford felt that he sometimes spoke to her as if she actually were a teenager rather than a young woman. Some have cited his rush to judgment when he believed others weren't behaving professionally, with increasing periods of frustration later on.

An age paradox is at work here. Hartnell remains the oldest actor cast for the part, but is, of course, actually the youngest Doctor. In the Big Finish audio drama "Quinnis," Susan flippantly remarks that the First Doctor was practically a teenager by Time Lord standards. In the 2007 miniepisode "Time Crash," the Tenth Doctor directly referenced this paradox: "Back when I first started, at the very beginning, I was always trying to be old and grumpy and important. Like you do when you're young."

THE NEED FOR OTHERS

> "Just promise me one thing. Find someone . . . 'cause sometimes I think you need someone to stop you. "
>
> —DONNA NOBLE TO THE TENTH DOCTOR,
> FROM "THE RUNAWAY BRIDE" (2006)

In the first story arc, curiosity and scientific interest motivate the Doctor, but he has little care for others around him and is, possibly, murderous. While fleeing from unfriendly cave people, the heroes come across an injured man. The schoolteachers insist on stopping to help, but the Doctor argues that their pursuers are closing in and it's best to hurry back to the TARDIS. They overrule him, but, while no one is looking, he picks up a rock—before Ian grabs his wrist a moment later. The startled Doctor stammers, claiming he intended to ask the injured man to draw a map. Was the Doctor telling the truth? Was he about to kill the man? Perhaps he only considered the man's death for a moment and would have ultimately decided against it.

In the BBC novel *The Eight Doctors* by Terrance Dicks, the Eighth Doctor revisits this famous moment, noting that his first incarnation's action in picking up the rock was indicative that he was still acting like a traditional Time Lord, so concerned with the big picture that he failed to see how each individual life had meaning. In the Big Finish audio drama *To the Death,* the Eighth Doctor discusses the same event with an older Susan.

> **DOCTOR:** "For one moment, just—I entertained the possibility. I picked up a rock and I—"
> **SUSAN:** "But you didn't do it. You didn't kill that man."
> **DOCTOR:** "Only because Chesterton stopped me."

This palpable element of danger continued into the second story arc, "The Daleks," which also began the Doctor's path to heroism. In that adventure, the Doctor sees how his inability to compromise can endanger the lives of the group members. His goal becomes escape, but the rest of the crew doesn't want to leave after encountering people who need help. Reluctantly at first, the Doctor agrees to help and finds the role fulfilling. By the end of the adventure, he admits to Barbara and Ian that he has underestimated them. He softens considerably toward the local inhabitants, confessing that he admires the opportunity they now have to build a better world, revealing that he was once regarded as a pioneer on his own planet.

By the end of the third story arc, "The Edge of Destruction," the Doctor openly extends friendship to his two human travelers, counting them as admirable comrades. He still has a compulsive curiosity, but now he wants to share the wonders of the universe with his companions for the joy of the experience, not to prove his superiority. While he starts fighting evil more, he dismisses violence as a primitive solution, believing that people need to seek out new knowledge and then employ reason, intellect, and imagination to solve (most of) their problems. In the program's fourth story arc, when asked by Marco Polo whom he serves, the Doctor proudly proclaims, "I serve the truth!" Late night TV host Craig Ferguson nicely summed up the philosophy behind the Doctor's personality in a song written to celebrate the show: "Intellect and romance over brute force and cynicism."

In the 1990s, the Seventh Doctor novels released by Virgin Publishing proposed that our alien adventurer relies on human companions and their

Earth-born morality to keep him on a heroic path. Without them, he soon falls into his old Time Lord ways. This idea recurred in the Eighth Doctor audio dramas and in the modern TV program. As we benefit from his presence, so he benefits from ours. The Doctor then is not just our hero—we are also his.

Of course, becoming more heroic doesn't mean the Doctor isn't dangerous. He still acts recklessly, and his obsessive curiosity puts himself and others at risk. The TARDIS also has a knack for bringing him to places where trouble is about to happen, making him a harbinger of chaos. These traits remain consistent through the hero's subsequent incarnations. The Ninth Doctor needed the influence of a teenage shop clerk to soften him, just as his younger self once needed the company of two altruistic schoolteachers.

The Hero with No Name

Sydney Newman never considered a real name for the Doctor. In "An Unearthly Child," Susan attends Coal Hill School under the alias Susan Foreman, apparently taking the surname from the fact that the TARDIS is parked in I. M. Foreman's scrap yard (some tie-in novels proposed that I. M. Foreman was a fellow Time Lord and friend of the Doctor). Naturally, Ian later addresses the girl's grandfather as "Dr. Foreman." The Doctor responds in confusion, "Eh? Doctor *who?*" This became a running joke in several episodes across the decades. While "Doctor Who" was originally meant to be the character's alias, it instead became a question for the audience.

In the episodes of *Doctor Who* he's written, Steven Moffat has repeatedly brought attention to the secret of the Doctor's real name. Yet the classic program didn't focus on this much. People found it strange at first that this person only used a title, but they all quickly accepted the matter (except in Seventh Doctor stories, where a larger mystery was implied).

By the program's tenth year, we meet other Time Lords with strange titles: The Monk, the War Chief, the Master. One might assume that the Doctor's people only used titles—but along with Susan, the classic *Doctor Who* program introduced us to Time Lords who did have names: Morbius, Borusa, Spandrell, Goth, Runcible, Romanadvoratrelundar, and others.

In 1972, Picolo Books published *The Making of Doctor Who*, the first nonfiction book to delve into the popular TV program. Written by Malcolm Hulke and Terrance Dicks, the book suggested that the Doctor's original name among his people was expressed as $\partial^3 \Sigma x^2$. Several readers accepted this as fact, while others were more skeptical, as tie-in materials didn't always agree with what became canon in the show. For instance, the Dalek comic strips gave a very different origin for the creatures than what was revealed in *Doctor Who*. They also said that Dalek armor was made of a metal called Dalekanium, whereas the classic *Doctor Who* program referred to it as "bonded polycarbide" and used the word "Dalekanium" to refer to an explosive capable of destroying Dalek casings.

In the 1977 story "The Deadly Assassin," it was said that the Doctor was a member of the Prydonian Clan of Time Lords and that Prydonians who turned their backs on society also knowingly forfeited their birthrights. This could mean that the Doctor and the other renegades he fought all lost the right to their own names, making them forbidden things. It would explain why other Time Lords only called him "Doctor," and only referred to other renegades such as the Master and the Rani by their chosen titles.

In the 1979 story "The Armageddon Factor," the Doctor runs into a former classmate named Drax who immediately calls him "Theta Sigma" ($\Theta\Sigma$) or "Thete," for short. The hero becomes annoyed, reminding Drax that he is now called "Doctor." Nearly a decade later, the Seventh Doctor story "The Happiness Patrol" in 1988 clarified that Theta Sigma was merely a nickname he'd earned while at Prydon Academy on Gallifrey. On-screen, this nickname only came up another time in the 2010 episode "The Pandorica Opens," when a message left for the Doctor on the side of a diamond cliff face included the letters $\Theta\Sigma$ in the last line.

Many times, the Doctor has fallen back on an archetypal alias: John Smith. On-screen, he first used this label in the Second Doctor adventure "The Wheel in Space" in 1968. The Third Doctor used the name habitually since he was working with a military organization that needed to file paperwork. In the 2010 episode "The Vampires of Venice," the Eleventh Doctor is seen holding a library card that he had obtained when he was still living in a scrap yard in Totter's Lane. The library card listed him as John Smith, so he had also used the name during his first life. The 1998 novel *The Witch Hunters,* by Steve Lyons, said that the Doctor adopted this moniker because he recalled that Susan's favorite band was John Smith and the Common Men (which she mentioned on-screen during "An Unearthly Child").

But where did the title of "Doctor" come from? In his first two TV story arcs, the hero remarks that he had been a research scientist on his planet and was not a doctor of medicine (though he did pick up medical knowledge in later adventures). So he did have the Gallifreyan equivalent of a doctorate in some field of science, perhaps several. The 2013 episode

"The Name of the Doctor" confirmed that he held this rank before leaving his home.

Yet, after choosing to leave behind his people (and even his name), the hero could have chosen any new epithet. Why stick with the academic title of "Doctor"? The modern program has proposed some ideas on the matter, which we'll get into later.

In the twenty-six seasons of the classic program and the past several years of the modern-day show, our hero has been specifically called "Doctor Who" on television only once, by an artificial intelligence called WOTAN in the TV story "The War Machines." In the spin-off pilot *K-9 and Company*, a young man asks, "Who is the Doctor?" and the titular robot dog responds, "Affirmative." There was also a TV story entitled "Doctor Who and the Silurians."

Fans have explained these instances, as fans often do. The title of the Silurian story, being only a title, doesn't cause any worry. As for WOTAN, the artificial intelligence could have decided to refer to our character as "Doctor Who" because, being a computer, it considered it inaccurate to refer to a man solely by a title that belonged to many professionals. As for K-9's response, perhaps he was noting that "Who is the Doctor?" is a question constantly surrounding the hero. Then again, maybe we just shouldn't take the occasionally limited robot dog too seriously.

At times the Doctor has joked about refusing to give his own name and about how often he's been asked "Doctor who?" after introducing himself. In "The Highlanders," the Second Doctor adopted the alias of Doktor von Wer, "wer" being German for "who" or "somebody." In "The Daemons," the Third Doctor claimed to be a wizard named QuiQuaeQuod, a merging of the masculine, feminine, and neuter forms of the Latin word meaning "who."

But despite the character's official name being "The Doctor," many BBC releases, along with the show's creators, staff, and actors over the years and up to today, have still referred to him as "Doctor Who." Many novelizations of the TV stories did this in their titles, the first of which being *Doctor Who in an Exciting Adventure with the Daleks*. In the first comic strip series in *TV Comics*, the hero introduces himself on multiple occasions literally as "Doctor Who."

Along with this, the end credits of the television program itself called him "Dr. Who" or "Doctor Who" from 1963 all the way until 1981, when then-producer John Nathan-Turner altered it to "The Doctor." When the modern program began in 2005, the credits again labeled the hero "Doctor Who," until David Tennant took over the role and it changed back to "The Doctor."

Moral of the story? The hero has used many names and it's not a crime to call him "Doctor Who" in conversation—despite heated claims in online forums and at conventions.

3

Rise of the Monsters

"The monsters and the Doctor, it seems you cannot have one with-out the other. . . . One may tolerate a world of demons for the sake of an angel."

—REINETTE, FROM "THE GIRL IN THE FIREPLACE" (2006)

"Absolutely no bug-eyed monsters."

So ruled Sydney Newman, and Donald Wilson agreed. The same 1962 report by John Braybon and Alice Frick that advised how the BBC could pursue new science fiction programming also concluded that "bug-eyed monsters" or "B.E.M.s" were to be avoided. Newman wanted to explore humanity, not deadly alien creatures.

Originally, Anthony Coburn was supposed to script the second *Doctor Who* story, the title of which shifted between "The Robots" and "The Masters of Luxor." But Verity Lambert instead produced a script featuring aliens called Daleks. The story was commissioned from writer Terry Nation, who had impressed Whitaker with his writing for ABC's science fiction program *Out of This World*. In later years, Nation would create the science fiction shows *Blake's 7* and *Survivors*. He had initially turned down Whitaker's offer to join *Doctor Who,* as he was working as chief writer for comedian Tony Hancock. When he and Hancock fell out, Nation called Whitaker and went to work on a script featuring strange aliens.

Nation didn't want these beings to look like actors wearing suits and makeup. While watching a performance of the Georgian National Ballet, he saw dancers glide across the stage like ghosts, an illusion created with long skirts and roller skates. Inspired, Nation made the Daleks legless beings living inside machines that floated across surfaces, their metal casings armed with mechanical limbs and a single eye-stalk. The true creature existed inside, the body completely atrophied except for a brain plugged into circuitry, making it a strange type of cyborg. The story proposed that Daleks had once been like humans but mutated because of radiation unleashed during a war that engulfed their entire planet. The metal shell was both a personal tank and life-support system.

David Whitaker worked with Terry Nation to flesh out the script, adding more characterization for the TARDIS crew and others. One initial idea was that the Daleks and Thals, a human-like race inhabiting the same planet, join forces to face a mutual threat from outer space. But very quickly the Daleks became the villains, symbolizing the dangers of prejudice and single-mindedness. Nation intentionally made them analogous to the Nazis, with their fascist behavior, distrust of individuality, and obsessive need to exterminate or enslave all "inferior" life forms that threatened them. The pacifistic Thals—who not coincidentally resembled the physical Aryan ideal—counterbalanced them.

Though they may have looked like robots, the Daleks didn't act as such. They were single-minded, true, but their debut story revealed their fear, impatience, and hatred. When the Doctor tells a Dalek that its plans amount to nothing more than sheer murder, the monster clarifies: "No. Extermination." Ian and a Thal named Ganatus discuss the narrow-minded purpose of the villains:

GANATUS: "Yes, but why destroy without any apparent thought or reason? That's what I don't understand."
IAN: "Oh, there's a reason. Explanation might be better. It's stupid and ridiculous, but it's the only one that fits . . . a dislike for the unlike."

Doctor Who designer Raymond Cusick first drew the Dalek casing as a tall cylindrical machine with robotic claws. But he realized he couldn't force the actors inside to stand for hours during filming and redrew the Dalek shell around the figure of a man seated on a plank of wood. When speaking with others, Cusick used a pepper shaker to demonstrate how the Dalek would move. Which of course led many to say later, inaccurately, that a pepper shaker had inspired his design.

The production budget allowed for four Daleks. There wasn't enough money to make proper mechanical claws, so simple plungers replaced them, with a magnet inside to take hold of certain objects. Later exposition explained that the plunger or "manipulator arm" used an intense vacuum or focused energy field to grab objects, interact with computers, and even crush a human's skull in moments. The plunger also shifted modes when required. In their debut story, one Dalek's arm alters into a blowtorch. In "The Dalek Invasion of Earth," several of the villains utilize flamethrowers built into their limbs.

The Dalek operators were cast for size (they had to fit inside the casing) and muscular ability, needing to endure long hours in cramped conditions. Along with the marks and cues for the characters, they had to coordinate their performances with the Dalek voice actors.

Since Daleks didn't have faces, their voices became a key character element. While operators manipulated the creature from within, voice actors stood elsewhere in the studio speaking into ring modulators. Over the years, Dalek voices shifted from sounding very stilted and robotic to resembling an enraged machine, both because of performer experimentation and because people kept forgetting to note which modulator levels were most effective. Notable early Dalek voice performers included Peter Hawkins, David Graham, and Roy Skelton.

When the directors and camera crew had difficulty identifying which Dalek was speaking at any given time, Cusick added lights to each of the monsters' headpieces that activated when they spoke. He had also wanted to add lights beneath each sensor sphere, which would illuminate chaotically when a Dalek panicked. However, this would have required a car battery housed within each monster, and the budget couldn't cope.

In tie-in media, it's been said that Dalek mutants have no true voice box, using computers to translate their thoughts into words that their prey may understand. Richard Martin, one of the directors of the monsters' debut story, later explained his thinking behind the sound of the Dalek voices and personalities: "The other thing that we thought . . . which I developed with the voices a lot, was that inside their metal machinery, they were nearly insane with claustrophobia. You only had to say one thing to them for them to lose their cool, and their only way out was to use this weapon."

THE STORY THAT ALMOST WASN'T

"No one can succeed who opposes the Daleks."
—A DALEK, FROM "DAY OF THE DALEKS" (1972)

Verity Lambert was proud of the Terry Nation story and happily turned it over to Donald Wilson . . . who hated the script. Sydney Newman, livid, agreed with Wilson that the story should be scrapped in favor of another already in production.

Lambert argued that the story wasn't just about one-dimensional monsters but had obvious moral value and worked as a social allegory. She also sagely pointed out that the Daleks were already built and production hadn't begun for any other script. If they dismissed the story, the program had to go on hold for a few weeks before they could prep another. Having already delayed once to reshoot "An Unearthly Child," Wilson and Newman conceded, and the second story arc went forward. The story was called "The Mutants" initially, but a Third Doctor adventure produced years later also used this title. To differentiate the two, the BBC officially renamed the earlier story "The Daleks."

When "The Daleks" debuted, the show's viewership almost doubled. Older viewers appreciated the science fiction take on a Nazi threat, and the inhuman creatures both frightened and fascinated children. A near instant outcry arose for Dalek toys and more stories. Playgrounds filled with children chasing one another while shouting in imitation Dalek voices. Suddenly the show entered the cultural mainstream. Over the next months, merchandising followed. In November 1964, David Whitaker adapted the first Dalek story into the TV program's first novelization: *Doctor Who in an Exciting Adventure with the Daleks* (later retitled *Doctor Who and the Daleks*). The public embraced these monsters so much that, seeing a parallel with four mop-top lads from Liverpool, the media referred to it as "Dalekmania."

Newman and Wilson conceded that they had been wrong. Audiences enjoyed monsters if the story was good. Moreover, the Daleks clearly had to return. Newman jokingly said in a later interview, "There again is the wisdom of being a great Head of Drama. . . . I didn't want any bug-eyed monsters and 'The Daleks' is what made *Doctor Who.*"

The mystery of the true appearance of a Dalek mutant captivated viewers. In the debut story, the Doctor and Ian open the metal casing of a dead Dalek and, visibly startled, quickly close it again. Needing access to the technology inside, they use a cloak to pick up the creature (hidden from view) and place it on the floor. As they leave, a strange, jelly-like claw emerges from the cloak. In other adventures, Daleks occasionally were destroyed, briefly revealing green blobs or brainlike creatures with tentacles. In "Genesis of the Daleks" in 1975, the Doctor visits a Dalek incubator room, spying several mutants resembling jellyfish. In "Remembrance of the Daleks" in 1988, a Dalek that had been further genetically engineered was seen to have a lobsterlike claw.

We don't see a fully revealed Dalek until 2005 in an episode starring Ninth Doctor Christopher Eccleston, who took a keen interest in the nature of the villains. As he said in *Doctor Who Magazine* #343, "As a child, I was absolutely fascinated by the episode where we saw what was inside a Dalek. . . . This great, cold, steel instrument of destruction, all that casing, all that armor, is actually to protect this very vulnerable, strange, frightened creature. So yeah, you can think about that on different levels, and think about what it is that actually frightens us."

Unable to travel outside their own city, relying on its metal floors to power them, the original Daleks seemed dangerous but limited. When it came time to bring them back in the show's second year, the production team gave them improved personal power sources so they could leave not only their city but the planet Skaro itself, traveling through the universe in spinning, flying saucers. Tie-in media later proposed that the first Daleks the Doctor met were a weaker tribe that had split off, while the others had largely left Skaro already to build the interstellar Dalek Empire.

Along with improved travel, the Daleks were more vicious now. The story "The Dalek Invasion of Earth" did not involve the TARDIS crew stopping the monsters from invading. They had already done so and won by the time the Doctor and his allies arrived on Earth in the twenty-second century, having used germ warfare to eliminate most human resistance. As if this weren't bad enough, the Daleks now also stole the souls of those they conquered, turning many human survivors into cyborg slaves called "Robo-Men" (a precursor to the Cybermen). It was a new level of evil and horror for *Doctor Who,* perhaps best summed up by the armor-plated monsters themselves when they later declared: "Daleks conquer and destroy!"

Less than a year later, the Daleks truly cemented themselves as uniquely dangerous arch-enemies of the Doctor in "The Chase." In this adventure, the monsters added solar panels to their armor and developed their own form of time travel.

DALEKS—IN COLOR!

"This is only the beginning. We will prepare. We will grow stronger. When the time is right, we will emerge and take our rightful place as the supreme power of the universe!"
—A DALEK, FROM "GENESIS OF THE DALEKS" (1975)

Terry Nation wisely made sure he had joint rights with the BBC to his monstrous creations. In 1964, he began a regular Dalek comic strip in *TV Century 21* magazine. These stories followed battles between the Dalek Empire and other races, with the Doctor conspicuously absent. Rare Daleks developed individuality, such as one that took the name Zeg. The strip also introduced the Dalek Emperor (and the narrative explained that this was only the first of such rulers). Although these comics ran for years, the *Doctor Who* TV program didn't reference them.

In 1965, the villains from Skaro hit the silver screen in full color. The theatrical film *Dr. Who and the Daleks* was loosely adapted from the first Dalek story. Peter Cushing played an English scientist literally named Dr. Who, who has invented a time machine that he calls *Tardis,* treating it as the ship's proper name rather than an acronym. He travels in it with his granddaughters, young Barbara and preadolescent Susan, as well as Barbara's boyfriend, Ian Chesterton.

The movie's full-color Daleks have proper mechanical claws and guns that release a deadly smoke. The production team originally intended to arm each monster with a flamethrower, but concern arose that this would frighten children, so fire extinguishers were used instead.

The film did well, and a sequel, *Daleks Invasion Earth: 2150 A.D.,* hit theaters the next year. With Ian and Barbara gone now, Dr. Who is accompanied by Susan and his niece Louise. Policeman Tom Campbell joins the gang just before *Tardis* takes them all to Earth's future, where the Daleks are in charge. Tom was portrayed by Bernard Cribbins, who later played Wilford Mott in several Tenth Doctor episodes.

The same year that the first Dalek film was released, David Whitaker and Terry Nation wrote a stage play entitled *The Curse of the Daleks* that premiered at the Wyndham's Theatre in London. The Doctor was nowhere to be found in this story, which ran for a month. In 1974, Terrance Dicks wrote *Doctor Who and the Seven Keys to Doomsday,* a stage play that introduced Dalek slaves called Clawrantulars and featured a quest for seven crystals that could control the universe. It ran for four weeks at the Adelphi Theatre in London, starring Trevor Martin as the Doctor, along with two new companions named Jenny and Jimmy. Jimmy was played by James Matthews and Jenny was played by Wendy Padbury, who years earlier had played the Second Doctor's companion Zoe.

With revenue pouring in from comics, toys, and films, Terry Nation became a millionaire. Despite having actually designed the Daleks, however, Raymond Cusick didn't get any royalties since he had no ownership rights.

EXPANDING MONSTER POPULATION

Doctor Who was originally supposed to present a number of stories that were historical fiction without science fiction elements added. But while viewers loved the slightly magical environment of the first episode, "An Unearthly Child," they generally didn't care for the next three chapters of the story that featured cavemen. It's an opinion that holds to this day.

Doctor Who novelist and audio drama writer Simon Guerrier works on *Doctor Who Adventures,* a popular magazine and website for children. On November 23, 2012, he watched "An Unearthly Child" with several young viewers. Despite its age, the episode met with such great approval that the kids asked if they could watch the next episode. As Guerrier said in an interview for this book, "We watched episode two, and they quickly got bored. So *Doctor Who* wasn't as good as it used to be from the very beginning."

The BBC saw how the program's popularity spiked when the second story arc introduced the Daleks and Skaro. The show started changing from educational stories about lost time travelers to a saga about heroes who fought monsters. Starting with the second year, historical fiction stories (often called just "historicals") happened less frequently. If the TARDIS landed in Earth's past, an alien force was now lurking about. Since the conclusion of the story "The Highlanders" (broadcast from December 17, 1966 to January 7, 1967), *Doctor Who* has only broadcast one pure historical, "The Black Orchid" in March 1982.

In an interview for this book, *Doctor Who* novelist and comic book writer Dan Abnett said, "I think the potential for having purely historical stories in *Doctor Who* is there as 'in case of emergency, break glass' to prove we're a legitimate television show that doesn't rely just on actors in rubber suits. The fact that it hasn't happened for so many years is a testament, I think, to the audience saying, 'It's already not a purely historical story because you have an alien scientist who got there in a blue box.' I think it's a serious challenge to have the Doctor have a story without any science fictional elements and make it as compelling as the stories that do. I think a pure historical declaws what *Doctor Who* is. There's a promise that there will be an unearthly threat, even if it doesn't seem unearthly at first, and the Doctor will be here to stop it."

In the commentary track for the "Rose" episode, Russell T. Davies spoke glowingly of the monsters, adding "[*Doctor Who*'s] unique quality is to take everyday things and make them scary." Ultimately, it's good story and characterization that make an alien villain successful. In the documentary *Doctor Who: A New Dimension,* Christopher Eccleston said about the monsters, "There's a danger of relying on them visually. To just think, *If we just roll them in with three heads, that's enough*—it isn't. They all have a relationship with the Doctor."

Many more monsters have populated the Whoniverse over the years, so what is it about the Daleks that so strongly enshrines them in viewers' minds as the hero's arch-foes?

Nicholas Briggs is the actor, writer, and director who has voiced the Daleks (and Cybermen) in Big Finish audio dramas and all their appearances in the modern TV program. When we discussed the villains, Briggs said, "The Daleks are time travelers like the Doctor, they possess a strange high intelligence like him, and he sees them as a genuine threat, so they're natural enemies. But also, I think people like certainty. Life is so full of gray, isn't it? . . . But the Daleks are certain about everything they do, and they are also certainly bad in everything they do. Symbolically, there are layers to them, but emotionally Daleks aren't conflicted at all, which also means you can't reason with them, and that's scary. That also throws the Doctor into sharp contrast because, even if other people don't believe him, we know how right he is that these things are pure evil; we see how good he is now in contrast to how bad they are—and there's always something fun about seeing true evil getting its ass kicked."

4

An Educational Crew

"As we learn about each other, so we learn about ourselves."
—FIRST DOCTOR TO BARBARA,
FROM "THE EDGE OF DESTRUCTION" (1964)

In the beginning, part of the Doctor's mystery revolved around his relationship with young Susan. When Anthony Coburn first revised Webber's script for "An Unearthly Child," Susan became "Suzanne," an alien girl from the same world as the Doctor. That draft also had the mysterious Doctor hinting that Suzanne was considered "royal blood."

David Whitaker liked the idea of this teenage girl coming from the same alien society as the Doctor, but he didn't want her to be royalty. Suzanne changed back to "Susan," and now used the assumed surname of "Foreman" during her stay on Earth, taking it from the owner of the junk yard that hid the TARDIS: I. M. Foreman. The idea of the Doctor adopting and raising a girl of Gallifreyan royalty would later inspire the character Miranda Dawkins, who appeared in Eighth Doctor novels from BBC Books and got her own comic book mini-series.

The script made clear that the Doctor was acting as a parental figure and guardian to Susan. Nevertheless, Coburn feared that some might still infer inappropriate reasons why this secretive, mercurial old man was traveling alone with a teenage girl. Others agreed, and Coburn made Susan the Doctor's granddaughter, which is explained in "An Unearthly Child" before the mysterious scientist even appears on-screen.

Carole Ann Ford, twenty-three at the time of filming, played Susan. Often cast in younger roles, Ford was happy to play an alien teenager, one who liked foggy streets at night, had an incredible knowledge of science and history, and possessed telepathic traits. As with the Doctor, Susan's odd remarks made the audience wonder at times whether she was deliberately witty or just honest and strange.

There was also the mystery of why Susan had joined the Doctor in exile. In the third story arc, "The Edge of Destruction," the Doctor falls unconscious for several minutes. When he wakes, he says, "I can't take you back, Susan! I can't!" Some viewers wondered if this meant Susan had never intended to travel in the TARDIS, perhaps forced onto the ship by her grandfather who didn't want to travel alone. Others thought that she chose to join him but regretted the decision later, and the Doctor was reliving an old argument.

In 2013, the episode "The Name of the Doctor" finally sheds a little light on the mystery. A flashback scene shows the Doctor selecting a TARDIS so he can leave Gallifrey, with Susan willingly entering the ship first.

Of course, this still doesn't answer another basic question. Who were Susan's parents? Which of them was a child of the Doctor? Did they approve of her leaving Gallifrey or did the family consider her and her grandfather as black sheep who were best forgotten?

The Big Finish audio play "Auld Mortality" refers to Susan as the daughter of the Doctor's daughter, but that story was meant to take place outside continuity and her exact lineage has never been confirmed on-screen. The television episodes "Fear Her" (2006) and "The Doctor's Daughter" (2008) confirmed that the Doctor was a father, but didn't say if he had a son, daughter, or multiple children. Behind the scenes, Hartnell suggested that Susan was the child of the Doctor's son and thought her father could be introduced as a villain who traveled in his own TARDIS. Hartnell even mused that he himself could play the Doctor's son, making him a twisted reflection of the hero. Though this character never appeared, the idea of such a villain presaged later enemies the Monk, the War Chief, the Rani, and the Master.

In the 1964 story "The Sensorites," we learned that while the Doctor's people had telepathic traits that could be honed through training, his granddaughter's were naturally stronger than his own. In the same story, Susan also gives the first description of their home world. According to her, "The sky is a burnt orange, and the leaves on the trees are silver." In 2007, David Tennant's Tenth Doctor repeats these words almost exactly in the episode "Gridlock," adding that the light of the rising sun made the forest look as if it were on fire.

In later years, some readers put forth the notion that Susan wasn't literally the Doctor's granddaughter but just his first traveling companion, whom he came to consider family. As far as the show's creators and cast were concerned, they were indeed directly related, and the writers made sure to say as much in their dialogue. Creators of the modern program share this belief. In the 2005 episode "The Empty Child," a man named Dr. Constantine remarks, "Before this war began, I was a father and a grandfather. Now I'm neither, but I'm still a doctor." The Ninth Doctor quietly replies: "Yeah. Know the feeling." To this day, when some have referred to Susan as the Doctor's "first traveling companion" or "first assistant," Ford openly objects, saying: "I wasn't a companion; I was the granddaughter."

Anthony Coburn, the writer responsible for making Susan and the Doctor family, never wrote another story for *Doctor Who* after "An Unearthly Child." When his scripts failed to be produced, he left the show in frustration. The script for "Masters of Luxor" was published by Titan Books in 1992. It was then adapted as an audio drama by Big Finish in 2012.

IAN CHESTERTON, MAN OF ACTION

William Russell—born Russell William Enoch—played Ian Chesterton. During his time in the Royal Air Force, he organized entertainment and after graduating from college went into repertory theater. In addition to appearing in *Hamlet* in London's West End, he appeared in several films, including *The Great Escape,* and was known as a heartthrob leading man.

Doctor Who's educational aspect determined the roles of the first two traveling companions. Ian the science teacher could prompt the Doctor to explain science fiction concepts more simply for the audience, grounding it in his own understanding. Ian was also there to be the man of action when needed, as the alien scientist was too elderly to fight. The Doctor's need for a younger and more physically able male companion continued until 1970, when the martial arts savvy Third Doctor arrived. Along with his physicality, Ian's morality became a driving force in the stories. In "The Daleks," the Doctor volunteers to lead the Thal people to victory. Ian overrules him, saying that it is better to inspire people to fight for themselves.

Russell appreciated this role of a romantic hero and the messages of the *Doctor Who* stories. In the commentary for "The Daleks," he summed up one of the program's recurring messages by saying, "You've got to make a decision, you've got to come to a conclusion. You can't just ignore it. You face it and you say, 'All right, then I'll stay. . . . You all run away.'"

Russell also enjoyed the relationship that developed between Ian and the Doctor, evolving from potential enemies to colleagues who liked each other more than they'd admit. Despite a desire to go home, Ian finds himself enjoying many of his adventures. In "The Reign of Terror," the Doctor insists that they've returned to 1960s London but is, again, wrong. Yet when Barbara asks if Ian is disappointed, he replies, "Funnily enough, no. I don't know."

BARBARA WRIGHT, VOICE OF REASON

Jacqueline Hill played Barbara Wright. She entered the Royal Academy of Dramatic Art on scholarship at age sixteen. In 1957, she starred in the BBC adaptation of Rod Serling's *Requiem for a Heavyweight,* convincing the director, Alvin Rakoff (whom she later married), to cast relatively new actor Sean Connery as well, believing he would be popular with female viewers.

Lambert personally approached Hill about playing Barbara, and the two discussed the character for some time before the producer officially offered her the role, which she accepted readily. Hill told *Doctor Who Magazine*:

> All I knew at first, all I was actually told, was that my character was a very learned history teacher and that I was there to represent the Earth point of view when we went back in time and did the occasional serial set in the past. I found that quite easy, as I liked history and those historical stories appealed to me anyway. Everything else I had to put in myself, and this meant taking it up with either Verity or the director concerned. I think there were times when I said, "Barbara wouldn't say this or she wouldn't do this," and they were usually very good and listened to me on those points because I knew the character better than anybody else.

The good thing about Barbara was that because she was older than most of the girls since, the writers were more hesitant about making her look silly or scream too much. That side of things was largely left to Carole Ann Ford, which is why she left earlier than Bill Russell and myself.

Some modern viewers have found it surprising just how realized Barbara's character is during the early adventures. While she does scream at seeing some of the monsters, she doesn't have emotional outbursts foreign to the circumstances (and Ian could get quite emotional during the stories, too). During their first journey through time, Ian refuses to accept the Doctor's stories as true, whereas Barbara—who considers Ian a friend rather than a mentor or a colleague with authority—instantly understands and seeks new answers. Even when the two teachers leave the TARDIS and discover that they have traveled to another place and time, Ian, visibly shaken, remarks that the situation is "impossible to accept." Barbara on the other hand says matter-of-factly: "The point is, Ian, that it's happened."

Barbara continues to stand out from many expectations in the next two stories. In "The Daleks," Barbara is the one to find a love interest on a strange new planet rather than Ian, and in "The Edge of Destruction," it's her imagination and insight that save the TARDIS crew from doom when she realizes the ship is alive and trying to communicate (something Ian can't quite believe). This third story finally convinces the Doctor that he has much to learn from these worthy human friends, meaning she is a major catalyst in making him a hero. We have producer Verity Lambert to thank, along with the writers, for the show treating Barbara so well in those early days.

Like Ian, Barbara's occupation had a purpose. Since the TARDIS "year-o-meter" broke in the second episode, it was sometimes left to the history teacher to determine where the ship had landed, noting various clues as she educated viewers on Earth's past.

Barbara also added drama by challenging the Doctor's authority in time travel. In the 1964 story "The Aztecs," she is mistaken for a goddess and decides to take this opportunity to influence Aztec society for the better. The Doctor immediately opposes this, declaring it both impossible and amoral to change history. In the end, Barbara's hopes come to nothing, and she regrets deceiving the Aztecs, particularly a kindly elder who defended her.

> **BARBARA:** "I gave him false hope, and in the end he lost his faith."
>
> **DOCTOR:** "He found another faith, a better one. And that's the good you've done. You failed to save a civilization, but at least you helped one man."

While Ian still challenged the Doctor openly, Barbara became keenly aware that the strange scientist had the final say in many matters as he alone could work the TARDIS and understood the full dangers of time travel. As she explained in "The Sensorites," "We're very dependent on the Doctor. He leads and we follow."

CHANGING ATMOSPHERE

As time went on, Carole Ann Ford cooled on the role of Susan. Some of the writers seemed to forget that she hailed from a society of long-lived time travelers, portraying her more as an ordinary teenager who easily startled and often suffered being a damsel in distress. The TV story "The Sensorites" became one of Ford's favorites, depicting Susan as inexperienced but also wise beyond her apparent years, musing, "Isn't it better to travel hopefully than arrive?"

Because of this difference in vision and the grueling schedule of filming a fifty-two episode season, Ford decided to leave the program early in the second year. The second story arc of that year was "The Dalek Invasion of Earth." When the TARDIS crew aids human freedom fighters, Susan grows close to a young man named David Campbell, and the Doctor takes notice. Despite her protests that she needs to stay with him, the Doctor tells Susan that she is no longer a child but a woman who needs to find her own life and home, as she's often wanted to. He locks the TARDIS doors, promises to return, and leaves.

In this pre-Internet era, viewers had no warning that Susan might leave. Some wondered whether the hero had left his granddaughter behind to protect her from the unseen forces he was fleeing. Simon Guerrier's novel *The Time Travellers* points to that as the main reason for the parting, once the Doctor knows she has someone who loves her and will aid her against danger.

The Doctor's farewell to Susan became one of the most famous speeches in the show: "One day, I shall come back. Yes, I shall come back. Until then, there must be no regrets, no tears, no anxieties. Just go forward in all your beliefs—and prove to me that I am not mistaken in mine."

After Susan's departure came the TV story "The Escape," which introduced Vicki, played by Maureen O'Brien, a sixteen-year-old human born and raised in the twenty-fifth century. Though she had no family name in the program, some tie-in media gave it as Pallister.

Along with the change in cast, the second year of *Doctor Who* seemed to go down a darker path. "The Dalek Invasion of Earth" had featured germ warfare and forced brain surgery. "The Escape" introduced Vicki in the middle of a mass murder mystery, her father one of the victims. In the same story, Barbara kills Vicki's pet "sand beast," mistaking it for a predator. With no family or home, Vicki forgives Barbara and accepts a place on the TARDIS.

By this time, the audience knew the Doctor well enough that there was no longer the fear of anyone inferring inappropriate reasons for his having an unrelated teenage girl traveling and living with him, so Vicki's presence was accepted. On the surface, Vicki paralleled Susan, being another teenager intelligent beyond her years, having obtained certificates in medicine, chemistry, physics, and computer sciences by age ten. But her manner was much more Earth-bound and playful, the girl teasing the Doctor whenever he was in a cranky mood. If she believed someone wasn't listening to her, she pointed out the mistake. Vicki willingly chose life on the TARDIS, symbolizing the children watching who wished they could join the Doctor.

While O'Brien enjoyed her cast mates, she disliked her character occasionally being a damsel in distress. It also annoyed her that some directors focused on filming as quickly as possible rather than discussing the story more with the cast. In a commentary track for "The Space Museum," William Russell offered an explanation. "I think that's one of the faults of being a regular in a series that brings in different directors. Because they think the character—whatever you do—is probably already established, and they don't want to interfere."

In an interview with *Doctor Who Magazine,* Jacqueline Hill remarked, "She inherited Carole's role of screaming all the time. . . . It was more or less her first big television part, and I think it was a bit of a rude awakening."

Fortunately, Vicki still stood out as a feisty and intelligent girl. As the second year went on, new script editor Dennis Spooner continued pushing the program's boundaries. Spooner told *Doctor Who Magazine:*

> After the first series, we realized that the show was destined to run a long time. And in a television show, you have to learn very quickly what you are going to get away with because once it becomes at all established you cannot change it. . . . With the second series of *Doctor Who,* we knew that whatever we could establish would make the boundaries for a long time to come. "The Romans" was done for comedy, and in "The Web Planet" we wanted to see how far we could go with being weird. And my God, that tested facilities and technical resources to the limit.

THE VOYAGE HOME

"The Chase," the penultimate story of the program's second year, became famous for a few reasons. Along with the Doctor learning the Daleks now had time travel, the first episode of the story had the TARDIS use a "time-space visualizer" to peek in on a performance by the Beatles. Due to legal rights, this small segment has sadly been removed from the DVD release.

Another thing that marked this story was that it ended with the departure of Barbara and Ian. The schoolteachers make it back to London by stealing a Dalek time ship, arriving roughly two years after they first found the TARDIS. Unlike Susan's departure, theirs is a happy one, the two shouting, "It was fun, Doctor!" before running through the streets together. Back on the TARDIS, the Doctor, solemn and stiff, quietly says, "I shall miss them. Yes, I shall miss them. Silly old fusspots." It's a rare display of emotion from the First Doctor, one of our first clues to how much he fears loneliness and the departure of friends.

Interestingly, it has been said by several who worked with him that William Hartnell became afraid of Daleks after finishing "The Chase," concluding that their presence meant someone in the cast was leaving. The next Dalek adventure followed suit.

"Jacqueline Hill and I left together, and Billy was absolutely furious," William Russell told *Doctor Who Magazine*. In another interview with *Doctor Who Magazine,* Hill added:

> We'd done two years of it, which was a strain . . . Everything that we wanted to do in the series had been accomplished, and we felt, and I think Verity sneakingly agreed with us, that it was time for the series to try and see if it could do something new. As for the question of going together, well, it all just seemed to come together at the right time for both of us. I think it had always been felt that Ian and Barbara, who had this slightly romantic side to their relationship, should go together much as they came—back to the London they left. They wrote us out well.

Russell often spoke fondly of his time on *Doctor Who* and continued acting on a regular basis, with roles in TV shows such as *Breaking Point, Harriet's Back in Town, Black Adder,* and *Coronation Street,* as well as a minor role as an elder of Krypton in *Superman: The Movie.* Hill left acting to raise a family, but returned to television roughly a decade later. She came back to *Doctor Who* in the Fourth Doctor adventure "Meglos," playing the character Lexa.

Unlike today, there wasn't much media attention surrounding the show's cast changes. As Russell told *Doctor Who Magazine,* "We all got up early, drove into London and rehearsed, and then went home; life went on." A Fifth Doctor TV story called "Mawdryn Undead" intended for Russell to return as Ian, but the plan didn't work out and the character's role was replaced.

Though tie-in media sometimes revisited Ian and Barbara, saying they married, the characters were never mentioned again in *Doctor Who* (although Barbara's photograph appeared in a scene cut from the 2010 adventure "The Vampires of Venice"). Just over forty-five years after last seeing them with the Doctor, fans finally got an answer during *The Sarah Jane Adventures* in 2010. In the two-part "Death of the Doctor," Sarah Jane Smith reveals that she has learned about two married professors in Cambridge, named Ian and Barbara Chesterton, neither of whom appears to have aged since the 1960s.

NEW CREW, NEW DOCTOR

"He's the crew. We're just the passengers."

—VICKI, FROM "THE TIME MEDDLER" (1965)

"The Chase" also introduced Steven Taylor, a combat pilot from Earth's future (some time after the Dalek invasion of the twenty-second century). Before meeting the Doctor, Steven has spent two years as a prisoner on the planet Mechanus, with only a toy panda called HiFi for company. During the story's last episode, he wanders into the TARDIS, seeking safety before he collapses from weakness, unintentionally becoming a stowaway as the ship takes flight.

Peter Purves, a young actor who had appeared in *Armchair Theater* and BBC's *Play of the Month,* played Steven Taylor. He originally appeared

Peter Purves (Steven Taylor)

as Morton Dill, a minor character, in an early episode of "The Chase" and impressed the director enough that he was asked to be the new companion. Purves was first in a long line of actors who appear in *Doctor Who* and then return as a different character.

With Steven's addition to the TARDIS crew, the next story, "The Time Meddler," served both as season finale and the first chapter of a new era. Originally, the Doctor had traveled with three people who all longed for home.

Now, he had two companions happy to embark on unpredictable adventures. As Vicki and Steven both recognized the Doctor's leadership rather than challenge it, they seemed to inspire the character to fill that role better, truly making him the hero fans know today rather than an occasional obstacle in the lives of his crew.

In 2013, Peter Purves made his first appearance at Gallifrey One, a fan-run convention held annually in Los Angeles since 1990, and spoke glowingly of his time on *Doctor Who*. "There was actually a while where I didn't want to do more conventions because I thought, *I don't like looking back.* But doing these DVD commentaries on the old shows and seeing them again, there's a lot I fondly remember and things I like much better now. 'The Gunfighters,' where the Doctor gets mistaken for Doc Holliday? I used to think it was quite bad . . . but now it's great fun to me. Bill was just enjoying himself. He loved the idea of a Western for the kids. He really wanted the show to be enjoyable for children. It bothered him if it got a little too dark or violent."

I pointed out to Purves what a unique crew he and Maureen O'Brien made. Rather than two ordinary people from the modern day, here were a soldier and a genius from the future. "Yeah, it became a different show in a way," Purves replied. "Now you couldn't ignore it was science fiction even if you just had a historical fiction story. . . . Vicki and Steven were from the future, and they could recognize ray guns and spaceships all by themselves.

"It was a great time, and Bill was marvelous," he added. "Looking back, I can still be critical of my performance. We were shooting so many episodes, and we had I think about ten weeks off in the year, so there was a rush. You didn't always have time to consider things you wanted clear about your character. But now I'm back doing Steven [in audio dramas] for Big Finish. . . . In The Anachronauts [audio drama], there's a bit there about Steven's guilt that he left a war to go have fun time traveling. He didn't mean to, but he did."

LAMBERT LEAVES

Soon after Peter Purves joined the cast, Verity Lambert left *Doctor Who*, though she remained at the BBC. She later explained,

I had been at *Doctor Who* for . . . probably more than eighteen months . . . and I just felt that, you know, it needed new blood. I think things do . . . especially something like *Doctor Who*. I mean, I'd had tremendous fun, and we'd been able to do so many different things, and I just needed to move on, really. And there was another idea that Sydney had called *Adam Adamant* which was equally kind of, sort of mad, and I was quite attracted to that.

The last episode that Verity Lambert produced was "Mission to the Unknown." It's the only story of the classic series that was one episode in length and is the only episode of both the classic series and the modern that doesn't feature or mention the Doctor or even any of his companions. The episode was a prelude to the adventure "The Daleks' Master Plan," though the four-part story "The Myth Makers" aired in between.

Lambert always spoke with pride about her time with *Doctor Who*. When people mentioned how often tight budgets or problems on set created obstacles, she offered that people learn more during times when things go wrong. She was happy with having worked on a show with such an atypical hero and a universal appeal to children and adults, though she did criticize some later eras during which she felt the program strayed too far from what she considered to be the core story. She died in 2007.

The Comic Doctor

At twenty-six years old, the classic *Doctor Who* program remains the longest running science fiction series in television history. Less known is that the *Doctor Who* comic strip, though it has changed publishers, is the longest running comic strip based on a TV series, starting in November 1964 in the pages of *TV Comic* and continuing to this day in *Doctor Who Magazine*.

TV Comic catered to a readership generally under the age of ten, so making stories that appealed to parents as well wasn't a concern. The narratives, drawn by Neville Main, were simplistic fare, much lighter than the TV show. There was still violence and death, true, but it didn't feel as dark as the show would become.

The first story, "The Klepton Parasites," features two preadolescent children named John and Gillian who decide to meet their mysterious grandfather, a man who calls himself "Dr. Who." They find a yard rather than a house, empty except for a police box that's bigger on the inside. The Doctor, drawn to resemble William Hartnell, looks up as the children enter his ship and says, "You must be John and Gillian! How nice to meet you!"

This Doctor wasn't sinister at all, in keeping with how the character had softened by the time the comic appeared. He was a curious, mischievous, occasionally reckless inventor with a bottomless black bag that held all manner of strange gadgets, rather like a science fiction Mary Poppins. The comic never addressed whether he was an alien or a scientist native to England. When their first adventure ended, Dr. Who suggested taking his grandchildren home, but John said he would be happy to continue traveling through space and time.

There was little concern for continuity between the strip and the TV program, although an early strip clearly provided a sequel to the TV story "The Web Planet." The comic had its own sense of fun, depicting aliens and stories not easily brought to life on television and even dabbling in experimental storytelling, including one adventure shown in reverse to indicate time running backward. *TV Comic* published the strip until 1971, at which point it moved to the pages of *TV Action* and featured the Third Doctor. This new and dynamic incarnation of the comic appealed to a broader fan base.

The strip moved back to *TV Comic* in 1973 and remained there until 1979. This second *TV Comic* era didn't match the quality of the *TV Action* era. In fact, some of the Fourth Doctor stories were just Third Doctor strips with Tom Baker's face drawn over Jon Pertwee's. In these republished stories, television companion Sarah Jane Smith was altered to become a new character named Joan Brown.

In 1979, the strip moved to *Doctor Who Weekly*, a new magazine dedicated to articles, reviews, commentaries, and interviews surrounding the show, published by the UK branch of Marvel Comics. The comic quickly shifted gears, hewing much closer to what appeared on screens. The hero became simply "the Doctor" rather than "Doctor Who" and was clearly identified as a renegade Time Lord from the planet Gallifrey. The first regular artist was Dave Gibbons, who gained greater acclaim later as co-creator of the comic book series *Watchmen*.

Doctor Who Weekly evolved into *Doctor Who: A Marvel Monthly*, then *The Official Doctor Who Magazine,* and later *Doctor Who Magazine.* To this day, it is the longest running magazine based on a television series and happily shows no signs of stopping.

5

The TARDIS and Time Travel

"Well, I came up with the name from the initials: Time and Relative Dimension in Space."
— SUSAN, FROM "AN UNEARTHLY CHILD" (1963)

In the first official pitch by C. E. Webber, he suggested that the Doctor's time machine be invisible due to light-resistant paint. He believed a futuristic spaceship would put off viewers disinclined to science fiction stories, while disguising the time machine as a common public object, such as a "night-watchman's shelter," would make it seem too much like a magic door in a fairy tale, putting off adults. Invisibility was his visual compromise.

Newman objected to an invisible spaceship—which Webber suggested be hidden in a van for the opening story—saying the machine needed to be iconic and visually interesting. The idea came that the Doctor's ship would have the ability to change shape, camouflaging itself wherever it landed.

Making the ship capable of disguise and saying it was larger inside (a quality the Third Doctor later described as "dimensionally transcendental") meant the production crew didn't have to film a large spaceship landing and taking off in each story. It was much easier to have a familiar object simply fade in and out of locations.

Over the years, different stories implied the TARDIS interior was out of synch with the outside universe. The Fourth Doctor called this a state of "temporal grace" and claimed it also prevented weapons from working inside (though this defense feature stopped working by the time the Fifth Doctor came along). Simon Guerrier's novel *The Time Travellers* delved into the ship's design strategy. In one scene, the First Doctor explains to Barbara, "The TARDIS is built specifically not to change history. We can visit, we can observe, and the ship can disguise itself so no one need ever know we were there. But only so long as we never step outside. We watch it all on the scanner." In the episode "The Parting of the Ways," the Ninth

Doctor echoes this sentiment, revealing that he becomes part of the local timeline once he leaves the TARDIS doors. This certainly explains why Time Lords, sworn never to interfere, would bother building time ships in the first place.

Susan said she came up with the name TARDIS, but we later learn that other Time Lords use the same term. Perhaps Susan started the trend many years before, when she and the Doctor still lived on Gallifrey. In the Fourth Doctor adventure "The Deadly Assassin," TARDISes are also known by the technical term "TT capsule," the initials standing for "time travel." Officially, the Doctor's ship is a Type 40 TT capsule, a model so old as to be considered obsolete by his lifetime, further explaining the unreliability of the ship's controls.

"IT'S ALIVE!"

In the third *Doctor Who* TV story, "The Edge of Destruction," Ian asks if it's possible that the ship can think on its own. The Doctor admits that it thinks not in terms a human being could understand but more as a computer processing various simultaneous operations. Nevertheless, the Doctor considers the ship a living thing and shows great affection toward it. Starting in his third incarnation, the hero sometimes addresses the ship directly as "old girl," and lovingly pats the console, particularly if he thinks the TARDIS has suffered insult.

After a few years, viewers couldn't ignore that the Doctor conveniently kept arriving in places where terrible things were about to occur. Many fans concluded that the TARDIS was deliberately taking the Doctor to such situations because it knew his help was needed and understood that he thrived on defeating evil.

"The Doctor's Wife" episode in 2011 confirmed this idea. A rare set of circumstances allowed the Doctor to speak directly to the soul of his ship. By the 2012 Christmas special "The Snowmen," the Doctor added a section to the TARDIS control console designed to enable more direct communication with his ship.

BROKEN CIRCUITS

For the opening story, Anthony Coburn thought that the TARDIS should disguise itself as a blue police phone box, a commonly seen object in London and other cities. For decades, police phone boxes provided direct communication with the police department before walkie-talkies. The light at the top flashed to alert police on patrol to call in. Prisoners could also be held inside temporarily, while the police summoned aid via the phone on the door.

As the police box prop was built, the concern arose of how expensive it was going to be to replace the time machine every few weeks with another large object that served no function except to wait for the adventurers to return to it at some point. To save money and time, Verity Lambert decided to keep reusing the police box model, remarking, "We'll just say the controls are broken."

This explanation was easy enough. Though Syndey Newman had initially imagined that the Doctor would not remember how to fly his ship, "An Unearthly Child" established that the TARDIS was not in top form. Moments after the audience first sees the interior, the Doctor mentions needing to rely on an "amateur" spare part to repair part of the machine. After the TARDIS makes its first on-screen flight, the Doctor says that the "year-o-meter," which apparently helps determine destinations, is broken (then, rather than fixing it immediately, he dismisses it and explores outside). Later on, Susan mentions on-screen that her grandfather often forgets a few steps in the ship's flight protocols, adding to the unpredictability of its flight. In "The Name of the Doctor" in 2013, we learned that the alien scientist had been warned that the ship's navigation system was not working correctly when he stole it, but was also advised that this would make his travels more fun. Which, of course, is why the writers made it an unpredictable time machine in the first place, along with the fact that it prevented the ship from being an easy cure for dangerous situations. If Ian and Barbara were imprisoned, the Doctor couldn't simply teleport the TARDIS into their jail cell because he might wind up on the other side of the universe instead, unable to return.

So with both ship and pilot quickly established as unreliable, it wasn't so surprising in "An Unearthly Child" when, after landing in prehistoric

Earth, the Doctor leaves the TARDIS and is alarmed to discover that his ship's disguise feature has failed, its outer shell still resembling a London police box from 1963.

The dramatic contrivance of such an advanced and seemingly magical form of technology also being imperfect adds to the charm of the show, as does the bizarre imagery of a British police box acting as a spaceship. In the commentary for "The Time Meddler," Verity Lambert said, "Like a lot of things that you have to do [for budget], I think it turned out to be a rather wonderful thing. The sort of incongruity of that [police box]."

The often beat-up looking police box became a fixed symbol of the program. Many years later, London's Metropolitan Police Service wanted to build new police boxes using this classic design and the BBC objected, saying that they had a trademark on the image. A judge ruled in the BBC's favor, as *Doctor Who* had used it for decades without complaint from the police.

In the 1965 TV story "The Time Meddler," the ship's disguise feature was called a "camouflage unit." The 1966 radio play "Journey into Time," written by Malcolm Hulke and recorded by Stanmark Productions, called it the "electronic chameleon system." In 1981, in "Logopolis," the Fourth Doctor called it the "chameleon circuit," which then became the official name. In a cut scene from 2010, the Eleventh Doctor explains how the chameleon circuit works:

> Every time the TARDIS materializes in a new location, within the first nanosecond of landing, it analyzes its surroundings, calculates a twelve-dimensional data map of everything within a thousand mile radius, and determines which outer shell would blend in best with the environment. . . . And then it disguises itself as a police telephone box from 1963. . . . Probably a bit of a fault, actually. I've been meaning to check.

In the 1981 story "Logopolis," the Fourth Doctor added that the TARDIS had been in a repair shop when he "borrowed" it in his haste to leave Gallifrey, and the technicians had not yet corrected certain things such as the "chameleon conversions."

The Fourth Doctor was the first incarnation who tried repairing the chameleon circuit, deciding in "Logopolis" that he wanted to travel more discreetly, but an adventure interrupted his efforts. The Sixth Doctor determined to solve the problem and partially succeeded, but now the ship took on the appearance of objects that stood out even more ridiculously than a police box. Frustrated, the Sixth Doctor let it resume its blue box setting.

Over the years it's become necessary to build a new police box for the program, which has led to minor cosmetic differences. The TARDIS used by the first two Doctors had a St. John's Ambulance badge on one of the doors, but this vanished by the Third Doctor's first appearance. It didn't appear on the door again until 2010 when the ship rebuilt itself in "The Eleventh Hour." Fans and creators alike have joked that the TARDIS exterior occasionally alters because the old time ship tries to change shape again but can't do more than tweak minor details. Simon Guerrier's novel The Time Travellers directly references this phenomenon, which also explains why the TARDIS key occasionally has a different design. As the Doctor reveals in "The Sound of Drums" (2007), the keys form part of the TARDIS itself and are connected to its abilities.

In the first episode of the spin-off show Torchwood in 2006, the character Jack Harkness refers to the TARDIS as having a "perception filter." This was then mentioned in the Doctor Who program itself as a feature that influenced people to not notice the ship, unless it's brought to their attention, they're already familiar with it, or they're directly watching the spot where it lands. Like everything else about the TARDIS, this feature doesn't work perfectly, so some people might still notice the ship after it's fully materialized.

The perception filter sounds a lot like the "Somebody Else's Problem" field used in the book Life, The Universe and Everything by Douglas Adams, a technology that influences people to ignore a bizarre spaceship. A fitting connection, as Douglas Adams served as a writer and script editor on Doctor Who in the 1970s.

THE SOUND

Brian Hodgson of the BBC Radiophonic Workshop created the famous wheezing, groaning sound of the time engines, often depicted in comics and novels as "VWORP." As he explained in the documentary *The Story of Doctor Who*: "I took my mother's front door key, and I put it down the bass strings of an old piano we had. We took the sound, we speeded it up, we slowed it down, we cut them together, and it became one of the great icons of sound effects."

The sound has remained relatively the same over the decades, married to the image of the TARDIS itself. In the 2006 episode "Love and Monsters," it is referred to as "the sound of the universe."

In 2010, time adventurer River Song tells the Doctor that the ship isn't supposed to make a sound when it lands, and that this results from not turning off the parking brake. But the classic *Doctor Who* program played the sound every time another TARDIS left or arrived. Perhaps the ability to travel quietly was an improvement made to TARDISes during the Last Great Time War, an update that the Doctor ignored. Perhaps River was just teasing, as she often does.

Speaking of sound, the question occasionally arose as to why so many people across the universe all seem to speak English—and with British accents, at that. In "The Space Museum," an alien display even had a sign with the word "Dalek" written in English. The original explanation for this particular sign was that the museum used a telepathic translation system for visitors, letting them hear and see what language they wished, but the dialogue revealing this was cut. This basic idea was later used in "The Mask of Mandragora" (1976), when the Fourth Doctor tells Sarah Jane that her ability to understand all languages is a Time Lord "gift" that he has extended to her. In the 2005 episode "The End of the World," the Ninth Doctor finally explains that the TARDIS's telepathic circuits extends a field that translates for its crew.

THE CONTROL ROOM AND THE CONSOLE

The control room was a strange sight from the beginning, with walls decorated by roundels and a hexagonal console that held a cylindrical time rotor at its center, beneath which lay the TARDIS's heart, a power source of dangerous energy, as we learned in "The Edge of Destruction." Originally, the room could hold a dozen people comfortably, and had a small section divided by a transparent wall that housed computer banks. This set proved too large to constantly rebuild—delaying filming and taxing the budget—so it soon shrank.

The console, though designed quickly, immediately stood out from traditional depictions of spaceships. In many films and TV programs, space ship controls occupied different areas of a room, similar to a naval vessel with separate posts. But the Doctor and Susan faced each other when they operated different sections of the console, indicating the ship was meant to have as many as six people operating in a communal manner, and tie-in materials said that this was definitely the case. The supposition became official in the 2008 episode "The Journey's End." No wonder the Doctor has so much trouble flying the ship, he's doing six jobs! (Not to mention, as we learn in "The Shakespeare Code," he failed his pilot's exam.)

According to William Russell, William Hartnell actually mapped out the console's controls and did his best to keep consistent with their use, believing that children would notice if the Doctor's operation of the ship showed no rhyme or reason. In later years, designs for the TARDIS console were released for fans, allowing them to build their own versions, complete with vector trackers, vortex loops, horizontal holds, dimensional stabilizers, dematerializers, force field generators, scanner screen controls, a fast return switch, mustard and ketchup nozzles, and other vital technology. Matt Smith has memorized the controls of his own TARDIS console.

BIGGER ON THE INSIDE

"Just how big is the TARDIS?"
"Well, how big's big? Relative dimensions, you see. No constant."
—SARAH JANE AND THE FOURTH DOCTOR,
FROM "THE MASK OF MANDRAGORA" (1976)

In the 1977 TV story "The Robots of Death," the Fourth Doctor attempts to explain the science of "trans-dimensional engineering" that makes the inner dimensions of his ship possible. He takes two boxes, putting the larger on the console, then brings his companion Leela to the edge of the room and holds up the smaller one in front of her. Of course, she understands that it's only her perspective that makes the smaller one look larger. The Doctor concedes, but adds that if you can keep the larger box a distance away while simultaneously having access to it, then you can "fit" it inside the smaller box.

"That's silly," Leela says.

In the early adventures, viewers saw that the TARDIS had sleeping quarters, hallways, a wardrobe, and a small section that housed a food machine. But as the crew spent more time adventuring through time and space, the more interesting locations lay beyond the ship's doors rather than within it, and so the control room became the main interior setting. In the 1970s, some of the Fourth Doctor's stories showed more of the TARDIS interior again, including a swimming pool, a jungle room with a man-eating plant, and a large drawing room with a pair of Wellington boots, which was called the "boot cupboard." There was also the cloister room, which housed an alarm that rang if the ship was in extreme danger. The cloister bell has rung several times in the modern series.

Tom Baker often suggested the ship's interior be explored more, believing it could have entire sections that resembled restaurants, cathedrals, and city streets. He joked that he could find someone who had stowed away for years, unnoticed because the Doctor had simply stopped visiting that part of the ship. In the *Doctor Who Magazine* comic strip, writer Grant Morrison created memory rooms within the TARDIS that simulate places the ship had visited.

Although the control room (which was renamed the console room in the 1980s) is what first comes to mind when people consider the interior, it constantly changes. When the Second Doctor wound up in the TARDIS of his third incarnation, he commented that he didn't like how the room had been redecorated. We had no explanation for these differences until the 1977 TV story "The Invisible Enemy," when the Doctor mentioned programming the TARDIS computer to alter the interior design.

On another occasion, in "The Mask of Mandragora," the Fourth Doctor wanders through his ship and stumbles across an entirely separate control room from the one he's been using, one with a wooden console. He first assumes this is the "secondary control room," but then finds the recorder he once used during his second life, along with one of the outfits he'd worn in his third incarnation. Since he's been here in multiple forms, he wonders if this isn't the original control room after all, which means he unknowingly began using the secondary version some time ago, while this one modified its design. In any event, he decides to use the wooden control room until further notice and the ship's main exit doors conveniently relocate to accommodate him.

This wooden control room, the only version without a time rotor in the center of the console, had been built to be a smaller, more manageable set. The design evoked a Jules Verne sensibility, making it seem timeless rather than trying to look like some idea of the future. When Graham Williams later took over as producer, he preferred something closer to the classic room with its white walls and space-age style, so he had the wooden set destroyed.

In the 1980s, script editor Christopher Bidmead's high interest in computers influenced the ship's capabilities. He compared the TARDIS and its many rooms to a database that held many files. Some files could be moved, some redesigned, and some deleted, depending on the programming. In a couple of 1980s stories, the Doctor jettisoned certain rooms of the TARDIS in order to gain thrust. The Eleventh Doctor showed us more of the ship's rooms and inner workings in 2013, including a technology tree that grew machines you needed.

I asked *Doctor Who* fans and writers how much we should see of the TARDIS. Is it a place to explore, or is it better to keep it as a mysterious means of travel?

Doctor Who novelist and comic book writer Dan Abnett: "My gut feeling as a writer is to say that the less we know, the better. It allows our imagination to roam, and the TARDIS is a plot mechanism. Although it is an enduring thing that has taken on, quite literally at one point, a life of its own. You can have fun with it without revealing all its secrets. You can have that moment of realizing, wait, there's a second console room?"

Electronics expert and *Mythbusters* team member Grant Imahara: "I enjoy every once in a while hearing references to other parts of the TARDIS, but I would rather they be kept out of the main narrative. I'm sure the rooms in my imagination are much better."

Big Finish Productions script editor, novelist, and past editor of *Doctor Who Magazine* Gary Russell: "I'd like to explore the TARDIS more. I think it's silly that fifty years later, we've still only seen a few rooms and corridors. This is a living, breathing craft. Let's see what it truly has in its walls."

THE RULES OF TIME

"You can't rewrite history. Not one line!"

—THE FIRST DOCTOR, FROM "THE AZTECS" (1964)

Originally, the BBC directed that major historical events and figures be depicted accurately, unaltered by the TARDIS crew. According to writer Dennis Spooner, Sydney Newman told them that, when it came to history or large-scale events, the Doctor preferred to observe, limiting how much influence he had. This explains why the First Doctor occasionally dressed like a native and assumed an alias that suited the location, unlike most of his later incarnations.

David Whitaker explained the philosophy behind these limits when he responded to mail from a viewer named R. Adams of Quinton, Birmingham. Whitaker's letter read:

> Undoubtedly one must look at time as a roadway going uphill and down the other side. You and I are in the position of walking along that road, whereas Doctor Who is in the position of being placed on top of the hill. He can look backward and he can look forward, in fact the whole pattern of the road is laid out for him. But you will appreciate of course that he cannot interfere with that road in any way whatsoever. . . . The basis of time travelling is that all things that happen are fixed and unalterable, otherwise of course the whole structure of existence would be thrown into unutterable confusion and the purpose of life itself would be destroyed. Doctor Who is an observer. . . . Where we are allowed to use fiction, of course, is that we allow the Doctor

and his friends to interfere in the personal histories of certain people from the past. We can get away with this provided they are not formally established as historical characters. We cannot tell Nelson how to win at the Battle of the Nile because no viewer would accept such a hypothesis. However, we can influence one Captain on board a minor ship in Napoleon's armada.

So when the Doctor warned Barbara that it was impossible to alter the major history of the Aztecs, he was speaking literally as far as the writers were concerned. However, by the end of the program's second year, writer Dennis Spooner succeeded Whitaker as script editor and decided to bring up the alteration of history as a real danger. Since the Doctor acted to keep history on its proper course (and educate children in the process), the BBC didn't object.

In the final story of the second year, "The Time Meddler," the TARDIS crew encounters a villain who seeks to alter British history. Unconvinced of the danger at first, Steven points out to Vicki that he remembers his history, and therefore the past is safe from the meddler.

> **STEVEN:** "What about the history books?"
>
> **VICKI:** "That's all right. They're not written yet. They'll just write and print the new version."
>
> **STEVEN:** "But that means that the exact minute, the exact second that he does it, every history book, every—well, whole future of every year and time on Earth will change, just like that, and nobody'll know it has?"

"The Time Meddler" certainly turned up the drama of life in the TARDIS and made the Doctor a protector of reality itself. In the same story, the Doctor tells his enemy the Monk that there are rules concerning time travel, an idea repeated in the 1973 story "The Three Doctors," in which a Time Lord notes that the First Law of Time says no one may visit a future or past version of his or herself (though another Time Lord argues this can be broken on occasion, in special circumstances). Paradoxes were things to avoid.

The potential to change history now also brought up new moral disagreements. When Steven asks why they can't save certain people in the past, the Doctor explains. "My dear Steven, history sometimes gives us a terrible shock, and that is because we don't quite fully understand. Why should we? After all, we're all too small to realize its final pattern. Therefore don't try and judge it from where you stand."

In the TV story "Pyramids of Mars" (1975), the Fourth Doctor and Sarah Jane are defending humanity from a powerful alien menace in 1911. At one point, Sarah Jane suggests they simply leave since she knows her planet wasn't destroyed in 1911. Humoring her, the Doctor travels to 1980 and opens the TARDIS doors: The Earth that lies outside is a lifeless wasteland, the result of a new timeline created by leaving humanity defenseless in 1911. Either their adventure in Earth's past is fulfilling a part of history that was always there or the presence of different time traveling races in the universe causes ripples that create new dangers in past and future that have to be vanquished to preserve reality. The Doctor admits, though, that most people can only influence the future, as it takes a powerful being to completely alter or destroy a planet's fate. Of course, history is much more delicate since the events of the Last Great Time War . . .

6

Violence and Endings

"It's a very difficult thing, time . . . Once you start to interfere with it, the strangest things start happening."
—THE THIRD DOCTOR, FROM "DAY OF THE DALEKS" (1972)

In the two years following Barbara and Ian's departure, change became the main theme of the show, which charged forward under the banner that nothing was static.

During a trip to Earth's past, Vicki found a new life for herself (and fulfilled a place in history otherwise vacant). She was succeeded by Katarina, a Trojan woman who at first believed the Doctor was a god traveling in a magic temple but who soon understood the basics of technology. Katarina (played by Adrienne Hill) became another example of the program's darkening atmosphere in the twelve-part story "The Daleks' Master Plan." While the heroes and new allies are escaping Daleks in a starship, a madman takes the young Trojan woman hostage in the airlock, demanding the ship land immediately on the nearby planet Kembel. Knowing that Kembel is ruled by Daleks, Katarina chooses to die rather than allow Steven and the Doctor to endanger themselves. Having learned how to operate the ship's airlock earlier, Katarina opens it, expelling herself and her captor into the cold void of outer space. The Doctor and Steven can only watch. The heroes didn't save the day and a traveling companion was dead.

As the adventure continues, the Doctor and Steven attempt to warn the people of the future that the Daleks are planning an all-out assault. A member of the Space Security Service, Bret Vyon—played by Nicholas Courtney, whom we'll see again—joins them. Vyon learns that Mavic Chen, his superior and appointed Guardian of the Solar System, has betrayed the human race to the monsters. Meanwhile, Chen dispatches Vyon's sister, Space Security operative Sara Kingdom, telling her that the man is a traitor. Never questioning her orders, Sara hunts down and kills her brother for the greater good, only learning the truth afterward. With her faith in the system shattered, she joins the Doctor and Steven, hoping to make amends by saving humanity.

Sara Kingdom (played by Jean Marsh) was the first militaristic character to join the Doctor's team. In contrast to young Katarina who had fallen into tropes of being a young damsel in distress, Kingdom was an adult and the first physically formidable woman on the TARDIS, which we wouldn't see again until the late 1970s with Leela. Terry Nation even intended for Sara Kingdom to spin off into a US TV series featuring an anti-Dalek task force. When that plan fell through, Nation absorbed some of the ideas into the "The Daleks' Master Plan" and, sadly, decided to end the character. In the final chapter, Sarah Kingdom is caught in the temporal onslaught of the Daleks' new weapon, the Time Destructor. She falls to the ground, aging rapidly into a skeleton, then dust. The Doctor defeats his enemies again, but the victory proves hollow in the wake of so many deaths.

As she appeared only in "The Daleks' Master Plan," some have argued that Sara Kingdom doesn't "count" as a companion. But during her stay, she visits multiple planets and time periods with the Doctor. What's more, the narrative implies that weeks pass during the 12-part story, and the novelization and various tie-ins state that Sara actually stayed on the TARDIS for months, leading to new stories produced later that filled in the gaps. In recent years, Jean Marsh—who was married to Third Doctor Jon Pertwee for a time before *Doctor Who* began and later fought the Seventh Doctor as Morgaine le Fey—has returned to the role of Sara Kingdom in multiple Big Finish audio dramas.

After "The Daleks' Master Plan" came "The Massacre of St. Bartholomew's Eve," the first television adventure to feature the Doctor with only one traveling companion at his side (and a male, at that). At the end of the story, the two must leave just before the event of the title takes place. The Doctor explains that many are fated to die, and admits he can't offer any evidence of the survival of Anne Chaplet, a servant girl whom Steven befriended. Steven challenges the Doctor, and leaves when the TARDIS next lands. The Doctor stands alone, musing aloud. "Now they're all gone. All gone. None of them could understand. Not even my little Susan . . . or Vicki. And as for Barbara and Chatterton . . . Chesterton . . . They were all too impatient to get back to their own time. And now, Steven. Perhaps I should go home, back to my own planet. But I can't! . . . I can't."

Then, a girl identical to Anne Chaplet walks into the TARDIS, believing it a real police box. Their new arrival confuses Steven, who has returned. The girl is Dorothea "Dodo" Chaplet of 1960s England, possibly Anne's descendant, which means she did survive. Filled with hope and amazement, Steve, the Doctor, and their new friend Dodo set off for adventure.

Jackie Lane—whom some sources have claimed was considered for the role of Susan years before—played Dodo, a friendly, jocular orphan who reminded the Doctor of his granddaughter. (Lane was later the theatrical agent for Fourth Doctor Tom Baker and Janet Fielding, who played the Doctor's companion Tegan Jovanka in the 1980s.) Dodo brought back a sense of fun after months of mostly darkness, but was it too little, too late?

GROWING DISCOMFORT

Doctor Who was taking its toll on William Hartnell. During "The Dalek Invasion of Earth," the ramp of a Dalek spaceship collapsed, and he fell to the ground, requiring complete bed rest for several days. The grueling production schedule that left little time for breaks exacerbated his arteriosclerosis, which made filming more difficult and prompted more line flubs. During "The Myth Makers," his beloved aunt Bessie died, but he couldn't take time off to attend her funeral.

Along with this, Hartnell grew concerned with the increasingly dark and violent storylines. Along with the obvious death and violence in "The Dalek Invasion of Earth," "The Escape," "The Daleks' Master Plan," and "The Massacre of St. Bartholomew's Eve," there had been an implication of rape in "The Time Meddler." Hartnell believed that the stories were dropping all educational and moral value for children and catering too much to the older audience. He argued over the matter with John Wiles, Verity Lambert's replacement producer, as well as with script editor Donald Tosh. Wiles argued that Hartnell took his role too seriously, adding that the actor was becoming more feeble and having increasing difficulty remembering his lines. Others have argued that Hartnell's health problems were exaggerated by Wiles to justify recasting the Doctor. Wiles and Tosh considered recasting the hero in the four-part story "The Celestial Toymaker," which aired halfway through the program's third year.

Michael Gough as the Toymaker, an immortal cosmic being, forced people into strange games where their lives and freedom were at stake. When the TARDIS crew found itself in the Toymaker's realm, the Doctor quickly recognized his surroundings and tried to leave. The Toymaker arrived and commented, "You're so innocent, Doctor. The last time you were here, I hoped you'd stay long enough for a game, but you had hardly time to turn around."

Tie-in media later expanded that the Toymaker had met the Doctor when the scientist was a young man, before he left his home planet. According to Donald Tosh, the original intention was that the Celestial Toymaker, like the Monk in "The Time Meddler," belonged to the Doctor's society. However, as we learned more about Time Lords, this became unlikely. Tie-in media expanded the character, and it became generally accepted by Whovians that the Toymaker is a cosmic force rather than native of Gallifrey, possibly a unique creature in the universe. The novel *The Quantum Archangel* refers to the Toymaker as an embodiment of a fundamental force in the universe, and, in the Big Finish audio drama *The Magic Mousetrap,* the Seventh Doctor calls him, "a spirit of mischief from the infancy of the universe."

As Wiles and Tosh originally intended for the story "The Celestial Toymaker," the villain makes the Doctor invisible. When he later returns the hero's visibility, we see the Doctor's appearance has been transformed, another of the Toymaker's tricks. Despite defeating the villain, the Doctor would remain trapped in his new body as he and his friends leave in the TARDIS.

The notion of replacing the lead of the program was surprising. Head of Serials Gerald Savory resisted the casting of a new Doctor and it was scrapped. During filming on "The Celestial Toymaker," Wiles and Tosh were replaced by new producer Innes Lloyd and script editor Gerry Davis, which led to several rewrites. This made filming more difficult, in addition to the fact that a legal issue arose when one character seemed to be based on Billy Bunter, the comedic lead character of a recent TV program that aired from 1952 to 1961. Despite this, the story was completed and Hartnell remained as the Doctor. There were later attempts to bring back the

Celestial Toymaker as a recurring villain, but they never came to fruition. Many older fans still hope that this strange trickster might appear again in the modern day show.

(Now here's a strange but fun bit of trivia. Peter Cushing once said in an interview that the existence of the Toymaker could explain how his film version of the Doctor could be part of the TV show's official continuity. According to Cushing, he actually played a future version of the Doctor who had been captured by the Toymaker and forced to relive his earlier adventures, his memory altered so he believed that he was a human literally named Dr. Who. It's not the strangest idea that's ever cropped up in the stories.)

Although Hartnell remained past the third season, Peter Purves didn't. In "The Savages," the second story after "The Celestial Toymaker," Steven Taylor helps bring peace between two warring races, after which he's asked to remain as leader of both. He thanks the Doctor for all their experiences and begins a new life. This made Steven the first companion who wasn't on his native planet when he joined the TARDIS crew and didn't return to his home when he left.

FAREWELLS

Despite the change in producer and script editor, Hartnell still protested that the show focused too much on villains and dark scenarios without also including educational value and morality. Lloyd and Davis claimed that the actor had become overly territorial about the program. Unlike Wiles, Innes Lloyd had more success in negotiating Hartnell's departure and the BBC decided that *Doctor Who* was successful enough to merit continuing even with a new lead actor. Varying accounts report the exact nature of Hartnell's exit. Rumors said he had finally grown too ill to continue and conceded to leave, but that ignores that he acted on stage afterward.

In BBC press releases, Hartnell said he left because he believed three years a good tenure to play the Doctor, and it was time for a change. Other BBC press releases and Innes Lloyd said it was a mutual decision due in part to Hartnell's desire to return to stage acting. Lloyd even claimed that Hartnell happily suggested Patrick Troughton as his replacement. But in a response to fan mail, the actor said, "I didn't willingly give up the part." In other interviews, he said that he had been sad to go but had been upset during the last few months of work and decided to leave because he couldn't agree with the direction of the show.

The final story of the third season was "The War Machines." After parting ways with Steven, the Doctor's time ship lands in 1966 London, just months after Dodo was first picked up. The two time travelers befriend sailor Ben Jackson and lab assistant Polly Wright, played by Michael Craze and Anneke Wills, the latter of whom was married to Michael Gough and was also once considered for the part of Susan. Following another fight against evil, Dodo goes away to the countryside to recuperate. Ben and Polly later arrive at the TARDIS and tell the Doctor that Dodo has decided to stay and sends her regards. Taken aback by this abrupt departure, the alien scientist storms into the ship. Curious about the man, and needing to return a TARDIS key he dropped earlier, Ben and Polly enter the police box. Before they realize that it's a time ship, the TARDIS is already taking flight as the show's third year ends.

Hartnell did only two stories in the fourth year of *Doctor Who*. When he left, Ben and Polly aided the audience in the transition from one Doctor to another.

BODIES WEARING THIN

Hartnell's final adventure aired in October 1966, entitled "The Tenth Planet" (before we realized that Pluto had fooled us all). The story, written by Kit Pedler and Gerry Davis, has the Doctor, Ben, and Polly discover a military station in Antarctica in 1986. The station is monitoring a space flight when suddenly a new planet appears, one with massive engines that make it a mobile fortress. The Cybermen are here, returning to a solar system that never knew of them until now.

In the third episode of their debut story, the Cybermen activate a weapon that begins draining half the Earth of its power. This weapon apparently affects the Doctor, who sways, moans, and collapses into unconsciousness. In the fourth and final episode, he recovers. Polly asks what happened, and the Doctor responds, "Oh, I'm not sure, my dear. Comes from

an outside influence. Unless this old body of mine is wearing a bit thin."
The adventure continues, and the Cybermen are defeated, but the old man
looks increasingly ill. As Ben assures him that the crisis is over, the Doctor
seems frightened and possibly delirious. "It's all over. That's what you said.
No, but it isn't all over. It's far from being all over . . . I must get back to
the TARDIS immediately!"

Back in his ship, the scientist activates the console. Some of the controls operate by themselves, as if the ship is preparing for what's about to
happen. The Doctor collapses to the floor, and Ben and Polly rush to his
side. As we hear the familiar sound of dematerialization—though we later
find out that the ship may not actually be flying this time—the hero's face
glows with a strange light. Moments later the glow is gone, leaving a new,
shorter, younger man in the Doctor's place, followed by a fade to black.

The Cybermen

"Aeons ago, our planets were twins. Then we drifted away from you on a journey to the edge of space. Now we have returned."
—CYBERMAN, FROM "THE TENTH PLANET" (1966)

The Cybermen debuted in "The Tenth Planet," going on to make several more appearances in the next few years. In the same story, we learn that their home planet Mondas had been a twin of our own world, sharing its orbit on the opposite side of the sun and giving rise to its own human race. But its orbit shifted, leading to environmental chaos. Before their planet completely broke free of Earth's solar system, the people of Mondas adapted to the new deadly environment by upgrading their bodies, finally becoming cyborgs wrapped in life-support suits, their brains surgically altered to remove pain and emotion. Now reborn as Cybermen, they converted Mondas into a planet-sized mobile fortress and set off to cyber-convert others.

The Cybermen were a quick hit with viewers, rivaling the Daleks. Sophie Aldred, who later played the Doctor's companion Ace, discussed the monsters in the documentary *The Story of Doctor Who*. "The Cybermen scared me [as a child] because they were vaguely human. They had these horrible mouths . . . and they were so sort of inhumanly human. I had nightmares about them, and my mum actually stopped me watching [*Doctor Who*] for a while."

"There's an almost vampiric quality to them," Peter Davison said at New York Comic Con 2012 in an interview for this book. "They were once like us, and now they're cold, and they want us all to be like them. Once it happens, once you become a Cyberman, you're not coming back. You can't just put your organs and the bits of your brain they took out back in. It's a terrifying idea, losing your identity as you become a killer."

Like the Daleks, they were monsters who couldn't be reasoned with. Seeing themselves as superior beings existing without fear or weakness, the Cybermen have often told their prey "You belong to us," and

"Resistance is useless." (On rare occasion, they said "Resistance is futile," which will strike a chord with fans of *Star Trek: The Next Generation*.)

While subtle details of the Daleks' appearance changed over the years, Cybermen have sported a wide variety of styles. The original version seemed like humans in life support gear, but starting with the second model the Cybermen were more robotic, with metal masks. A couple of models added a teardrop design to the eyes, reflecting the tragedy inherent in each Cyberman.

In the 1980s, the villains started to lose their robotic nature. Cyber-Leaders now gleefully declared, "Excellent," when things went well. Their life support coverings loosened and their helmets now had transparent portions that showed part of the human face underneath.

In the modern-day program, comic book artist Bryan Hitch helped design new Cybermen, who came from a version of Earth in a parallel universe. Aside from their brains and synthetic nervous systems, these Cybermen had no organic parts and often told their enemies, "You will be deleted." In the 2013 episode "Nightmare in Silver," they became more formidable than ever, now able to instantly upgrade themselves during battle. The episode also established that Cybermen now exist as part of a collective intelligence network called the Cyberiad.

As with all technology, the Cybermen are sure to continually evolve, making them threats for years to come.

7

Life Is Renewal

"There are some corners of the universe which have bred the most terrible things, things which act against everything we believe in. They must be fought."

—SECOND DOCTOR, FROM "THE MOONBASE" (1967)

For decades, it has been traditional on *Doctor Who* to end a lead actor's tenure at the close of a season, giving the audience months to prepare for a fresh start with the next Doctor. But this was the first such change to happen and the audience didn't yet know about the concept of "regeneration" (which wouldn't even be named until 1974). Viewers needed to be quickly sold on this new plot contrivance, so only a week passed after Hartnell's final episode before viewers learned what happened. When the next story, "The Power of the Daleks," starts, Ben is confused about the stranger who somehow has switched places with the Doctor. But Polly realizes the truth.

> **POLLY:** "Ben, do you remember what he said in the tracking room? Something about, 'This old body of mine is wearing a bit thin.'"
> **BEN:** "So he gets himself a *new* one?!"
> **POLLY:** ". . . Well, yes."

The stranger rises, groaning as he holds his head, stumbling around like a toddler unfamiliar with gravity. His clothes are too large, and the First Doctor's ring slips off his finger. He looks into a mirror; the First Doctor stares back but then the reflection changes to his own face. This new Doctor explains that he has undergone a process similar to when a caterpillar becomes a butterfly. "Life depends on change and renewal," he points out.

The TARDIS lands, and the Doctor ventures out, testing his new body and realizing that his vision has improved enough not to need glasses anymore. Only a few minutes pass before he finds himself involved in a new mystery. Ben parallels the skeptical viewer, not yet convinced that he likes this new version of the hero. As the story goes on, things start to feel familiar again, especially when Daleks appear and recognize the Doctor, despite his new face. By story's end, Ben and Polly accept that this man is indeed the same strange scientist they know and love, helping many viewers to do so as well. The era of the Second Doctor begins.

THE SAME TIME LORD

"I was dying. To save my own life, I changed my body, every single cell. But it's still me."

—THE TENTH DOCTOR,
FROM THE 2005 CHILDREN IN NEED MINI-EPISODE

In the hours following his transformation, the Second Doctor not only suffers partial amnesia—reading over a 500-year diary to remind himself of his past—but he also initially refers to his previous incarnation in the third person. By the end, he connects to his old memories and identifies as the Doctor, the same man as before. But why the initial confusion?

Dr. Travis Langley, a professor of psychology at Henderson State University, is also an avid *Doctor Who* fan and author of *Batman and Psychology: A Dark and Stormy Knight*. When we discussed the Second Doctor's initial identity confusion, Dr. Langley said, "We know from 'The Three Doctors' that Hartnell's Doctor is the first one; he didn't have previous versions of himself we didn't see. So when the Second Doctor arrives, this is someone who's just experienced regeneration for the first time and wasn't really expecting it that day. It makes sense that, at least at first, he feels disconnected from his old self. People who've had serious facial reconstructive surgery can experience a depersonalization effect. When people change their names, it can take a while to adjust to that concept emotionally. The temporary, partial amnesia that usually happens during regeneration can also enhance this. People who've suffered amnesia or brain damage will sometimes refer to who they were before the change as a different person. As his memories settle back into place, he feels more connected to his past."

ENTER PATRICK TROUGHTON

Today, people are far more used to recasting roles. But this was 1966, before anyone argued about the best James Bond and soap operas made a regular practice of replacing actors. While adults might understand, would the children react badly to a new Doctor?

If the Doctor were centuries old and came from a race of time traveling telepaths, who was to say he couldn't also alter his appearance under the right circumstances? Perhaps a side effect would be a slight alteration in personality, giving the next actor some freedom to do his own take on the character. You couldn't complain that the new Doctor wasn't exactly like the previous one if he wasn't supposed to be. Newman approved the idea and the team came to forty-six-year-old Patrick Troughton, who had been considered for the role of Johnny Ringo in the First Doctor adventure "The Gunfighters."

Born just north of London, Troughton attended the Embassy School of Acting at Swiss Cottage and entered the Leighton Rallius Studios on Long Island, New York, on scholarship. When World War II broke out, he took a ship back to Britain, but it hit a mine and sank. Fortunately, Troughton escaped on a lifeboat and enlisted in the Royal Navy in 1940. After the war, he delved into theater and television, becoming the first man to play Robin Hood on the small screen in 1953. Producer Innes Lloyd contacted Troughton about *Doctor Who* while the actor was shooting the film *The Viking Queen* in Ireland. He refused repeatedly, saying the audience wouldn't accept him and thinking the show couldn't last much longer than three years. As he told *Whovian Times* in 1984, "The phone kept on ringing, and they were saying, 'Come and play Doctor Who.' And I said, 'No, no, I don't want to play Doctor Who. . . . It wouldn't last more than six weeks more with me!' In the end, they kept on pushing the money up so much every day that at the end of the week I said, 'What am I doing? Of course, I'll do this part!'"

WHO IS THE SECOND DOCTOR?

They had their actor, but now the production team had to figure out what kind of man this new Doctor was. The new incarnation's debut story was "The

Power of the Daleks." Writer David Whitaker had to write it before Troughton had been cast, so he left much of the Doctor's actions and dialogue vague. Once on board, Troughton suggested becoming a bearded figure, so he could shave when the role finished and avoid typecasting. The production team veered toward an alien version of Sherlock Holmes, a sardonic, suspicious man fond of disguise, disconcerting to his companions, haunted by memories of the galactic war that had inspired him to flee his own people. These traumatic recollections were now fresh in his mind again, thanks to the experience of his transformation into a new man—which at that point was described as a "metaphysical change which takes place every five hundred or so years" for members of his race, when their bodies wear out with age.

Troughton wasn't keen on this new characterization, arguing it made the Doctor a verbose autocrat. He saw the figure as a great listener, attentive to everything and everyone around him, quickly sorting out information to draw his conclusions. Newman also disliked the idea of an outer space Sherlock Holmes and suggested that the new Doctor be a joking, whimsical "cosmic hobo" to contrast against Hartnell's gruff, serious nature. Troughton agreed and developed the idea with the production team, adding that he wanted to do a Charlie Chaplin-esque character that his own children would find entertaining. The Second Doctor would be mercurial, prone to outburst when excited, sometimes playing the coward or fool to manipulate his enemies. He would be warmer than his first incarnation, more a patient uncle than a moody grandfather.

At the same time, Troughton didn't want to dismiss completely the arrogance and danger Hartnell established. As he told *Doctor Who Magazine* in 1984, "I don't think [the Doctor] was a goody. He was a bit naughty, wasn't he? Of course, you've got to be on the right side when there's a villain about, but he was naughty all the same. If you're going to be totally moral, it's boring, so you have to color it a bit."

Script editor Gerry Davis later explained: "I thought it would be very interesting to have a character who never quite says what he means, who, really, uses the intelligence of the people he is with. He knows the answer all the time; if he suggests something, he knows the outcome. He is watching, he's really directing, but he doesn't want to *show* he's directing like the old Doctor."

Many changes happened behind the scenes during Troughton's second year. During "The Evil of the Daleks," Davis had worked with Peter Bryant as co-script editor. Davis then stepped down, with Victor Pemberton taking over for the fifth season's first story. Bryant took over as script editor for three stories before replacing Innes Lloyd as producer for the rest of the fifth season. At the same time, Derrick Sherwin became new script editor. In the middle of all of this, Sydney Newman left as head of Drama in 1967. Shaun Sutton, who had been one of Newman's first choices to produce *Doctor Who*, replaced him.

Newman joined the Associated British Picture Corporation as a producer, but after eighteen months none of his projects had been produced, and he counted the experience a waste of time. The BBC offered him a position as executive producer, but he decided instead to return to Canada, quickly gaining attention for his battles against content regulations on TV and radio. He died in 1997.

THE NEW LIFE BEGINS

"Our lives are different to anybody else's. That's the exciting thing, that nobody in the universe can do what we're doing."
—SECOND DOCTOR, FROM "TOMB OF THE CYBERMEN" (1967)

"I was shy to tell him while he was alive," Colin Baker, the Sixth Doctor, admitted to me at New York Comic Con 2009, "but Patrick was my favorite Doctor. We had stern Old Grumpy for a while, and we quite liked him. But suddenly, ooh, look at this. It's strange, old, impish Fun Uncle! And he had the hardest task of any of us later Doctors because he was the first who had to convince the audience that you could have a different version of the character suddenly appear—with a different actor—and it was still all right. That was quite a big thing, especially when people, young or old, can be quite territorial with an actor playing the role."

At San Diego Comic-Con in 2011, I asked Matt Smith, "Who is your favorite Doctor?" Without hesitation, he answered: "I love Patrick Troughton. 'Tomb of the Cybermen' is one of my favorite stories. It's so creepy. What I think is wonderful about Troughton is he's weird and peculiar, but he never asks you to find him weird and peculiar. He was a great actor, and I think the Cybermen are as scary as they've ever been in that one story. . . . There's something to love about all the Doctors, but when I went back and watched the older stories finally, Patrick Troughton quickly became my favorite. He's always prodding people into action and smiling as he thinks ahead."

Writer Dan Abnett reflected, "It's funny to think now what a risky idea that must have been to try. Because, of course, debating which version of the Doctor works for you and understanding that other people will have their own favorites, which is perfectly fine, is part of the joy of being a fan of *Doctor Who*. Anyone who thinks there's only one version that properly works is really saying they want to limit their enjoyment of the program."

While the First Doctor often double-checked the TARDIS console readings to make sure that the outside environment was safe, the Second Doctor absorbed this information with barely a glance and simply walked outside. The First Doctor occasionally tried to blend in, but the Second Doctor never minded standing out with his odd wardrobe.

The Second Doctor also carried a handy tool that hadn't been seen before: a sonic screwdriver. Through the use of sonic manipulation, it acted as a handy lock pick and cutting tool. In "The War Games," he actually used it simply as a screwdriver.

THE NEW COMPANIONS

In his second adventure, "The Highlanders," the Second Doctor befriends Jamie McCrimmon, a feisty Scottish bagpipe player from the eighteenth century. Jamie stayed with the Second Doctor for the rest of his incarnation, which, including a few later appearances, put 117 episodes under his belt, more than any other companion. In the 2006 episode "Tooth and Claw," the Doctor arrives in nineteenth-century Scotland and says his name is "Dr. James McCrimmon."

From the get-go, actor Frazer Hines gave a new take on the companion, acting more like a younger brother rather than an assistant. While he did occasionally long to return home, Jamie enjoyed his strange adventures and felt an obligation to keep the Doctor out of trouble.

In addition to Cybermen and corrupt humans, the Second Doctor and his crew fought fish people, shape shifters who had lost their identities, giant crab conquerors known as the Macra (encountered again in 2007), a group of robotic yeti, and a non-corporeal being called the Great Intelligence.

During the penultimate story of the program's fourth season, "The Faceless Ones," the TARDIS lands in London just before Ben and Polly had left with the First Doctor. Realizing they are now home and have lost no time at all, the two say their goodbyes. In the next story, "The Evil of the Daleks," the archenemies find Professor Waterfield, a nineteenth-century scientist developing his own form of time travel through the use of mirrors. This adventure was intended to serve as the possible last story of the Daleks, as Terry Nation was trying to sell the Daleks as a stand-alone series for US television and thought he needed to end their association with *Doctor Who*. The story also introduced the Dalek Emperor for the first time on-screen (with a very different design from the Emperor seen in the Dalek comic strips). The monsters force the Doctor to help with their experiments in improving their race. The Doctor winds up introducing a "human factor" into a select group of Daleks, granting them full emotional capacity. These friendly, peaceful Daleks even adopt names: Alpha, Beta, and Omega. The Doctor hopes they will spread the human factor to the rest of their race, but learns that he has been tricked. The Emperor will now use his research and time travel to introduce a "Dalek factor" into humanity's past, rewriting Earth history and making it another Dalek world.

The epic story ends with the Doctor and Jamie escaping as the three peaceful Daleks rebel against the Emperor, sacrificing themselves as their city is destroyed. During the chaos, Professor Waterfield is killed, leaving his daughter Victoria an orphan. The Doctor welcomes her aboard the TARDIS and the season ends with them all leaving, wondering if this is truly the end of the Dalek Empire. It would be five years before the monsters were seen again.

Deborah Watling played Victoria, a sweet girl longing for a new home. The Doctor was now traveling with two people who predated the twentieth century, making it a reversal of the team of Steven and Vicki. In the fifth season's premiere story, "Tomb of the Cybermen" (1967), considered by

Deborah Watling (Victoria) at Gallifrey One 2013

many to be Troughton's finest adventure, Victoria brought out a softer side of the Second Doctor when they both spoke of remembering the families they had lost.

As viewers saw romance developing between Barbara and Ian and then Ben and Polly, they also saw an emerging relationship between Jamie and Victoria. But Victoria wasn't suited for TARDIS travel and left in the 1968 story "Fury from the Deep," despite Jamie's protests.

In the final story of season five, "The Wheel in Space," the Doctor and Jamie meet and recruit Zoe Heriot, a young twenty-first-century scientist whose math skills seem to trump the Doctor's. Trained to listen only to logic, her imagination and understanding of risk are sorely lacking, so she still has much to learn. Wendy Padbury played Zoe, and in later years, as a theatrical agent, she represented Nicholas Courtney, Mark Strickson, and Colin Baker. She's also credited for helping to discover an actor at the National Youth Theater named Matt Smith.

Along with introducing Zoe, the fifth season is notable for the story "The Web of Fear." Along with bringing back the Great Intelligence, it featured the return of actor Nicholas Courtney, now playing Colonel Alistair Gordon Lethbridge-Stewart, a military man initially skeptical of the existence of aliens but who comes to see the truth and learns to trust the Doctor. No one realized at the time just how big a role Lethbridge-Stewart would become.

WRAPPING THINGS UP

Despite well-received characters and imaginative stories, including a journey to the Land of Fiction, there were increasing reports of scriptwriting problems, and viewing figures were falling noticeably. The members of the cast enjoyed working with one another, lightening the mood with practical jokes on occasion, but the shooting schedule exhausted them more and more, and rehearsal time reduced to just about nil.

The BBC decided to film the seventh season in color, but they didn't increase the production budget. This development worried producer Peter Bryant and Derrick Sherwin, who had become coproducer. The expense of monsters and special effects was becoming harder to handle now that the show didn't have historical adventures to buffer costs between visits to alien worlds.

Sherwin came up with the idea that the seventh season be Earthbound to save money on location shoots, costumes, and set constructions, adding that this would also make the stories easier for the audience to relate to. The Doctor would be exiled to Earth and paired with a military organization, ensuring a constant supply of action and drama.

Bryan and Sherwin discussed this new direction with script editor Terrance Dicks, and they decided this military organization would be led by Alistair Gordon Lethbridge-Stewart. To set things up, Lethbridge-Stewart appears again in the sixth season story "The Invasion," explaining that he's been promoted to brigadier and now heads the UK branch of UNIT—the United Nations Intelligence Task force. While the public believes UNIT to be intelligence gatherers, they actually deal with strange menaces and alien attacks. Tie-in media later suggested that Lethbridge-Stewart himself had spearheaded the creation of the organization after his first adventure with the Doctor.

Now, when the Doctor met up with UNIT during his exile, the familiarity of the organization would help ease fans into the new era. But while the creative team was setting the stage for the seventh season, Troughton decided that three years was a good run as the Doctor and staying longer increased the risk of typecasting. He spoke with Frazer Hines and Wendy Padbury, and all three decided to leave together at the end of the sixth season. Troughton later said that he also worried that *Doctor Who* was running its course as a program.

Along with starting the Doctor's exile, the producers decided to mark the end of Troughton's run with a story that finally revealed some secrets about the hero and his home planet.

"I WAS BORED . . ."

When one of the last two stories of the sixth season had to be scrapped, the Second Doctor's final tale, "The War Games," wound up extending into a ten-episode adventure. (It also featured Patrick Troughton's son David in the minor role of Private Moor.) The Doctor, Jamie, and Zoe land in what seems to be World War I, but they find soldiers from many other wars of Earth's history, all separated into different zones of this strange place where time is corrupted. A group of aliens has caused this chaos for their own ends, led by a man called the War Lord. One of the villains is a strange scientist called the War Chief, who has made his colleagues limited time travel units called SIDRATs—a backward play on TARDIS.

When the Doctor and War Chief lay eyes on each other, there is instant recognition. Later, the War Chief confronts the hero and remarks, "You may have changed your appearance, but I know who you are." This encounter gives us the first time since the Monk's appearance in January 1966 that we meet another of the Doctor's people. The conversation between the two alien scientists revealed yet more.

> **DOCTOR:** "I had every right to leave."
> **WAR CHIEF:** "Stealing a TARDIS. Oh, I'm not criticizing you. We're both two of a kind."
> **DOCTOR:** "We most certainly are not."

> **WAR CHIEF:** "We were both Time Lords. We both decided to leave our race."
>
> **DOCTOR:** "I have reasons of my own."
>
> **WAR CHIEF:** "Just as I have."
>
> **DOCTOR:** "Your reasons are only too obvious. Power."

It had taken six years, but now we finally knew the name of the Doctor's people: Time Lords. And at last, Newman's idea that the Doctor had stolen the TARDIS finally made it on-screen. As the story continues, the Doctor knows he can't fix this situation on his own. Realizing what the hero intends, the War Chief panics and warns him that they will both be punished by the Time Lords. The Doctor ignores this, transmitting a telepathic message into a cube that he sends off into space. He then tells Jamie and Zoe to hurry. He can't be there when his people arrive.

The War Chief is killed by his colleagues, and the Doctor races to the TARDIS, but this time there's no escape. The Time Lords warp time around them and seize control of the Doctor's ship, forcing him to return to his home planet. He materializes in a TARDIS docking bay, surrounded by time ships not bothering to disguise their outer shells.

Jamie and Zoe don't understand why the Doctor fears his own people, and he finally explains. Time Lords hardly ever use their great power and technology, usually choosing only to observe the universe from afar. That wasn't enough for the Doctor. "I was bored," he says. So he stole a TARDIS and left. But the Time Lords don't care for interfering in the development of other races, and, as the Doctor reluctantly admits, "I do tend to get involved with things."

After removing the War Lord and his colleagues from existence, the Time Lords put the Doctor on trial. He argues that, while he has interfered, he has done so in positive ways and has helped to preserve life in the universe. Using telepathic screens, he displays the many monsters he has faced, including the time traveling Daleks. The Time Lords admit they have much to consider. Before passing sentence, they allow Jamie and Zoe to say goodbye to the Doctor. The humans are returned to the moment just after the Doctor recruited them. After they each say a heartfelt goodbye, we learn what the Doctor has already realized: The Time Lords will wipe their memories. They will have no idea of the many adventures they shared nor of the strong friendships they developed.

The Doctor is criminal and yet has done good things. The Time Lords also note that the Doctor has a great interest in Earth, a planet which seems to come under threat often. So rather than execution, they sentence him to exile on Earth (perhaps as a form of community service, helping to protect the human race). His mind will be altered so he can't recall the secrets of the TARDIS and the ship will have its travel abilities removed. As part of the sentence, the Doctor will adopt a new body. To show they're not heartless, they offer him several possible new faces.

The hero stalls by protesting each face and the Time Lords grow weary. The room goes dark and we hear the Doctor cry out, "What are you doing? NO! STOP!" All fades to black, and so ends the show's sixth year. Six months will pass before we meet the Third Doctor.

LOST IN TIME

William Hartnell introduced us to the Doctor, the Daleks, the Cybermen, and the TARDIS. Patrick Troughton convinced us that it was all right to have multiple versions of the same hero, and introduced us to UNIT and the Time Lords. Together, they starred in 253 episodes during the first six years of *Doctor Who*, totaling fifty stories. Sadly, to date only twenty-three of these stories are preserved in their entirety.

During the 1960s and 1970s, the BBC and ITV had a regular practice of destroying and "junking" footage they saw no need to preserve, freeing up limited storage space. This affected many shows, including Sydney Newman's other creation *The Avengers*. Whovian and record producer Ian Levine was able to stop the junking of *Doctor Who* footage, and the wiping policy ended in 1978. Some Third Doctor episodes were missing, but over the years they were all recovered (though copies only existed in black and white). Unfortunately, Levine's efforts were too late to save most of the program's first six years. Because of *Doctor Who*'s popularity and international broadcasts, several copies were found in different countries and in private collections, but the recovery has not been complete. To date, there are still 106 episodes missing from the First and Second Doctors, including ten full stories.

With other shows, it's bad enough to miss an entire episode, but since classic *Doctor Who* dealt in multi-episode arcs, this meant that many stories had gaps or were missing their final chapters. Out of Patrick Troughton's first two years as the Doctor, only one story "Tomb of the Cybermen" was preserved entirely, thanks to a copy found in Hong Kong in 1992.

But while episodes for many programs were lost entirely, the audio of all *Doctor Who* adventures was preserved because many fans recorded the sound off their television sets so they could listen again later and remember the story (as this was before reruns). These recordings were remastered by the fan-run group the Doctor Who Restoration Team, initially formed in 1992 to restore some of Jon Pertwee's episodes. The BBC converted the remastered soundtracks into audio plays released on CD, with an actor narrating what the audience couldn't see. Some of the missing episodes were presented on VHS by playing the audio reel while displaying photographic stills and recovered clips, with a ticker tape at the bottom describing the action. In recent DVD releases such as "The Reign of Terror," "The Tenth Planet," and "The Invasion," the missing chapters have been animated.

For years, the BBC, the Doctor Who Restoration Team, and many fans have made efforts to locate copies of missing *Doctor Who* episodes, occasionally with success. These efforts have led to the complete restoration of eight stories that were previously incomplete or lost. The children's show *Blue Peter*, which has had a long association with promoting *Doctor Who* and counted Peter Purves as one of its early hosts, offered life-size Daleks to anyone who recovered a missing episode. In December 2012, the magazine *Radio Times* announced that it was on the hunt for the remaining missing footage, inviting readers to join the effort.

Time will tell if fans will one day have access to a complete library of classic *Doctor Who*.

8
Time-Locked!

"I wouldn't like to have to order you, Doctor."
"I wouldn't advise you to try."
—BRIGADIER LETHBRIDGE-STEWART AND THE THIRD DOCTOR,
FROM "THE GREEN DEATH" (1973)

In January 1970, the seventh season opened by reintroducing the audience to UNIT. In "Spearhead from Space," Brigadier Lethbridge-Stewart recruits scientist Dr. Liz Shaw, played by Caroline John—whose husband, Geoffrey Beevers, later played an incarnation of the Master. The Brig explains that aliens exist and are coming to Earth more often now that it's drawing attention to itself with radio transmissions and satellites (an idea the Tenth Doctor repeats in 2005's "The Christmas Invasion"). Before he can convince Dr. Shaw, though, Lethbridge-Stewart discovers that the Doctor has returned, with a new face and gaps in his memory.

After the soldier and the scientist stop another alien threat, Lethbridge-Stewart asks if he can rely on the Doctor's continued help. The Doctor agrees to act as UNIT's scientific advisor, "Dr. John Smith." In exchange, he wants to use UNIT's labs and resources, hoping he can repair the TARDIS despite his memory gaps. Also, he has grown quite fond of an old roadster during this latest adventure, and now wants a car of his own. The deal is struck and a new era of *Doctor Who* begins.

Though Terrance Dicks remained as script editor, Bryant had left as producer just before "The War Games." Sherwin produced that story and "Spearhead from Space" but then left, turning the reins over to Barry Letts. The Third Doctor became a true product of the collaboration between Letts and Dicks, though sometimes they disagreed on the character. Letts enjoyed utilizing character flaws to drive the drama, whereas Dicks wanted to highlight the Doctor's heroism. The man who made it work in the end was actor Jon Pertwee.

Growing up, Pertwee was expelled repeatedly from schools for his behavior. At the Royal Academy of Dramatic Art, he was accused of writing about tutors and teachers on bathroom walls and was expelled finally for his attitude. Pertwee joined the Royal Navy and served as a naval intelligence operative during World War II, reporting directly to Churchill and working alongside Ian Fleming, author of the James Bond novels. After the war, Pertwee became a character actor and comedian, often performing on radio.

Hearing that Troughton was leaving the show, Pertwee suggested his agent look into the role, and was surprised to learn his name was already on a short list of candidates. When first choice Ron Moody turned down the part, Peter Bryant approached Pertwee, explaining the show's new direction: more James Bond than the Wizard of Oz. In an interview for the *Jon Pertwee Fan Club News* (1975), Pertwee explained: "I asked Shaun Sutton, Head of Drama at the BBC and an old friend of mine, how he wanted me to play [the Third Doctor]. He said, 'Well, as you.'"

In this incarnation, the Doctor becomes quite the gadget man, cobbling together devices to sense time-field disturbances or sedate dinosaurs. He alters the sonic screwdriver to have more uses, such as measuring for radiation, scanning for alarm systems and traps, and acting as a hypnotic aid. His Edwardian roadster, affectionately called "Bessie," is modified with extra features and increased speed. Though William Hartnell's dear departed aunt shared the name Bessie, it seems unlikely to be more than a coincidence, as the creative team of the time didn't know the actor well, it now having been over three years since he'd left.

Costume designer Christine Rawlins deliberately went for a very different look to contrast Pertwee from the previous Doctors, seeing him as an elegant, romantic adventurer who might have left a dinner party early to stop alien invaders. Pertwee approved of the direction, and so the Third Doctor wore bright frilly shirts and colorful velvet coats, assuming the Edwardian revival fashions of Carnaby Street and Kings Road that had infiltrated the fashion mainstream in the 1960s. As a result, some fans nicknamed him the Dandy Doctor. Not averse to wearing capes from time to time, he seemed a gentleman superhero.

Frustrated by his exile, the Third Doctor was as short-tempered as his first incarnation, snapping at people when they questioned him, criticizing planet Earth as an annoyance to tolerate. This impatience also affected how he confronted danger. When attackers proved immune to reason, the Third Doctor disarmed them through martial arts, claiming he had mastered Venusian aikido, occasionally calling it Venusian karate. (Earth's form of aikido was introduced to Britain in 1955 and karate began its popularity there in 1965).

THE UNIT FAMILY

Derrick Sherwin said that UNIT was partly created in response to how taking on most of the show's lines had unduly exhausted Troughton. To avoid this with Jon Pertwee, UNIT included the Brigadier, the jocular Captain Mike Yates (played by Richard Franklin), the sweet and deferential Sergeant Benton (played by John Levene), and Liz Shaw.

Like Zoe, Shaw was a scientist, but she was actually paid to act as the Doctor's assistant. While the character came to appreciate the Doctor's intellect, Shaw didn't care for having her beliefs constantly put into doubt by his claims of alien life forms and advanced technology. Writers created Dr. Shaw as a contrast to the female companions of the past few years, criticized by some as weak characters serving primarily to ask questions and fall into danger. Terrance Dicks thought Liz's confident disposition made for interesting drama with the Doctor, though some viewers found her unnecessarily argumentative. Caroline John later joked that she had prepared for the role by learning many scientific concepts and terms only to discover that she'd done more research than the writers themselves.

Along with Liz, the character who spent the most time with the Third Doctor was the Brigadier. The two clashed often in how they approached matters, yet did take time to listen to one another and respected each other's experience. A major rift occurred in the story "Doctor Who and the Silurians," when a tribe of reptilian humanoids decided to wage war on humanity. The Doctor failed to broker peace, so Lethbridge-Stewart had the tribe bombed. The Doctor was appalled but later came to trust the Brig again, the two becoming friends who enjoyed an odd camaraderie. When the soldier saved the Doctor's life, he complained that the man always waited until the "nick of time," prompting the Brig to smile and remark, "I'm happy to see you too, Doctor."

Since viewership had been declining, producers understood that the BBC would cancel the program if this seventh season didn't do well. But the new premise succeeded, not only bringing some old fans back to the fold but also attracting new viewers who preferred an action scientist with military backing over a strange homeless traveler in an unreliable ship. Not everyone cared for these changes, though. Verity Lambert often said that having the Third Doctor recognized by humans as an authority and trusted advisor to military forces was a mistake. In the commentary for "The Time Meddler," she explained: "I think the whole thing about *Doctor Who* and one of the things why kids really responded to him is he was completely anti-establishment, and they could actually relate to the fact that . . . he went his own way."

Ninth Doctor Christopher Eccleston later recalled seeing this Doctor as a young child and not caring for what an authority figure he seemed to be.

But the Third Doctor struck a chord with many, as evidenced by the viewership, and writer Dan Abnett argues that this unusual new premise is what made Pertwee's incarnation so interesting. As he sees it, "The Third Doctor was given authority and a UNIT ID, but he was still someone who thought people should've listened to him more anyway. He was working with the military but it was under protest. He argued against the Brigadier and UNIT policies. Seeing him angry at being in a situation he didn't want to be in and couldn't escape, but still be able to put his issues aside and save the day when he had to, that made him a proper hero to me. He wanted to be anywhere but Earth sometimes but he'd still risk his life to save it. And his humor was different from the first two Doctors, but it was still there."

A phrase that has become associated with the Third Doctor is "Reverse the polarity of the neutron flow." In actuality, he only said this line twice on-screen, though he did often solve problems by reversing a device's polarity in some fashion. As Pertwee disliked technobabble, he had complimented Terrance Dicks on writing the phrasing, thinking it sounded good and scientific enough without being complicated. Pertwee made sure to use the line again when he reprised his role for the 1989 UK touring stage play *Doctor Who: The Ultimate Adventure*. When Sixth Doctor Colin Baker later took over the role, the line was altered to say "Reverse the linearity of the proton flow."

The phrase has been referenced in other science fiction franchises. In 2000, a *Fantastic Four* comic used it, only for a child in the story to point out that neutrons have no polarity.

A NEW ASSISTANT

Producer Barry Letts didn't like having an opinionated adult as the Doctor's aide. Caroline John's contract was not renewed and in the eighth season's premiere story, "Terror of the Autons," the Brigadier informs the Doctor that Shaw asked to be reassigned, feeling she can be more valuable elsewhere. Lethbridge-Stewart assigns a new assistant, young Jo Grant, skilled in lock picking, self-defense, and piloting helicopters. Jo remained for three more seasons.

Katy Manning, who played Jo Grant, had begun her television career just the year before. She was quickly welcomed by Pertwee and their rapport was clear on-screen. Though nearsighted, Manning didn't tell anyone and didn't wear glasses on set. During filming one day, she ran across a field and crashed into a tree, knocking herself unconscious. From then on, the Doctor usually held Jo's hand whenever they ran across a field.

Jo wore her heart on her sleeve and her empathy helped bring the Doctor back to a softer disposition. Though she occasionally joked about being a bad student, she showed cleverness on several occasions and understood alien science better than the Brigadier. Nevertheless, some criticized the character for stepping backward in the evolution of the female companion.

TEMPORARY ESCAPES

"If I could leave, I would, if only to get away from people like you. And your petty obsessions!"

—THIRD DOCTOR, FROM "THE CLAWS OF AXOS" (1971)

Although he didn't wish to end the Doctor's exile too soon, Barry Letts worried that having only UNIT stories each season risked predictability and could veer too far from the original idea of an alien traveler. As a result, the eighth and ninth seasons involved the Doctor occasionally leaving Earth either because he forced the TARDIS into an uncontrolled test flight, or the Time Lords sent him on a mission. This could explain why the Time Lords sent him to Earth in exile yet allowed him to keep his time ship rather than just stranding him completely. The Doctor didn't appreciate this treatment, saying he felt like a "galactic yo-yo."

But Jo Grant's debut story also introduced a new recurring enemy who would keep him quite busy. Many had compared the odd friendship of the Doctor and the Brigadier to that of Sherlock Holmes and John Watson. Now, the Doctor would meet his Moriarty.

9

The First Master

"I have so few worthy opponents. When they're gone, I always miss them."

—THE MASTER, FROM "TERROR OF THE AUTONS" (1971)

"There are so many great monsters, but I loved the original Master," Peter Davison told me at Gallifrey One in 2011. "I didn't work with him, of course; I worked with Anthony Ainley. He did a great job, and so did John Simms. But Roger Delgado, he was the Master of my childhood. He was just so perfect, and he brought something new to the program, which I'd been watching since the first airing. I hope we get a new Master. *Doctor Who* has to have the Master, don't you think?"

There are different types of arch-enemies, and the best heroes tend to have more than one. In the past, the Doctor had encountered the Monk and the War Chief, but neither hit the right note to become a major recurring character. This new villain derived directly from Sherlock Holmes's opposite number. Although Professor James Moriarty remains the most notorious enemy of Doyle's famous consulting detective, he died in the same story wherein he debuted. He didn't have time to develop into an archenemy in the way we often expect now. One day Holmes simply explained to Watson that for several years he had been waging a hidden war against a criminal mastermind named Moriarty and that the villain had organized some of the cases that he'd solved. With this bit of retroactive history, Doyle quickly gave his readers a character who had a brilliant, calculating mind like Holmes, but who chose the darker path.

The Master debuted in a similar fashion. Though we'd never seen him before, he and the Doctor clearly had a history, much more personal than the relationship between the great detective and the professor. The creative team originally considered making this villain a female—perhaps evoking Irene Adler instead—but decided against it, believing that casting a man enhanced the chilling sense of similarity to the Doctor. They also doubted whether the audience would accept a woman as such a powerfully evil force.

This male enemy would seem almost a physical manifestation of our hero's dark side. While the hero had a sonic screwdriver, this villain wielded a cylindrical device known as a tissue compression eliminator. The weapon, which resembled a magic wand, shrank its target, causing victims to scream as their organs compressed. The painful method of killing left doll-sized corpses as a bizarre calling card.

Like the Doctor, this villain wouldn't have a name but rather an academic title, one that also declared his ultimate goal. His catchphrase became, "I am the Master and you will obey me."

CASTING EVIL

The role of this dark enemy went to Roger Delgado. Born in London to French and Spanish parents, he had acted onstage during the '30s and served in the war starting in 1940. He appeared in Charlton Heston's 1972 *Antony and Cleopatra,* among other films, as well as numerous television programs. Producer Barry Letts personally selected Delgado for the role, believing he would imbue the character with the proper gravitas and sinister authority. Letts knew the audience would have no trouble believing he could match wits with the Doctor.

Sadly, Delgado gave few interviews before his untimely death, but he did speak to *Doctor Who Magazine* about his character:

> I love playing villains. I am chosen by directors to play wicked men because I have a beard, a menacing chin, and piercing eyes. I was thrilled to be offered the part of the Master as I had tried three times to break into *Doctor Who,* but the scope offered by the part was way above any other I had considered.
>
> I enjoyed this chap who was really more than just a Moriarty to the Doctor, and I could tell from fan letters that I was the man they loved to hate. There were even one or two kids who complained that I wasn't wicked enough!

Fans may have loved to hate the character, but Pertwee felt rather differently about the man who played him. "Roger was one of the most gentle men I've ever known," Pertwee told his *Fan Club Newsletter* in 1975. "He was the most courteous person—he had a temperament, but always it was at himself in rehearsals. He would go absolutely berserk with anger if he couldn't get something right, but always at himself, never at anyone else. He was charming, polite, kind, and considerate."

At this beginning of the program's eighth year, in the story "Terror of the Autons," we hear the sound of a TARDIS landing. But instead of the familiar blue box, a horsebox trailer materializes and the Master emerges, dressed from neck to toe in black. Using hypnotic abilities, he quickly gathers henchmen and hatches his plans, while the Time Lords warn the Doctor about his presence on Earth.

Eventually, a face-to-face confrontation occurs. Like Holmes and Moriarty in their first meeting, the two respectfully and politely threaten each other, the Master remarking that he will regret having to kill the hero because "You see, Doctor, you're my intellectual equal. Almost." "Terror of the Autons" ends with the Master escaping UNIT but not Earth. The Doctor sabotages the villain's TARDIS, waylaying them both on the planet. The war has begun.

As the adventures progress, we learn a bit more about their relationship. The Doctor reluctantly admits that the two attended "the academy" on Gallifrey together, and during the story "The Mind of Evil," the two enemies must temporarily join forces. Seeing how easily they fall into a partnership gives us a glimpse into what they must have been like years before.

The Master's schemes were more majestic than those of other monsters that plagued the program. In "The Time Monster," he tries to control a creature born outside physical reality, native to the space-time vortex through which all TARDIS ships travel. In "Colony in Space," the villain uncovers a doomsday weapon that could wipe out solar systems. In "The Claws of Axos," he again joins forces with the Doctor, this time against the cunning Axons.

PEELING THE LAYERS

Pertwee and Delgado, friends off-screen, developed an even closer relation-ship through *Doctor Who*. In a 1993 reunion special, *Return to Devil's End*, Pertwee commented on their friendship.

> He was one of my greatest personal friends. One thing I've said many, many times before is that Roger Delgado was the bravest man that I ever knew because he was basically a coward. And I don't mean that in a derogatory fashion, he was just a natu-rally very, very nervous man. Roger was frightened of his own shadow, yet look at that face. I mean, he terrified the bejeezus out of anybody.

Many felt Delgado's positive influence, in particular John Levene, who por-trayed UNIT Sergeant Benton, and who spoke, also in *Return to Devil's End*, of how the actor helped him find his footing on the show.

> I had a bit of a problem with my own decision as to whether I was a good actor or not. Not that I necessarily needed to be good, but I used to worry the other cast by saying I don't think I can handle certain scenes. And one day we were on the set of "The Daemons" here, and I said to Roger, "You know, we have a couple of scenes together," and he said, "John, just let the day take its own course. Just play it as you feel it."
>
> I always remember the scene where he said, "the resourceful Sgt. Benton." He made me feel very important and made me like myself a little better.

Indeed, in multiple stories the Master remarked on the resourcefulness of UNIT and of Sergeant Benton in particular. He even regarded the Brigadier as a worthy opponent. These touches kept the Master from devolving into a one-dimensional villain, along with the character's Doctoresque sense of humor—suggesting the Brigadier take precautions against a nuclear explo-sion by placing "sticky tape on the window" and once remarking flippantly,

"I don't know, rocket fire at long range . . . Somehow it lacks that personal touch."

THE THIRD LAW

"The universe needs me and I need all that it has to offer. I am the Master! That is who I am, what I am, and what I need to be!"
—THE MASTER, FROM THE BIG FINISH AUDIO PLAY *MASTER* (2003)

Barry Letts and Robert Sloman, a playwright, journalist, and friend of Letts's wife, wrote the five-episode story "The Daemons," closing the eighth year. Letts had originated the concept of the story as an audition scene written for the character of Jo Grant, eager to take the Doctor into a different kind of danger. He thought a story of supernatural evil would nicely shake up the usual science fiction style of the show. At the time, the BBC frowned on producers and other production staff writing for their own shows, so Letts and Sloman used the pen name "Guy Leopold." Sloman's son was named Guy, and Letts's middle name was Leopold.

The plot revolved around the Master taking up residence in the village of Devil's End, posing as a vicar named Mr. Magister, the Latin word for his name. Originally, the Master was to perform a ceremony at the altar of the church to summon a demon named Azal. He would demand this demon's power, becoming an invincible conqueror. The Doctor, used to scientific realities, would find himself unnerved by the magical forces he couldn't predict.

But script editor Terrance Dicks feared this plotline would induce religious viewers—not keen to see the Master conducting a demonic ritual in a church—to target the show, which was already criticized on occasion for frightening younger viewers. The church setting became a church crypt and then an underground cave that merely resembled a crypt. Rather than call Azal a genuine demon, the narrative explained that he was an alien from the planet Daemos, roughly sixty thousand light-years from Earth.

Azal and his people the Daemons had technology that only seemed supernatural, an idea taken from science fiction writer Arthur C. Clarke's Three Laws, the third being: "Any sufficiently advanced technology is indistinguishable from magic." An ancient race, the Daemons traveled across the universe, interacting with sentient races of many worlds. They visited Earth roughly one hundred thousand years ago and inspired many myths about supernatural creatures.

But these science fiction explanations still weren't good enough for the BBC, which said that *Doctor Who* was not allowed to reference God in the script on the chance that viewers would find it blasphemous. Despite this, it was still acceptable to reference the Devil, for the Master to masquerade as a vicar, and for the Doctor to claim he was a wizard.

Despite the BBC's concerns, "The Daemons" became an instant classic and attracted over eight million viewers for each episode. Months later, on December 28, 1971, BBC One rebroadcast the five-part story in its entirety, the first repeat of a *Doctor Who* adventure. This attracted 10.5 million viewers, the highest rating the show had received since 1965.

"The Daemons" also features Brigadier Lethbridge-Stewart's most famous moment. Confronted by a living gargoyle, a deadly creature animated by Azal's power, the Brig, not showing a hint of concern, calls over a man named Jenkens and nonchalantly says, "Chap with the wings there. Five rounds rapid." Jensen fires, and this hilariously fearless moment captured many fans. Years later, Nicholas Courtney titled his memoirs *Five Rounds Rapid!* Terrance Dicks had initially cut the line but brought it back at Letts's request.

"The Daemons" also enabled later writers to delve into supernatural themes without disrupting the Doctor's insistence on rational explanations for seemingly supernatural events. In "The Pyramid of Mars," the Fourth Doctor explains to Sarah Jane Smith that Egypt's ancient deities were actually aliens known as the Osirans, whose powers dwarfed those of the Time Lords. In the Seventh Doctor TV story "Battlefield," our hero fights the witch Morgaine le Fey and another demon-like entity. In the 2007 episode "The Shakespeare Code," the Tenth Doctor fights three witches, explaining at several points how their magical powers are just a different form of science hidden behind superstitious ritual. The Tenth Doctor episode "The Satan Pit" directly referenced the planet Daemos, as the Doctor wondered if he'd met the very creature that had inspired the Daemons' preference for devil-like forms.

ENDINGS

The Master had debuted at the beginning of 1971 and had starred in all five stories that year. "The Daemons" ended with UNIT capturing the villain at last. "We decided his regular appearance was a mistake," Pertwee said in the third issue of his *Fan Club Newsletter*, "because I was always defeating him, which just made him look stupid. I think sometimes the Master should have defeated me temporarily at the end of a story—such as in 'The Sea Devils,' but on a grander scale."

During his interview with the *Jon Pertwee Fan Club Newsletter*, the actor revealed an idea discussed behind the scenes. "It was suggested by Nick Courtney that the reason we didn't kill each other was that fundamentally we knew there was some connection between us. Then we wanted it to turn out by a Time Lord giving the game away that we were, in fact, brothers, which would have been a rather clever idea." But the creative team decided not to pursue this.

After appearing only occasionally over the next two years, Delgado decided to leave the role of the Master behind and focus on other work. Discussing it with Letts and Dicks, the actor had a choice between vanishing and leaving it open for his character to return at some later date or ending the Master in an epic final battle. Delgado eagerly chose the latter.

Around the same time, Pertwee had decided to leave the program after his fifth year as the Doctor, so a plan formed. The final story would involve yet another confrontation with the Master and would end with his death. But it would be ambiguous whether the villain had been destroyed by his hubris or if, at the last minute, he had sacrificed himself to prevent the Doctor from dying instead. Either way, the Doctor would survive, but would be so injured that he had to regenerate his body to survive. Pertwee and Delgado would leave at the same time, marking the end of an era together. The adventure would be called "The Final Game," a reference to Arthur Conan Doyle's "The Final Problem," in which Holmes and Moriarty first meet and then seemingly die in battle.

But none of this came to pass. On June 18, 1973, while shooting the never-completed movie *Bell of Tibet* in Turkey, Roger Delgado, age fifty-five, died along with two film technicians when their chauffeur-driven car went off the road and over a ravine. His sudden and unexpected death shocked family, friends, and fans. "He and his wife, Kismet, were very close friends to Ingeborg and me, and we loved them dearly," Pertwee said. "I was desperately shaken when he was killed. We looked after Kismet until she managed to get herself together, and we still see a lot of her . . . I loved working with him, and still miss him tremendously."

Even though regeneration meant they could recast the Master without much explanation, writers waited over three years before bringing the character on-screen again, and from then on they used him more sparingly. Delgado's version of the Master is remembered fondly to this day, his incarnation appearing in different novels and comic strips. One story has the evil Time Lord journey to the Land of Fiction and confront Professor Moriarty, criticizing him as a one-dimensional antagonist introduced for the sake of convenience. It's an interesting villain indeed who can overcome the character that inspired him.

With his old adventures now on DVD, a new generation of fans is discovering the original Master, who set the path that the rest have followed. In *Return to Devil's End,* John Levene spoke about his departed friend, who had helped him feel more secure as an actor. "I love Roger because he was the most honest and decent man I'd ever met. His morals were very high, and it's ironic that someone who loved God and loved the world should play the most evil man in the world."

10

Doctor Meets Doctor

"Ah, the Doctor. Wonderful chap. All of them."
—LETHBRIDGE-STEWART, FROM "THE FIVE DOCTORS" (1983)

After three years of having the Doctor largely time-locked on Earth, Barry Letts was ready to give the hero his freedom again and phase out UNIT's dominance in the program. Each of Pertwee's seasons began with a major story: The seventh season started with the Doctor's exile and joining UNIT; the eighth season opened with the debut of the Master; and the ninth season had begun with "Day of the Daleks," in which the Doctor dealt with alternate futures and fought the monsters for the first time in five years. Letts wanted the tenth season to involve a menace that threatened all of the Time Lords. The story would also feature a new TARDIS interior, since Letts hadn't liked the previous one that Pertwee used and it had warped in storage anyway.

But the ideas didn't stop there. For years, many fans had written to suggest that Hartnell or Troughton return for a story, arguing that the Doctor could visit his younger selves through time travel. Barry Letts had habitually dismissed this but now considered it a good way to celebrate the tenth anniversary.

The original story was called "Deathworld," revealing a conflict between the Time Lords and a powerful group known as the Federation of Evil, led by a living avatar of Death itself. The Time Lords, wishing to avert all-out war, send the Doctor and his first two incarnations to Underworld, a strange realm that the Federation calls home. There, the three Doctors fight their way through reanimated corpses as well as representations of the mythological cyclops Polyphemus, the Hindu goddess Kali, and the Four Horsemen of the Apocalypse before finally joining forces against Death itself.

Letts decided that the Underworld setting and its inhabitants were too bizarre for the show. Another suggestion conjured a villain called Ohm, a name taken from the measure of electrical resistance, which also spelled "Who" upside down and backward. Letts disliked this idea as well since the Doctor's real name wasn't "Who." So "Ohm" evolved into "Omega," a reference to the Greek letter (Ω) that represents Ohms and has been used at times as a symbol for Death, following a passage in the Book of Revelations: "I am the Alpha and the Omega, the first and the last, the beginning and the end."

STRANGE REUNION

As the story "Deathworld" changed, it was retitled "The Three Doctors" and opened the tenth season of *Doctor Who* on December 30, 1972. The next three episodes followed in January. The adventures featured forces from an antimatter reality invading our universe and placing Gallifrey under siege. Unable to leave their world, the Time Lords decide that only the Doctor can save them. But he'll need help and no other Time Lords can aid him, so they must break the First Law of Time, which states that no one should encounter an older or younger self. Using great amounts of energy, the Time Lords snatch up the First and Second Doctors from other points in history and transmit them to the Third Doctor's side.

The adventure offered more detail about Gallifrey, showing hints of the Time Lord government and bringing back one of the Second Doctor's judges in the role of Chancellor. Viewers were introduced to a special security force on the planet that ignored the laws of non-interference and the First Law of Time when the circumstances warranted it. We also learned how, long ago, the Gallifreyan named Omega had been a solar engineer whose experiments in harnessing a supernova created the power source for Gallifrey's original time ships.

Behind the scenes, Hartnell and Troughton happily returned for the anniversary. Initially, the script gave each Doctor an equal part to play in saving the day, but Hartnell's declining health prevented him from coming to the studio. To involve him still, the script changed so that the First Doctor was caught in a time eddy—a distortion in space and time. The Time Lords couldn't expend any more energy to free him; he could only advise his two future selves through the TARDIS scanner screen. Although Hartnell was able to meet Troughton and Pertwee for a promotional photo shoot, his scenes were filmed entirely separately at BBC's Ealing Studios, with someone holding cue cards for him. A common fan myth is that they were shot at his home in his garage.

Some thought that Jamie and Zoe might return with the Second Doctor, and Terrance Dicks apparently suggested a romantic attraction between Jamie and Jo. But Frazer Hines had a conflict in his schedule, and Pertwee objected to too many characters in one story.

While some criticized the anniversary story for being padded in areas and simplistic, many fans loved seeing the three Doctors interact, particularly as they engaged in many amusing arguments. Along with adding humor to the story, these interactions highlighted the differences in each Doctor.

The convergence of Doctors became a tradition. On the twentieth anniversary, the TV special "The Five Doctors" aired. Hartnell had died in 1975, so Richard Hurndall played the First Doctor in the story, joining forces with Pertwee, Troughton, and Peter Davison's Fifth Doctor. Tom Baker had decided not to participate, so footage from the unaired story "Shada" explained that the Fourth Doctor was trapped outside of space and time. The TV story was also the first to feature both Daleks and Cybermen (though sadly, they didn't fight).

Doctor Who was off the air during the thirtieth anniversary, but the surviving Doctors appeared together on the charity special "Dimensions in Time" (more about that later). In 2003, Big Finish Productions celebrated the fortieth anniversary with *Zagreus,* an Eighth Doctor audio drama starring Paul McGann in which every cast member was a former companion. Peter Davison, Colin Baker, and Sylvester McCoy played all-new characters before reprising their roles as previous Doctors. A recording of Jon Pertwee brought in a bit of him as well.

The anniversaries haven't been the only times different Doctors meet. Numerous team-ups have happened in the tie-in media. In 1985, then show runner John Nathan-Turner tried to repeat the success of "The Five Doctors" by producing "The Two Doctors," featuring the Sixth Doctor meeting the Second. In 2007, the charity Children in Need broadcast the mini-episode "Time Crash." Written by Steven Moffat, the story has the Tenth Doctor accidentally merge his TARDIS with the Fifth Doctor's, leading to a comedic meeting and a love letter to the past.

"Time Crash" seems to be the only time the later Doctor remembered a team-up from his younger counterpart's perspective. Perhaps this is because the Time Lords were around all the other times, placing memory blocks on the younger Doctors as they had with Jamie and Zoe.

Since the advent of the modern-day program, some have requested repeatedly that classic Doctors appear. "I'd love for it to happen," said Matt Smith in an interview for this book. "How amazing would it be to see Tom Baker? Can you imagine seeing him back in the scarf? And Paul McGann is a great actor and a great Doctor. I say bring back Chris and Dave, too! How many Doctors can we get into one story? Imagine if there were five or six of us in one ep and we could all look at one another and judge one another."

FAMILY TIES

Having saved Gallifrey (with the help of his earlier selves), the Third Doctor is given a new dematerialization circuit and regains his memories concerning his ship's operations. Either because his memory's been refreshed or since the ship has new, better circuits now, the Doctor at last has a greater deal of control over the TARDIS, whereas the first two incarnations were always flying blind. But rather than rush off without a second glance, he takes Jo on a few trips, always returning to the UNIT lab that he has called home for years. The season ended with the story "The Green Death," in which Jo falls in love and decides to leave UNIT. Hurt, the Doctor tells her to save him a slice of wedding cake and quietly departs. (A few years after leaving the show, Katy Manning caused quite a stir when she posed nude alongside a Dalek in photos for *Girl Illustrated*. "Typical Katy!" said Pertwee. Decades later, Manning rejoined the Whoniverse in Big Finish audio dramas as Iris Wildthyme, a hard-drinking, flirtatious Time Lord first introduced in prose.)

Jo Grant returned to the screen in a two-part story of *The Sarah Jane Adventures* in 2010, now using her married name, Jo Jones. In the two-part "Death of the Doctor" story by Russell T. Davies, she meets the Doctor's eleventh incarnation and finally encounters her successor, Sarah Jane Smith, a woman who changed what it meant to be the Doctor's friend.

Season 6B

Many fans worship continuity.

In "The Five Doctors," the Second Doctor navigates his TARDIS to visit the Brigadier in retirement. Yet the show had always shown that the hero had no control over his destination until after the Third Doctor's exile had ended. Later in the story, it became clear that this version of the Second Doctor had already experienced separation from Jamie and Zoe, commenting on their memory loss and remembering the battle with Omega. How was this possible when Jamie and Zoe were sent away just before his exile and forced regeneration?

The matter grew more complicated still in "The Two Doctors." Though generally regarded as a fun adventure, some fans noted continuity contradictions. The story features the Second Doctor and Jamie on a mission for the Time Lords and able to control the ship's destination. Along with this, the TARDIS doesn't look like the one he used before and has a remote unit that allows the Time Lords to take control. None of this corresponds with the Second Doctor's adventures where Jamie didn't even know about the Time Lords until the trial.

Several viewers pointed out that we never actually see the Second Doctor regenerate. We hear that his sentence is about to begin, and then something happens as the screen fades to black. When "Spearhead from Space" begins, the change has already occurred. Along with this, the Third Doctor possesses equipment that the Second Doctor didn't, such as a device that tracks his ship. It seems odd the Time Lords would give him these devices and explain their uses while he was regenerating. Perhaps *more* than a few minutes had passed between the end of "The War Games" and "Spearhead from Space."

The *TV Comic* adventures of the Second Doctor had already used this idea. During the six months between Troughton's last adventure and Pertwee's first, the strips depict the Doctor exiled to Earth but still wearing his second face. He has several adventures until finally he is lured to a farm where a group of scarecrows controlled by the Time Lords captures him. He is forced to regenerate and sent off in the TARDIS, leading into the Third Doctor's debut.

By the time "The Five Doctors" aired, these comic strip adventures were largely forgotten. But some Whovians still believed an untold adventure or several may have occurred between the Doctor's trial and exile. The TV story "The Deadly Assassin" fueled this possibility, mentioning that the exile was "subsequently remitted" by the Celestial Intervention Agency (CIA), introduced as a Time Lord black ops group. The remark led many to conclude that the Time Lords who had circumvented the First Law of Time in "The Three Doctors" had belonged to this agency. Perhaps it wasn't the first time they'd recruited the Doctor for special operations, either.

The book *The Discontinuity Guide*, published in 1995, suggests that following the end of the hero's trial, the Celestial Intervention Agency dispatched him on several missions, improving his TARDIS and providing the new equipment the Third Doctor had. During this time, the Doctor temporarily regained an older Jamie and Victoria as companions. Eventually, these assignments stopped and the exile and forced regeneration began, either because the hero proved too difficult to control or because the CIA had accomplished its goals. Along with his knowledge of time travel, the agency also blocked his memories of the missions for security reasons.

This period became known as "Season 6B." Fans quickly adopted it, and tie-in media started directly referencing it, but many still considered it just a fan theory or "fanon." Terrance Dicks liked the idea, though, and in 2005 he expanded on it in the novel *World Game* for BBC Books. The novel reveals that the end of "The War Games" seen on-screen was a "re-edited" version of events released for the public record. Now the true story could be revealed under the provisions of the Gallifreyan Freedom of Information Act.

World Game details the Second Doctor learning that his sentence of execution can be commuted to exile if he performs a task, possibly several, on behalf of the Celestial Intervention Agency. The Time Lords overhaul his ship, explaining the different interior in "The Two Doctors" and why the TARDIS is more reliable following his trial. The novel's epilogue establishes that the stresses of CIA missions cause the Second Doctor to age faster (a nod to Troughton being noticeably older in his later appearances). The novel's end leads directly into "The Two Doctors."

Since Terrance Dicks wrote the story, which the BBC issued via its publishing arm BBC Books, many fans took *World Game* as the official version of what occurred between "The War Games" and "Spearhead from Space." The BBC even adopted "Season 6B" into the official record on the classic *Doctor Who* website.

Fanon had become canon.

11

"I Walk in Eternity"

"There's no point in being grown up if you can't be childish sometimes!"

—THE FOURTH DOCTOR, FROM "ROBOT" (1974–1975)

As he prepared for his fifth year in the role, Jon Pertwee expressed to Barry Letts that he was finding it harder to land other roles because many thought of him as the Doctor. With Katy Manning and Roger Delgado gone, it was time to move on. According to Pertwee, he approached the BBC about staying if he received more money—only to be told that this wouldn't happen. Letts later denied this version of events; if Pertwee had wished to stay with more money, then he as producer would have moved funds around to make it so.

In December 1973, the eleventh season opened with "The Time Warrior," which introduced the warrior clone race known as the Sontarans and marked the debut of journalist Sarah Jane Smith, played by Elisabeth Sladen.

As a young girl, Sladen had performed with the Royal Ballet. As an adult, she appeared on *Coronation Street, Doomwatch,* and *Z-Cars.* At twenty-eight, she auditioned for *Doctor Who,* not realizing that the show was looking for a new companion. Sladen's performance and chemistry with Jon Pertwee impressed everyone.

Sarah Jane quickly proved to be a different sort of character. She had used her aunt's credentials to sneak onto a military base, hoping to get a news story. Though the Third Doctor occasionally condescended to her, as was his habit with people in general, she made it clear that they were equals as far as she was concerned. After their second adventure, she decided to stay close to the Time Lord. The previous Doctors had traveling companions who, whether they joined willingly, stowed away, or were accidentally kidnapped, found themselves stuck on the TARDIS until they found a new life or returned home by chance. Liz and Jo were both paid UNIT employees assigned to the Doctor. No one was paying Sarah Jane, and the TARDIS was working well enough now that she could leave any time. She was the first companion who was unquestionably there because she truly wanted to be there. After facing a Sontaran, she helped the Doctor and UNIT against an invasion of dinosaurs in modern-day London, met the Daleks on what was supposed to be a trip to the beach, and visited Peladon, where the Doctor and Jo had shared a strange caper.

Along with introducing Sarah Jane and the Sontarans, "The Time Warrior," which was broadcast ten years and a few weeks after "An Unearthly Child," finally gave the Time Lords' home planet a name: Gallifrey. Though Robert Holmes wrote the story, it is not known for sure if he came up with the name himself. In several subsequent adventures, a running joke would be that when humans learned the Doctor came from a place called Gallifrey, they would assume it was in Ireland.

THE ACTION SCIENTIST LEAVES

The eleventh season ended with "Planet of the Spiders," wherein the Doctor's hubris endangers both himself and others. The story itself had caused disagreement; Letts wanted the story to be about responsibility and redemption, with Captain Mike Yates returning after having betrayed UNIT in a previous story and the Doctor having to face consequences of his arrogance. Dicks feared this focus on hubris made their star seem less heroic, but he conceded.

The story introduces a new Time Lord, K'anpo—the name referencing a period in seventeenth-century Japanese history or the Japanese adaptation of traditional Chinese medicine. In the 1972 story "The Time Monster," the Doctor had spoken of a monk on Gallifrey who had taught him as a boy to expand his mind and appreciate the small things in life. Letts wanted K'anpo to be that monk, viewing Time Lord philosophy as similar to Buddhism. "Planet of the Spiders" also has the Third Doctor finally explain his previous changes in personality and appearance as a process that Time Lords undergo when their bodies wear out or are injured. Starting with this story, the change is called "regeneration."

Though the Doctor knows that the planet Metebilis III possesses highly radioactive crystals that could kill him, he journeys there to face a powerful enemy. Sarah Jane and the Brigadier don't see the Doctor for weeks before he finally materializes in the TARDIS, dying from radiation poisoning. "Don't cry," he weakly tells Sarah Jane. "While there's life, there's—"

The Doctor then slumps lifelessly to the floor. But K'anpo appears and gives the Doctor's cells "a little push" to jumpstart the regeneration process, ensuring all will be well . . . although he admits that the man's brain cells will jumble in the process, making him quite erratic.

K'anpo directs energy toward the Doctor, then vanishes as our hero's form changes for the third time. Exactly what he did to jumpstart the regeneration isn't explained. (Some compare it to a scene in 2011 where the regeneration energies of another are used to save the Doctor's life. Perhaps K'anpo made a similar sacrifice.)

While many appreciated the heartfelt and tragic goodbye, the regeneration itself was widely criticized. Unlike Hartnell's change, there was no glowing light, no sense that strange Time Lord energies were spreading over the body. Pertwee fast-dissolved to Tom Baker in a moment.

"I loved Jon Pertwee, but that regeneration was rubbish," Gary Russell said to me. "Pertwee was such a heroic Doctor, and he was my favorite. But for me it was a little too quiet and esoteric an end. He faces his fears, then falls on the floor and dies. I would rather that such an assertive, heroic Doctor rushed into a loud, big ending. I could deal with it, but then the regeneration is just badly done and badly shot."

Recalling the regeneration in her autobiography, Elisabeth Sladen said,

> The whole regeneration was such a cold affair. Tom simply dashed in and back out again because he was already rehearsing for his debut story. And Jon—Well, I don't know what was going through his mind exactly, except he refused to be in the same room with his successor. . . . The penny had finally dropped, I think. Jon was leaving—and the show was carrying on. I know later on [David Tennant] found handing over to Matt Smith harder than he'd possibly imagined. From star to history in a

matter of seconds; it's a phenomenal fall. No other show does this to an actor.

Indeed, Pertwee didn't exchange any words with Baker during the regeneration scene. The latter actor said in various interviews that he saw no hostility in this and understood the feeling years later when he filmed his regeneration into the Fifth Doctor, often saying the experience was similar to attending one's own wake.

In any event, Pertwee departed, and the new version of the hero arrived. But Pertwee wasn't quite done with the franchise. In 1989, he reprised the Third Doctor in *Doctor Who: The Ultimate Adventure*, a stage play that toured the UK. Written by Terrance Dicks, the traveling production featured the hero and a new French companion named Jason getting caught up in a conflict between the Cybermen and the Daleks (with a cameo by Margaret Thatcher). With Sladen, he also did two *Doctor Who* dramas for BBC Radio in 1993 and 1996.

THE BOHEMIAN

Robert Holmes had scripted the debut stories of the Third Doctor, the Master, and Sarah Jane, along with other Second and Third Doctor stories. In 1974, he took over as script editor starting with the twelfth season. After the Fourth Doctor's first adventure "Robot," Barry Letts left the program and was succeeded by Philip Hinchcliffe as producer. To many fans, Holmes and Hinchcliffe defined a key era of the show, aided by their leading man.

Tom Baker had shown an interest in acting at a young age. When he was a teenager, his mother forbade him from accepting a job at the Abbey Theatre in Dublin. Soon afterward, at age fifteen, he left school to live in a monastery as a Roman Catholic monk. He later said that in part he did it simply to escape his home and family. After six years, he left, saying he'd lost his faith. In later interviews, however, he admitted that the experience helped him as an actor: "If you can believe in the Christian religion, you can believe anything."

Weeks after leaving the monastery, Baker was called up to do his national service in the Royal Army Medical Corps. During this time, he took up acting as a hobby. By the late 1960s, he joined Laurence Olivier's National Theatre company, and in the '70s he started getting film roles, known in particular for his villains and character work.

For the Fourth Doctor, Letts initially considered older actors but found that several weren't interested in the role or couldn't do it. Letts saw Baker's performance in *The Golden Voyage of Sinbad* and spoke with him afterward, concluding that the actor would bring a sense of gravitas, as well as eccentricity, that the Doctor needed. At the time, Tom Baker was making ends meet by working part time as a builder. Entering his forties, he'd begun to think he would never have a steady career as an actor and joked that he largely accepted the role out of sheer desperation. When he got it, he couldn't tell anyone for at least two weeks until the official announcement, a task he found quite difficult.

Not knowing who would be cast for the role and how he would play it, Dicks had decided that the Fourth Doctor would act comically bizarre during "Robot" as a side effect of his regeneration, setting this up with K'anpo's remark about brain cells at the end of "Planet of the Spiders." But as it turned out, this fit Baker's own ideas about the character.

While the previous incarnation had grown fond of his place in UNIT, the new Doctor would have a strong wanderlust, harkening back to the idea of a cosmic tramp. Baker also wanted to emphasize the character's alien nature, giving him strange reactions and mood swings. This Doctor would grin at danger if it meant a good mystery, welcoming others to share in his joy. If he met scientists conducting dangerous experiments, he applauded their ingenuity only to then scold them for not accepting total responsibility for the consequences. When he praised people, he often quickly added that he was still somehow more impressive or perhaps was even responsible for the quality he had just complimented.

A key part of the Fourth Doctor was his look. In discussions with Baker, the creative team decided that this Doctor would look like a bohemian, similar to paintings that Henri de Toulouse-Lautrec did of Aristide Bruant in his dark hat and red scarf. The wardrobe department assembled an outfit consisting of a sport coat, large hat, sweater vest, traveling boots, and old-fashioned tie. In later seasons, this look reduced down to a white shirt and long coat—but the now-famous *Doctor Who* scarves linked the outfits.

Henri de Toulouse-Lautrec's iconic posters of Aristide Bruant served as the visual inspiration for Tom Baker's incarnation of the Doctor.

Begonia Pope was hired to knit a multicolored scarf for Tom Baker. She was so excited to be part of *Doctor Who* that she forgot to ask for the length of the scarf and then was too nervous to double-check. When she turned it over, she had used all of the wool she'd been given, resulting in a scarf roughly fourteen feet in length—over twice the height of Tom Baker, who stood six feet, three inches tall. Baker instantly loved the scarf and adopted it for his Doctor. In his second story, "The Ark in Space," our alien hero remarks that Madame Nostradamus had gifted him the item, referring to her as a "witty little knitter." Throughout Baker's tenure, he wore other versions of the scarf in various lengths, the shortest around eleven feet and the longest—a burgundy and crimson version used in season eighteen—said to be roughly twenty-four feet long.

Baker's Doctor also became famous for offering people jelly babies, a confectionery beloved in the UK. This had previously been done by Troughton in "The Three Doctors," but it became the Fourth Doctor's trademark.

Tom Baker and Louise Jameson (Leela) would like you to
have a jelly baby. They're quite good!
Photograph courtesy of Big Finish Productions

Whether inviting a character onto the TARDIS or finding himself confronted
by a deadly villain, this hero often thought candy was an excellent idea and
loved sharing. It fit in quite nicely with the Fourth Doctor's odd disposition.

THE ACTOR BEHIND THE ROLE

The Fourth Doctor's nature impressed Verity Lambert, who said that Tom
Baker came closest to her vision of the character apart from William Hartnell. She acknowledged, though, that her criticism of other Doctors often
reflected the stories they were given more than the actors.

Terrance Dicks and others have often joked that the strange and bizarre
Fourth Doctor was really just a slightly exaggerated version of Tom Baker. In
the documentary *Adventures in Time and Space,* Dicks said, "Tom impresses
you as being completely mad. . . . If you say something to Tom like, 'Good
morning, nice day,' he says, 'Is it? . . . Yes! Yes, it is, it's a wonderful day!'
. . . It's quite natural and unforced." In a 1982 interview with *Private Who,*

Baker said, "I didn't know how I was going to do Doctor Who. I had no idea at all—not until the very first rehearsal, and even then I didn't know . . . I just did it. I just played the script, and something evolved, and the audience liked the way I did it, obviously, so we kept it like that."

Philip Hinchcliffe was excited to have his first job as producer on a show as famous as *Doctor Who*. Baker had been cast before Hinchcliffe had been hired, so he understood that the actor would already have ideas about how to approach the role. The two had several conversations about how to portray the Doctor and his world and delighted in how much they agreed.

"He had an incredibly expressive face, those wide, intense eyes, and that grin," said Hinchcliffe in an interview for this book at Gallifrey One 2013. "He was tall and gave a real physical presence to the Doctor. He had a voice that spoke with authority and earnestness. You believed him when he said the universe was in danger; he projected urgency, especially when he instantly changed from being friendly to having this righteous anger. I thought he gave such a marvelous performance, a person you believed had been alive for centuries, who was ancient and not human, and had seen things across space and time."

"I wasn't the finest authority on all things Whovian," Elisabeth Sladen wrote in her autobiography, "but the word on set was that he was the first Doctor who really 'got' the fact that he was alien. I would read the script and try to predict how Tom would attack certain lines. Nine times out of ten, I was wrong. Whatever I predicted, he would find another way. And it would be perfect. *For a Time Lord*."

Tom Baker spoke of the challenge of finding his Doctor during those first few adventures, when the scriptwriters fell into habits that complemented Pertwee's strengths, such as his irritability and sarcasm. He told *Doctor Who Magazine*, "Jon Pertwee was absolutely brilliant at putting people down and being sarcastic, whereas I'm not very good at that. Sarcasm doesn't much interest me, really. I much prefer a kind of benevolent lunacy . . . because I'm an alien."

During the *Doctor Who @40 UK Gold* celebration, former editor of *Doctor Who Magazine* Clayton Hickman said, "Well, Tom Baker *is* Doctor Who, there's no denying it. Whether he's playing Doctor Who or whether he's walking down the streets going to the shops, he's Doctor Who. . . . If you've met the guy, he's insane. In a good way."

Baker himself often admitted that he was largely playing an idealized version of himself who was smarter and always knew what to do. In *Adventures in Time and Space,* he said, "My trade, such as it is, is to try and be convincing . . . but to play someone from outer space . . . how do you suggest he is alien? And so I felt the best way to suggest that I was an alien and came from somewhere else and had secrets—dark thoughts and wonderful thoughts—I thought the way to do that is just to be Tom Baker."

There have been reports of Tom Baker being difficult to work with, mostly in his later years on the program (discussed in the next chapter). But according to Hinchcliffe, "I found Tom to be very professional. He cared about the role and spoke up when he thought a scene could be better or wanted to add a line, and sometimes we agreed and sometimes we didn't. During my time, he never tried to take over and was never impossible to direct. I never had a cross word with him at all. If he had an idea that I thought wasn't going to work, he conceded."

Tom Baker had not been prepared for how much *Doctor Who* would change his life, despite warnings. When people stopped him on the street just weeks after his first episode, he decided it was his responsibility not to disrupt the fantasy for any children. Baker chose never to smoke or drink in an open, public area, lest a child see him. If young fans encountered him on the street, he responded in character, enthusiastically explaining that he was taking a stroll before his next adventure. During filming for "The Face of Evil," Baker noticed a production staffer's child on set and introduced himself as the Doctor before offering to show her the TARDIS.

Once, by chance, production of the show left Tom Baker with a few free days in his schedule. Rather than take a holiday, he visited schools in Belfast, which had recently suffered IRA bombings. Baker showed up in full costume, greeting schoolchildren, playing with them during recess, and reassuring them that they didn't need to be afraid.

"Children were very important to Tom," Hinchcliffe said. "He realized he was a hero to many of them, so he considered it a responsibility not to disappoint them. It led to a change in the first Leela adventure, where the script originally had him pretend to take a hostage by holding a knife to their throat. Tom didn't wish children to see the Doctor with a knife to anyone's throat, even if they knew he wouldn't hurt that person, so he substituted the knife with a jelly baby and still made the threat with deadly seriousness. It made for a funny scene and a better scene. It's how the Doctor would think."

FAMILIAR FOES

Hinchcliffe wanted to get away from Earth-bound stories for a while. He and Holmes also wanted stories involving small casts of characters in danger rather than full-scale alien invasions and cosmic threats where the stakes might be quite abstract. The Fourth Doctor's first season also featured the return of not one but three familiar races of monsters.

After the first script by Terrance Dicks, the Doctor rushes off with Sarah Jane and UNIT physician Dr. Harry Sullivan, played by Ian Marter, who also wrote many *Doctor Who* novelizations for Target and had appeared in the Third Doctor story "Carnival of Monsters." Harry is a posh Royal Navy surgeon who doesn't have a high enough UNIT security clearance to realize that the Brig's scientific advisor is actually an alien with a working time ship. Harry, Sarah Jane, and the Doctor find themselves thousands of years in the future on a space ark. Most of the ark's passengers are in hibernation, giving a great feeling of isolation as only the Doctor, his two friends, and a few humans realize that an intruder is stalking them. In fact, to magnify this, the first episode of the story featured no other speaking characters beyond the TARDIS crew.

At the conclusion of "The Ark in Space," the Doctor decides to check on how Earth is doing in this future era rather than take off in the TARDIS again. His quick visit leads to another encounter with a small group of astronauts and a Sontaran scout eager for battle. Although invasion was a looming threat, the main stakes of this story involved the group being captured or experimented on by the Sontaran warrior.

The fourth story of the season, a six-part tale, became a landmark and influenced the modern-day program. "Genesis of the Daleks" begins when a Time Lord, possibly an agent of the Celestial Intervention Agency, forcibly sends the Doctor and his friends to ancient Skaro, without the TARDIS. The Time Lords foresee a future in which the Daleks threaten Gallifrey's existence and become the dominant life form in the universe. The Doctor has been sent to when the race first rose. The Doctor can use this opportunity to learn secret weaknesses of the monsters, slow down their evolution instead, or even avert the birth of the Daleks entirely. Either way, he is without his ship and can't leave until the Time Lords consider his mission complete.

"Genesis of the Daleks" returned Terry Nation's creatures to their fascist roots and reminded viewers just why the Doctor feared them. The Doctor and his friends find themselves in the middle of a war between the Thals and a society called the Kaleds. The dark-haired Kaleds speak of "total extermination of the Thal race" and their uniforms evoke Nazi Germany. The Doctor meets their chief scientist, Davros, who believes in biological purity and survival of the fittest despite being dependent cybernetic implants and a life support unit that visually portends the Daleks. Davros has foreseen that his race will die and has created the Dalek race from the mutated ashes of the Kaleds, eliminating their psychological capacity for sympathy and pity while increasing their survival instinct.

Hinchcliffe and Holmes didn't care for the Daleks and had agreed to this story because Letts and Dicks had already commissioned it. They'd brought the Doctor to the origin of the genesis of the race because this could finally bring an end to the monsters. As Elisabeth Sladen tells it, the story originally was faster paced and ended with the Doctor averting the creation of the monsters by planting explosives in their incubator chamber and setting it off with two wires outside. But Tom Baker protested to director David Maloney, "I'm the Doctor—I can't go around wiping out entire civilizations. Have I the right?"

Baker's dilemma with the Doctor committing genocide led to rewrites that invited viewers to ponder the same moral conflict. In the new version, Sarah Jane tells the Doctor that he needs to set off the explosive, but the hero can't bring himself to destroy a race for crimes it has yet to commit. Furthermore, he knows many civilizations become allies due to mutual fear of the Daleks. Would he undo all the good that came of this evil?

The Doctor doesn't wipe the creatures from existence, though he does slow down their progress, and now understands them better. The story received praise for addressing such moral conflicts, along with other social and political arguments. Decades later, Russell T. Davies revealed in *Doctor*

Who Annual 2006 that the Doctor's mission to alter Dalek history represented the first attack in what led to the Last Great Time War.

Following this, the year ended with the return of the Cybermen, who hadn't appeared on-screen since fighting the Second Doctor, nearly seven years earlier. The twelfth year was a success in the ratings and the best was yet to come.

THE SCRATCHMAN

Before Tom Baker had been cast, the *Doctor Who* production team had considered that the next incarnation might be an older gentleman who wouldn't be as physical as Jon Pertwee. Troughton and Hartnell had been accompanied by young men of action, so Ian Marter was cast as Dr. Harry Sullivan to fill this role for the Fourth Doctor.

But after filming was in full swing, it became clear that Tom Baker could play the action hero well, and Sullivan was deemed unnecessary. In the thirteenth season, "Terror of the Zygons" features the Doctor helping out UNIT again, with Sullivan deciding to stay home at the end. After the thirteenth year of *Doctor Who,* UNIT vanished from the show until 1989. The Brigadier wasn't seen again until the Fifth Doctor story "Mawdryn Undead," seven years later.

Along with starring alongside each other on-screen, Ian Marter and Tom Baker worked together on a script for a proposed feature film, *Doctor Who Meets the Scratchman.* The story involved scarecrows coming to life and rampaging on Earth. Before the Doctor could properly handle the situation, an army of Cybermen would rise from the sea and attack Earth's shores. It would be revealed that all this chaos and more was caused by the Scratchman, a reference to an old name for the Devil, who created destruction for the sheer joy of it.

With a film budget, Baker wanted to take advantage of scenarios too costly for the TV stories. "I remember the ending," he told *Doctor Who Magazine.* "We were going to turn the whole studio into a giant pinball table. The Doctor and his companions were stuck on this table, and Scratchman was firing these balls at us. The balls disappeared down holes that were sort of gateways into other Hells. It was a very violent film, but very funny, too. The production office saw it and hated it, but I thought it was marvelous."

A TOUCH OF HORROR

For the program's thirteenth season, Hinchcliffe and Holmes took influence from the atmosphere of the famous Hammer horror films. "Terror of the Zygons" involved whispering villains in the dark and the Loch Ness monster. Stories followed featuring a geological dig threatened by a hidden menace, an Egyptian god who commanded reanimated cadavers and robot mummies, a Time Lord version of Frankenstein's monster, an abandoned village where all the calendars are on the same date, and alien seed pods found in Antarctica.

Some argued that the program was becoming too violent for children. One major figure who rose against the show was Mary Whitehouse, first president of the National Viewers' and Listeners' Association, now called Mediawatch-UK. She regularly protested that *Doctor Who* had become "teatime brutality for tots." She argued that the Nazi overtones of "Genesis of the Daleks" and certain cliffhangers—such as one in "The Deadly Assassin" wherein a villain tries to drown the Doctor—were too frightening and potentially damaging to children. Concerning the story "The Seeds of Doom," Whitehouse complained about one scene in which the Doctor holds a gun to his enemies in order to save Sarah Jane, and another that featured a strangulation. She suggested that *Doctor Who* might as well educate children on how to make a Molotov cocktail.

The BBC addressed these concerns from time to time, and the production team pointed out that for several years now the program had aimed toward children above the age of ten. Elisabeth Sladen occasionally addressed the matter as well, pointing out that if a parent found a child easily upset by violence or frightened by *Doctor Who,* then that parent had the power to change the channel. As far as the *Doctor Who* production office was concerned, though, Whitehouse did little beyond increasing the program's visibility and viewership.

Despite Whitehouse's protests, the new era of *Doctor Who* was considered a success by many, and ratings continued to rise. The Fourth Doctor was just starting.

1 2

The Journalist, the Warrior,
the Lady of Time

*"The Doctor loves being challenged and the best companions
are strong, intelligent, adventurous women who challenge him
constantly."*

—MATT SMITH, ELEVENTH DOCTOR

(2011 INTERVIEW WITH THE AUTHOR)

In casting Sarah Jane Smith, producer Barry Letts had a scene written specifically for the auditions, telling actors it was for a part in one *Doctor Who*
story. Elisabeth Sladen had no idea that she was auditioning for a regular
cast role. After seeing many others do the scene, Letts was impressed with
Sladen, saying later, "She could be frightened and brave at the same time.
The others could either be frightened or brave. . . . I made up my mind on
the spot." Rather than send Sladen home and have her wait to hear the
news, Letts told her that Pertwee was on his way to say hello. Sladen didn't
understand why but was happy to meet the actor. After introducing himself
and speaking to her, Pertwee discreetly gave Barry Letts a thumbs-up behind
Sladen's back, and the producer knew that he'd made the right decision.

Then script editor Terrance Dicks admitted in interviews that he had
an "old-fashioned idea" that the Doctor's assistants were there to ask for
plot clarification, get captured, and provide a good scream when a monster
showed up. He also said that he generally believed people didn't find *Doctor
Who* interesting during scenes that didn't showcase him or the villain, so
he never saw call to develop the companions. But Letts told him that Sarah
Jane wasn't to be an "assistant" but the Doctor's colleague, paralleling the
rise of feminism and women's lib.

Despite this intention, the character did seem like a sidekick at first,
and Dicks often joked that her career in journalism simply legitimized her

acting as an exposition prompt: "What is this creature, Doctor?" "What's happening, Doctor?" "What will your gadget do, Doctor?" "How is it possible that dinosaurs are randomly teleporting in and out of London, Doctor?"

But with Hinchcliffe, Holmes, and Baker on the scene, Sladen evolved Sarah Jane into a different kind of character.

THE JOURNALIST

"There's nothing 'only' about being a girl, your majesty."
—SARAH JANE SMITH, FROM "THE MONSTER OF PELADON" (1974)

As Elizabeth Sladen explained in her autobiography:

The arrival of a new Doctor actually gave me the freedom to regenerate Sarah Jane as well. If someone comes in who's the same person but is actually totally different, they do things differently. And that in turn makes you react differently. So I discovered all sorts of new things I could do; it gave me a new lease of life and allowed me to expand. I loved that.

When Harry Sullivan joined the TARDIS, he held openly old-fashioned views toward Sarah Jane, attempting to be chivalrous in ways that annoyed her as sexist. Sladen appreciated these scenes because they showed the kind of person Sarah Jane often encountered in life and also contrasted against how the Doctor trusted her.

Sladen and Baker instantly clicked, spending much of their time during breaks sharing jokes and discussing old movies. Sladen said they had a near-instant trust and understanding, and Baker claimed that she compelled affection. "There was this understanding between Tom and Lis," Philip Hinchcliffe commented. "They trusted each other, and they loved their own characters, and they pushed each other in the way good actors do. You could see that the Doctor and Sarah Jane understood each other on different levels, you could feel that special relationship and how they balanced each other."

Sarah Jane became more assertive, which Sladen credited to the quality of the new scripts and Tom's insistence that the companion must be capable and special if the Doctor had chosen her to join his adventures. In interviews, Sladen spoke of occasions on which Tom protested scenes that he thought weakened Sarah Jane. "He said, 'Look, I don't think Lis should do that because that makes her look stupid.' And he said, 'I would not go round in space with someone who is stupid!' I thought, *Oh, yes, Tom. Go, Tom!*"

Sarah Jane adopted a bit of the Doctor's fashion sense, dressing in odd, colorful outfits more youthful and playful than anything she had worn during Pertwee's final year. Sladen involved herself in these costume choices, wanting to display just how much Sarah was becoming more like the Time Lord. As the stories continued, the Doctor and the journalist became an inseparable pair. In the story "The Seeds of Doom," Baker added a line in which the Doctor gleefully introduces Sarah Jane as his "best friend." In all the years of *Doctor Who,* the hero had never before referred to anyone with such familiarity or affection, but Baker believed it fit the relationship developing. In contrast to previous companions, some fans wondered if their connection didn't have a subtle undertone of romance.

As her third year on the show wrapped up, though, Sladen decided that it was time to leave. Like so many before her, she counted three years a good run and wanted to end on a good note, while Sarah Jane was popular. Writers floated the idea that Smith might die at the end of an adventure, but Hinchcliffe didn't care for how the story was written, and Sladen met with him to protest that the character's death would upset many young fans. Along with this, she said that she didn't want her departure to be the focus of the story, as it was still the Doctor's show, and she didn't want Sarah Jane married off, as Jo Grant had been, as it would have been out of character and would, as she saw it, go against the relationship established in the TARDIS.

Holmes and Hinchcliffe discussed the matter with Tom Baker and Elisabeth Sladen, telling the two actors that only they knew for sure how the Doctor and Sarah Jane would say goodbye. A new script was given to the pair, who altered the finale scene's dialogue to fit the two characters' experience. According to Hinchcliffe, "They were right to object. The ending we had in mind didn't work. They weighed in, and we elongated the final scene to give Sarah Jane a proper goodbye and acknowledge how connected she and the Doctor had become."

Sarah Jane's final story was "The Hand of Fear," broadcast in October 1976 and written by Bob Baker (no relation to Tom or Colin) and Dave Martin. After saving the day again, Sarah Jane decides she's being taken for granted and threatens to leave. To seem serious, she packs her bags while the Doctor receives a telepathic summons to Gallifrey. As Sarah Jane returns to the control room with her luggage, the Doctor uncomfortably reveals that they must part ways, possibly because he fears for her safety on Gallifrey after what happened to Jamie and Zoe. (In 2006, we also learned that humans weren't permitted on the planet at this time.) The last time the Doctor went home, he was forced to regenerate and Sarah Jane asks if this will happen again. He doesn't know, but must face it alone. The two share a farewell that many still consider one of the saddest companion departures of the classic program.

Baker later said that during the farewell scene he focused on the Doctor's discomfort and inability to say goodbye directly, experiencing an emotion he wasn't altogether used to. Sladen said in an interview, "I would love to think that the audience gets a subtext from it, that it's the things that are not being said . . . how they felt about each other."

Sarah Jane's final episode attracted over twelve million viewers. She had been the show's longest running companion in terms of broadcast seasons, with three full years plus two extra stories under her belt. Fans often hoped that Sarah Jane would return. In different ways, they got their wish, first with her appearance in the failed pilot *K-9 and Company* (more about that in Chapter 14), then in radio plays and an unofficial spin-off video, and finally with a return to *Doctor Who* itself in 2006. This led to further appearances on the program and her own spin-off television show *The Sarah Jane Adventures* in 2007. Fans never had enough.

Sadly, Sladen was diagnosed with cancer in February 2011 and then died on April 19, 2011. Her autobiography appeared posthumously, seven months later. In 2010, she had filmed a crossover with the Eleventh Doctor in her own show, entitled "Death of the Doctor." At one point, Elisabeth Sladen remarked that she had a sense this would be the last time she stood on the TARDIS set.

THE WARRIOR

*"I too used to believe in magic, but the Doctor has taught me about
science. It is better to believe in science."*

—LEELA, FROM "THE HORROR OF FANG ROCK" (1977)

After Sarah Jane's departure, the Doctor had no companion at his side for
his next adventure. "The Deadly Assassin" took place entirely on Gallifrey
and featured the return of the Master after an absence of three years (more
about this in the following sidebar).

Baker had expressed a desire that the Doctor not have a companion
anymore, believing the character seemed just fine working only with those
he encountered when he arrived in places that needed his help, like a cosmic Western hero. If he had to have a companion, he joked that it might
as well just be an alien talking cabbage. But Hinchcliffe told him that the
companion was necessary for the audience to have a consistent character
with whom to connect and to provide humanity to the Doctor through
interaction.

The next adventure, "The Face of Evil," introduced the new traveling
companion. The Doctor, having wandered alone for some time and now
accustomed to talking to himself, lands on a savage world where primitive
people live in the ruins of advanced technology. A ship of humans crashed
here generations before, and the technicians and survey team went their
separate ways, evolving into two tribes called the Tesh and the Sevateem.

The Doctor soon befriends Leela, a fierce warrior of the Sevateem,
who at first thinks he is a god of evil. By the end of the adventure, Leela
realizes that what she believes to be magic is just science she doesn't yet
understand. Wishing to learn more about the universe, she decides to join
the Doctor, pushing her way into the TARDIS and activating the controls
as he protests.

Louise Jameson played Leela. She watched *Doctor Who* as a child, and
Patrick Troughton was her Doctor of choice. Jameson had attended the
Royal Academy of Dramatic Art and spent two years with the Royal Shakespeare Company. She'd also appeared regularly on the TV series *Emmerdale*
and was happy to join *Doctor Who* as a warrior rather than a hostage in

waiting. In contrast to the Doctor's manner, Leela had no problem suggesting "knife them in the neck" as a solution to danger.

According to Hinchcliffe, "Instead of a companion who became brave by meeting the Doctor, she was already quite brave, and he had to teach her to hold back, that there were ways to defeat evil without automatically killing people. It was sort of like *My Fair Lady*. Leela still challenged him and quickly came to see him as a man rather than a god. And it was important that she was the one who chose to go with him, she was the one who wanted to learn. Louise added humor and a playfulness at times and an impatience with some of the Doctor's attitude."

"I think it [Leela's violence] could have gone a lot further," Jameson said in an interview for this book, "but Tom was very clear that violence had to be used with great integrity. He was always aware of the younger audience."

Along with always carrying a knife, Leela donned a leather outfit considered pretty revealing for *Doctor Who*—and originally even more revealing before Jameson suggested the addition of leather flaps hanging from her belt. "The reactions were varied," according to Jameson, "from a four-year-old writing to ask me to put some clothes on to women my mother's age acknowledging that power and sex appeal can go together. In fact, sexy women are indeed very powerful because of what they are endowed with, not necessarily that they have to use it overtly in a gratuitous way. It is perfectly all right to look terrific and be political."

Jameson enjoyed playing the character and wanted her to rely on instinct in contrast to how the Doctor relied on science. She noted how her dog perked up at certain sounds how it turned its head when investigating a room and copied some of these traits. The name Leela, a variation of Leila, means "dark beauty" in Arabic, and the production office thought Jameson's blue eyes would jar with the character's skin tone and outfit. Jameson was given red contact lenses, making her eyes brown, but they bothered her and exacerbated her nearsightedness, so they were eventually abandoned. At the end of "Horror of Fang Rock," Leela witnesses a bright explosion, and the Doctor notes that her brown eyes have turned blue as a result.

While many fans welcomed Leela, there was tension behind the scenes. Baker hadn't wanted a new companion, and Jameson sensed his dislike for her character. In an interview for *Doctor Who @40,* Jameson said, "Tom Baker's an extraordinary man to work with . . . but along with that could come some tensions in a rehearsal room. You know, when someone is that talented and that high profile, sometimes they can be just a little bit difficult to work with."

In later years, Baker has spoken with regret of his occasional bad attitude toward Jameson, admitting that he had not initially cared for the violence that Leela's character seemed to represent and confessing that by this point he felt "drunk" on the fame that the Doctor had brought to his career, which made him resistant to change.

Leela's three adventures in the fourteenth year marked the end of Hinchcliffe's tenure as producer. Graham Williams took over, with Holmes staying as script editor until handing the reins to Anthony Read. Holmes's final story as script editor was "The Sunmakers," Jameson's favorite. Some scripts made her interchangeable with other companions, but she believed that Holmes and writer Chris Boucher brought out other dimensions in her character and let her display her instinctive tendencies. Holmes would occasionally write other *Doctor Who* stories in later years, making him the author of more scripts for the classic program than anyone else.

In *Doctor Who*'s fifteenth year, the story "The Invisible Enemy" turned the TARDIS crew into the rather unorthodox trio of a Time Lord, a warrior, and a robot dog. K-9 was conceived of by writer Bob Baker, and introduced in "The Invisible Enemy" as the robotic creation of Professor Marius in the fifty-first century (a century that was also said to be the home of the Time Agency). Some fans found the robot a bit silly, while others celebrated it as another example of the kind of character that only *Doctor Who* could get away with. Jameson loved K-9, and during many interviews she recalled with laughter times when voice actor John Leeson would rehearse with them on all fours since the robot cost money every time it was in use.

By the end of the fifteenth season, Jameson decided to leave the program, having been offered the role of Portia in *The Merchant of Venice* at the Bristol Old Vic. The season ended with "The Invasion of Time," in which the Doctor brings Leela to Gallifrey and declares himself president of the High Council of Time Lords (a title he actually did have some right to, due to the events of "The Deadly Assassin"). While the Doctor works a manipulative plan inside the capitol, Leela explores the wild open plains of Gallifrey, which even many Time Lords had never done.

At the story's conclusion, the Doctor is ready to leave but finds that Leela has chosen to stay, having developed romantic feelings for another Time Lord named Andred. K-9 remains with her, and, as the TARDIS takes flight, Leela wonders if her friend will be lonely. But we see the Doctor grin as he pulls out a box labeled "K-9 MARK II."

Hinchcliffe didn't know how Leela departed the show until his interview for this book. On hearing the details, he shook his head. "No, I don't like that. She should have had a noble warrior's death. Then her spirit could live on. How do we know what her thoughts were of an afterlife? Maybe her spirit could have lived on literally. How do we know what mysterious things there might have been where she came from? We never fully explored that."

Jameson herself wasn't terribly satisfied with the ending and its reliance on sudden romance to remove a female character. When I asked her about it, she said she would have preferred for Leela to die while saving the Doctor's life. She is glad today, however, that her character survived. For several years now, she has starred in the Big Finish audio drama series *Gallifrey*, which takes place after she left the Doctor. On Leela's ultimate fate, Jameson said, "It would be wonderful to see her [in the modern *Doctor Who*] as a huge Mother Earth figure with a football team of children and grandchildren, who all revere her and her stories, half of which they believe are made up, although we know the truth."

In 2012, Big Finish Productions released the first of several audio dramas in which Tom Baker and Louise Jameson reprise their roles as the Fourth Doctor and Leela, taking place just after "The Talons of Weng-Chiang," the last story that Hinchcliffe produced. The stories continue with Hinchcliffe's theme of Leela being educated about the universe. "I absolutely adore working with Tom Baker now," says Jameson. "He has apologized very sincerely and very publicly about the treatment I received back in the day and we have more [audio dramas] planned." Jameson also considers her brief tenure on the TV show as time well spent. "To this day, the fact that a ten-month job in 1976 and '77 can still get me work is amazing. Because the fans who watched then are now running the business and remember and are very movingly loyal to that era."

THE LADY OF TIME

"My name is Romanadvoratrelundar."

"Well, I'm terribly sorry about that. Is there anything we can do?"

—ROMANA I AND THE FOURTH DOCTOR,
FROM "THE RIBOS OPERATION" (1978)

Before *Doctor Who,* Mary Tamm worked onstage with the Birmingham Repertory Company and appeared in several films. When approached to play the Doctor's new traveling companion, she initially refused, but Graham Williams assured her she wouldn't be a damsel in distress. To counter Leela, the new companion would focus on scientific reason and intellect, a female Time Lord sent to the Doctor's side to help him protect the universe. Tamm accepted the role.

The show's sixteenth season tried something new. All six stories worked on their own but also served as parts of a season-long arc called "The Key to Time." In the first story, the Doctor and K-9 Mark II have been traveling alone for some time when suddenly a cosmic being called the White Guardian halts the TARDIS. This avatar of cosmic order charges the Doctor's with finding the Key to Time, a cube with power over reality that is divided into six segments scattered across reality. The Doctor must assemble it before agents of the Black Guardian do so. The Doctor returns to the TARDIS and meets Romana, who has been sent to aid his quest.

For the first time since Susan, the Doctor is traveling with another of his own people. Rather than see him as a mystery, Romana's done some reading on the Doctor. She knows how old he is, when he stole his TARDIS, and that he barely passed his final academy exams on the second try with a 51 percent score, whereas she (as she's quick to point out) ranked third in her class. The two quickly develop a teasing friendship.

But while Romana quickly gained many fans, Mary Tamm thought her character regressed into unwanted female tropes as the season went on. She decided not to continue for a second year. In her final story, "The Armageddon Factor," actor Lalla Ward appeared as a character named Princess Astra. The production team thought her quite good and decided that Ward would step in as a regenerated Romana for the seventeenth season. Fans later dubbed Tamm's incarnation as Romana I and Ward's as Romana II.

Tamm has said that she stated her willingness to return for Romana's regeneration scene for the sake of giving fans a smooth transition but wasn't invited back to do so. She also said that rumors that she left due to pregnancy were invented by producer Graham Williams. Following her departure, Tamm made regular television appearances for years, later acting alongside Lalla Ward in the *Gallifrey* audio dramas released by Big Finish, allowing for a meeting of sorts between the two Romanas. In July 2012, at the age of sixty-two, Tamm died from cancer. Her husband, Marcus Ringrose, died of a heart attack—some say a broken heart—just hours after giving the eulogy at her funeral.

According to Big Finish producer David Richardson, Tamm "eagerly embraced the opportunity to return as Romana for this series. 'Nothing will keep me away,' she told me when I first approached her, and she was true to her word. Even cancer and months spent enduring treatment didn't quell Mary's passion for the project. We, as colleagues and as fans, are indebted to her for seeing the series through under awful circumstances. She came to every studio recording full of enthusiasm, laughed endlessly, and—on the last day I saw her—told me that doing the recordings had helped her get through it. She was a fantastic lady, and this season is dedicated to her."

A FEMALE COUNTERPART

"Shall we take the lift or fly?"
"Let's not be ostentatious."
"All right. Let's fly then."
—ROMANA II AND THE FOURTH DOCTOR, FROM "CITY OF DEATH" (1979)

Season seventeen brought forth a new version of Romana and temporarily replaced K-9 voice actor John Leeson with David Brierly, explained as a side effect of the robot dog developing a mechanical version of laryngitis. The seventeenth season also brought writer Douglas Adams into the position of script editor. Adams had gained critical acclaim for his 1978 radio comedy *The Hitchhiker's Guide to the Galaxy,* which he later adapted into books. He embraced the strange, alien attitudes of the Fourth Doctor and Romana, tweaking scripts to emphasize the humor between the two. Lalla Ward and Tom Baker both very much enjoyed Adams's sense of storytelling.

Lalla Ward's stage name came from how she had mispronounced her given name, Sarah, as a young child. She made her acting debut in the Hammer horror movie *Vampire Circus*. She had appeared on the BBC series *The Duchess of Duke Street*, and during her time on *Doctor Who* she also played Ophelia in the BBC TV production of *Hamlet* starring Derek Jacobi, her first Shakespearean performance. During the production, actor Patrick Stewart, who played King Claudius, asked Ward why she wanted to waste her time working on a science fiction show rather than legitimate theatre—an irony not lost on her years later.

Lalla Ward (Romana II)
Photograph courtesy of Big Finish Productions

When Ward appeared in "The Armageddon Factor," she already knew director Michael Hayes, who had worked with her on *The Duchess of Duke Street*. But she was completely surprised when, in just a few weeks, she learned that Mary Tamm was leaving and she had been suggested to take her place. "I just couldn't be the same as Mary. It wouldn't have worked. I had to approach it differently. I kept thinking that I was in somebody else's shoes, and they didn't quite fit. So it was weird—but a challenge. Besides, when Time Lords regenerate, they don't stay the same, do they?"

In the seventeenth season's first story, "Destiny of the Daleks," the Doctor is relaxing after the Key to Time affair, his TARDIS now using a "randomizer" to make their trips unpredictable, ensuring that the Black Guardian can't track him down and exact revenge (although, one might imagine that an avatar of chaos wouldn't be foiled by chaotic travel plans). As the TARDIS is in flight, the hero looks up and sees Princess Astra standing before him, only to realize that it's actually Romana in the process of regenerating. She rather liked the Princess's appearance and has decided to adopt it. Perhaps as a joke, she donned a feminine take on the Fourth Doctor's costume, complete with a pink overcoat and a very long white scarf. The Doctor now truly had a female counterpart aboard his ship.

Romana's regeneration scene, written by Douglas Adams, had her try different bodies before deciding on one. She also didn't seem to suffer any amnesia or physical stress as the Doctor usually did. Years later, the story "The Mark of the Rani" confirmed that women Time Lords (Romana often identified as a Time Lord rather than a Time Lady) had greater control over regeneration and could even determine what their next incarnation looked like. Since the Doctor was presented with choices for his next face in "The War Game," males apparently only gain such control with the help of special equipment on Gallifrey. The modern program again indicated how women had better control over regeneration in the 2011 episode "Let's Kill Hitler," when we saw a genetically engineered Time Lord/human hybrid regenerate with relative ease and remark that she was focusing on a specific dress size (though she was still a bit surprised by her new appearance).

Romana II was notably more effervescent and mischievous than her previous incarnation. Her fashion choices alone landed her many fans, and Ward took an active role with her costume designs in each story. This Romana was much more a kindred spirit to the Doctor and employed a similar sense of humor, such as when she explained that she had two hearts because one was "casual" and one was "best." At the same time, she found the Doctor's over-the-top arrogance occasionally tiresome, and was happy to tell him so.

Some fans had seen a glimmer of a romantic undertone between the Doctor and Sarah Jane, but Romana II seemed a stronger possibility for a genuine romantic interest to the Doctor, even though on-screen they never did more than share smiles and sometimes hold hands when they ran together. As far as Tom Baker was concerned, the Doctor wasn't really a sexual creature, and the program was more innocent than that.

Both actors reprised their roles for TV commercials in Australia advertising the new Prime computer. These ads had more overt flirtation from Romana. One showed her being quite affectionate with the hero before he finally asks her to marry him—or attempts to ask since she accepts before he can finish the question. These commercials lay outside the official canon, of course, but it did make sense for the Doctor and Romana to have such strong chemistry, considering events off-screen. Tom Baker and Lalla Ward were dating. And then they weren't. And then they were again. It was a stormy relationship.

The Time Lords

"I renounced the society of the Time Lords. Now I'm simply a traveler."

—THE FOURTH DOCTOR, FROM "PYRAMIDS OF MARS" (1975)

It's amazing how slowly the mythology of the Time Lords evolved. Their name and basic nature as guardians of reality were first revealed in "The War Games" at the close of the sixth year. Then they were largely unseen again until the tenth year anniversary when we met one of their founders, Omega, and learned that at least one faction would break the laws of time in certain cases. We also saw throughout the program that Time Lord society could create dangerous villains, such as the Monk, the War Chief, and the Master.

As writer Dan Abnett saw it, "In the early days, it was wonderful that there was mystery. When the phrase 'Time Lord' itself was finally mentioned, it immediately made us wonder, *What does that title mean?* And when the Master shows up as a renegade Time Lord, you wonder, *Well, how does that work?* And his alias reminds you and makes you realize, *Wait, we still don't know the Doctor's name, either.* Why did the Time Lords only call him the Doctor during his trial instead of using an alien name? Why did they refer to the Master only by that title instead of using his name?"

Hinchcliffe saw the Master's introduction as an important step in characterizing the Doctor's people. "The Master added a new quality to the idea of the Time Lords. We'd seen them as these aliens who stood above us, almost like gods or angels, but then here's this one who's cast out like Lucifer. Was he always bad, or was he good like Lucifer and then fell from grace? And the Doctor is often the only one who can stop him, but he's not praised for his efforts. His people still treat him as a renegade. So what does that say about them?"

Hinchcliffe and Holmes decided to reveal more. In "Pyramids of Mars," written by Holmes and Lewis Grefier, the Doctor says Gallifrey is located within a constellation called Kasterborous. The subsequent story "The Invasion of Time" added that there were five other planets in Gallifrey's solar system. It later became a common belief that the constellation design on the Fourth Doctor's TARDIS key was, in fact, Kasterborous. The modern program added that Gallifrey was warmed by a binary star and was considered the "shining world of the seven systems," which corresponds to the constellation of seven stars that decorated the Fourth Doctor's key. Two of those stars could have been Gallifrey's suns.

Weeks after "Pyramids of Mars," Sarah Jane and the Doctor visited another planet in Gallifrey's solar system in "The Brain of Morbius," a script by Terrance Dicks that was rewritten by Robert Holmes (under the pseudonym Robin Bland). The world was called Karn and inhabited by self-styled witches called the Sisterhood who evidently had a long history with the Time Lords. Though the Sisters did not trust the people of Gallifrey, they still occasionally provided them with an Elixir of Life that could ease difficult regenerations. The same story tells of an ancient Time Lord of legend named Morbius, who tried to conquer the universe and achieve immortality.

But the biggest revelations concerning the Doctor's people came in "The Deadly Assassin," written entirely by Robert Holmes. The four-part story took place on Gallifrey and featured no companion, the Doctor having just left Sarah Jane behind. We learn just how mortal the Time Lords really are behind their ceremonies. The capitol is patrolled by Chancellory Guards who don gaudy and ineffective outfits, likely meant for show, and don't seem to have the experience of dealing with true criminals and threats. A Castellan serves as chief of police and the Celestial Intervention Agency handles secret operations. There's a lower class of some sort, while above them are the cardinals, chancellors, and a ruling High Council with a president at its head. A computer system known as the Matrix contains the encoded brainwave patterns of dead Time Lords, allowing it to predict the future and major events of the universe.

We also learn that Time Lords have different clans and houses. The Doctor belongs to the Prydonian clan, known for cunning and manipulation. The Master was evidently from this same clan, as was the villain known as the Rani. According to the tie-in media, Romana and the Time Lord founder Rassilon were both Prydonians as well.

The story shows that Gallifreyan society has become detached from its own history. Most know only legends of Lord Rassilon, whose seal became the official seal of the Time Lords and who harnessed the power of an object called the Eye of Harmony (also called Rassilon's Star), which ensured that the power of the Time Lords would "neither flux nor wither." It just takes a little effort and curiosity from the Doctor to realize that the Eye of Harmony is the stabilized nucleus of a black hole hidden within the planet, the true power source of Gallifrey.

More of Rassilon's secrets could be deduced with a little research and thought, but the Time Lords had no motivation to do so. In "The Deadly Assassin," the Doctor criticizes that Gallifreyan technology has lost innovation and would be considered primitive compared to some worlds he's visited. He also notes with a mixture of disappointment and cynical expectation that his people manipulate truth for the sake of public image and what they see as the greater good. Indeed, how the Time Lords see their place in the universe can be inferred from the name of their great ceremonial hall, the Panopticon, a word that means "all-seeing" and refers specifically to a prison in which all cells are viewable from a central vantage point.

"The Deadly Assassin" also established that Time Lords had a limit of twelve regenerations, giving them thirteen lives. This limit became a plot point in not only "The Deadly Assassin," but several other stories in classic *Doctor Who,* as well as the TV movie. In these stories and others, different Time Lords said there was no way to extend this limit. The Master found a deadly loophole years later by stealing an alien's body, after which he was offered a new "set" of regenerations. It was unclear if this was possible because he possessed a body that had never been granted the ability before or if it was because of cosmic energies he'd absorbed.

Many fans embraced "The Deadly Assassin," while others said it ruined the concept of the Time Lords by sacrificing their mysticism. Hinchcliffe himself admitted that a few aspects of the story made the Time Lords too human. "Barry Letts saw the Time Lords as inscrutable mystics, and Bob Holmes hated that. I didn't quite realize how ironic he was going to be. I wasn't 100 percent happy with it. But as for the corruption you see on Gallifrey and the fact that their powers are almost entirely technology-based, well, that makes sense to me, and that's what I wanted. The Doctor and the Master are Time Lords, and we see that, except for hypnosis, two hearts, and regeneration, any powers they have are based on technology, so that must be true of the Time Lords, too. The fact is, this is a society the Doctor turned away from, ran away from, even. He stole a TARDIS and ran off, and he hates it whenever they show up, and he's our hero. So there must have been something he found rotten with this society to give up his whole life and become a renegade . . . We called the Celestial Intervention Agency the CIA, but really, in their methods, I saw them as the KGB."

Writer Dan Abnett thinks "The Deadly Assassin" came at the right time. "If you have any story that's ongoing, there comes a point where you either dig into your own background and start saying new things, or it just keeps floating on the surface. It probably would have been a mistake not to give us more about the Time Lords and Gallifrey—by that point, the Doctor had been around for more than a decade. Yes, we learned that there's this Eye of Harmony that gives them power, but we don't know exactly how it works, and we were told almost nothing about Rassilon. . . . Even when we learned more in later stories, we never got the whole picture, so there's still mystery, just like there's still mystery with the Doctor even after you see Gallifrey. Besides, realizing that Time Lords have human frailties isn't spoiling anything when we've already met the Doctor and others."

"Societies go through changes," added Hinchcliffe. "The Time Lords can be mystic for a while, and then more technological and pragmatic, and corrupt for a while, and then maybe be mystical and very Zen again later on."

"The Deadly Assassin" greatly influenced all later stories concerning the Time Lords. Over the years, we learned that Rassilon had led Gallifrey in wars against the ancient vampire race, with battles so bloody that the Time Lords were inspired to turn away from violence afterward. The Doctor later told his companion Leela how long ago the Time Lords sought to improve and help other societies, sharing advanced knowledge. They helped the people of the planet Minyos, who then turned against the Time Lords before tearing their own planet apart with the new nuclear weapons they had developed. The Minyans were also said to have developed machines that allowed for unlimited regenerations, though at the cost of intense pain and trauma.

Time Lords, despite their arrogance, seemed to want peace and made treaties with other time traveling societies. Yet we learned of a dark side too. Once, they'd used time scoops to kidnap random people from space and time to fight for survival in the Death Zone, an isolated place where the Tomb of Rassilon stood in the center. This was called the Game of Rassilon.

As we learned more about Rassilon, the first Gallifreyan to discover time travel (with help from Omega's experiments), it turned out he may have been a vicious tyrant who kept the workings of some of his seemingly magical technology secret from others. Tie-in media proposed the founder of the Time Lords was xenophobic, exiling the Sisterhood of Pythia to the planet Karn because he distrusted their magic. An audio drama said he was responsible for many races being humanoid in appearance, having used time travel and genetic mutation agents to alter evolution across the universe after concluding that the Gallifreyan physical form was superior.

In "The Five Doctors," it was suggested that the Time Lords finally rose against the villain and defeated him, but some believed Rassilon found a way to survive through "perpetual bodily regeneration," achieving what many of his people desired: immortality.

Tie-in media have made even more revelations about Time Lord society, particularly the Big Finish audio drama series *Gallifrey*. In the comics of *Doctor Who Magazine* and in the Eighth Doctor audio dramas produced by Big Finish, it was said that, before he died, Rassilon created a copy of himself to inhabit the Matrix of Gallifrey. This psychic echo of the first Lord of Time was a manipulative figure who occasionally influenced events from afar, desiring to one day return to power and extend his dominion. He saw the Doctor as a weapon, eventually earning the hero's hatred.

If the real Rassilon had been anything like his Matrix echo, then he must have been a madman; and Time Lord society was, in a way, corrupt at its foundation.

13
A New Style

"Entropy increases. . . . The more you put things together, the more they keep falling apart."

—THE FOURTH DOCTOR, FROM "LOGOPOLIS" (1981)

In several interviews, Tom Baker explained that by his seventh year as the Doctor he felt he knew better than others how to produce the show. "Graham got on my nerves a lot," he said, concerning his relationship with producer Graham Williams. "He was a good man. . . . He had a strong will, and he overrode me sometimes, which irritated me. I did at one point offer to resign and then was persuaded to go on for a good time afterwards."

As the seventeenth year of the program came to an end and a Douglas Adams story called "Shada" was unable to finish production due to a technician strike, Graham Williams decided to leave. Tom Baker was fighting regularly with Lalla Ward, which led to a very tense working environment for all. Baker was no longer having fun as he had in the early years, and he realized that his unwillingness to take notes from others was becoming an obstacle. As he later said in the documentary *A New Body at Last,* "I thought to myself, *I can't go on like this, disagreeing with people and thinking I know more than they do.* Because people who are in charge of things are entitled to make creative decisions that will change certain emphases."

Production unit manager John Nathan-Turner was hired to produce *Doctor Who* for the next year, though officially the BBC considered him a unit manager who was filling in until he proved himself. Nevertheless, Nathan-Turner—known to his friends as JNT—decided to make major changes. Aiming for an older audience, JNT reduced the show's humor considerably and involved more complex science fiction in the storylines. Barry Letts returned as executive producer for the season, and Christopher Bidmead joined as script editor, replacing Douglas Adams.

The title sequence was redone, and Delia Derbyshire's musical arrangement was redone with synthesizers by Peter Howell. Dudley Simpson, who had been composing the incidental music on the show for years, was let go. The Radiophonic Workshop itself now arranged all incidental music, using new electronic instruments. A fiberglass model replaced the wooden TARDIS prop.

To enhance the marketability of the characters, Nathan-Turner wanted the Doctor and his companions to wear the same clothing consistently, like a uniform. Ward insisted on retaining a say in Romana's costume choices, but the Fourth Doctor's look received a total overhaul: burgundy overcoat with matching trousers and hat and a new twenty-four-foot scarf in various shades of crimson. Topping it off, question marks now decorated the collar of his shirts. Baker disliked the costume and loathed the collar question marks. Though JNT defended the marketability of a shirt with question marks over a plain white shirt, Bidmead agreed with Baker and later argued: "He doesn't see himself as 'Doctor who?' The Doctor knows who he is."

The eighteenth season began with "The Leisure Hive." A trip to Brighton Beach results in K-9 Mark II exploding, prompting a petition by fans to save their beloved robot dog. Repaired, K-9 appeared later in the season, but John Nathan-Turner still intended to remove him by the end of Baker's run, thinking the character was too silly. "The Leisure Hive" also featured the removal of the randomizer unit in the TARDIS, restoring the Doctor's ability to navigate.

But the real conflicts lay behind the scenes rather than in the plotlines. Ward and Baker were still fighting, director Lovett Bickford went seriously over budget—thereby dunking JNT in hot water—and ratings dropped with each new episode of "The Leisure Hive." The trend continued with the next story, and for the first time in years *Doctor Who* episodes weren't making Britain's top 100 TV charts. One cause for the dip in ratings was rival network ITV now airing the US program *Buck Rogers in the 25th Century* during the same time slot, attracting many viewers with its superior production values. However, even when ITV stopped airing the American show, *Doctor Who* figures didn't really pick back up.

Baker didn't care for JNT's changes, objecting that the atmosphere was darkening and the stories were becoming too reliant on complicated techno-babble rather than moral arguments. Believing that the dialogue was hemorrhaging personality, he regularly tried to change it, shouting, "This doesn't sound like anything, it's just audible print!" He also believed many of the new scripts were overwritten: "We don't need that line, we can *act* it!"

Baker's outbursts caused tension with Bidmead, who argued that people had spent time crafting the scripts and their work deserved respect. Ward sympathized with the pressure under which the writers were working, but she agreed with Baker that characterization was suffering in many scripts presented over the past two years.

As she said in *Doctor Who Magazine* in 1991, "We used to have the most awful problems with our writers. Tom and I used to have to rewrite most of our dialog with the director usually because it wasn't right for the parts we were playing, and it happened from the very start. Our actual rehearsal time, which was incredibly tight, was reduced still further as a result. So the program was always a heavy workload—we had this responsibility for the show, and we were doing so many a year against the problems of a small budget and scripts that we wouldn't have done without at least an element of rewriting."

JNT and Letts also had increasing creative differences. Nathan-Turner wanted to mark a change in the show by using only new writers and directors rather than veterans. But looking over new scripts, Letts argued that several didn't make sense and weren't consistent with established ideas about the program. According to Letts, JNT exhibited an unwillingness to discuss this, relying entirely on Christopher Bidmead to rework the scripts. Bidmead worked late many nights, occasionally finding himself locked in the BBC offices after working hours ended, concluding that he wasn't receiving the respect or payment he deserved.

In later interviews Letts often criticized JNT's working style, suggesting that Nathan-Turner didn't focus on scripts because he was more interested in pursuing marketing. Letts saw this as a serious mistake, pointing out that he and Terrance Dicks had successful seasons because they discussed every story. Bidmead later commented: "The problem was, at any stage, John might leap in and say, 'Oh, no, we can't do that.' . . . He clearly wasn't very interested in the scripts. He was interested in somehow keeping control of the process."

On the other side of the coin, different writers and directors spoke well of Nathan-Turner and how he encouraged them to bring their own take on the stories and trusted them to do their jobs. In any event, Baker decided this would be his last season.

STATE OF DECAY

The announcement that Baker was leaving shocked many fans. After nearly seven years, many children truly didn't consider that other Doctors had come before him (as this was before the old adventures were regularly rebroadcast and available for personal ownership). In other countries that had been importing the show only in the last few years, Baker was the only version of the hero many viewers knew. But others felt that it was definitely time for a change, as this incarnation had become so familiar that he was now predictable. In his interviews, the actor assured fans that his departure wouldn't ruin the show, which itself had no reason to stop.

Asked on the TV show *Nationwide* what he would do after leaving the role, Tom Baker answered, "I'm going into oblivion, I suppose. . . . We've now reached 100 million viewers around the world in about thirty-seven countries, and I've done the best I can with this, and I don't think I can do any more with it, which is a good enough reason to leave and give someone else a chance to nudge it on a bit. . . . I think it's probably good for everybody to have changes every now and then."

When asked what sort of man might take over the role, Baker smiled and remarked "You're making the assumption that it's going to be a man anyway that's taking over."

Years later, Baker admitted that he hadn't been joking about fading into oblivion. Knowing this was his last season, he began to worry about what to do after leaving a seven-year role that had brought him much fame and respect. This fear added to his terseness on set.

After two stories, the Doctor and Romana embarked on a trilogy of adventures known as the E-space trilogy. After learning that the Time Lords wanted Romana to return to Gallifrey—lest she become further corrupted by the Doctor's influence—viewers saw the TARDIS lost in a pocket universe, designated "E-space" (as opposed to the Doctor's universe of

"N-space"). There they fought literal vampires, who regarded Time Lords as "the ancient enemy," and met young math prodigy Adric, who helped them during an adventure that resulted in his brother's death. With no other family, Adric stowed away on the TARDIS.

Twenty-one-year-old Matthew Waterhouse played Adric. He later said that the tension between Baker and the rest of the production team surprised and affected him. He described Baker as "a difficult man," but he added, "to be fair, he has never pretended otherwise. . . . Tom's not a fake."

In various interviews, Waterhouse said he felt guilty about intruding on the strong duo of Ward and Baker, but otherwise he had a good experience, getting along well with Ward in particular. In an interview with *Doctor Who Magazine,* Lalla Ward had a very different opinion of her colleague.

> Matthew was a little brat. He threw his weight around because he thought that playing a so-called second leadish type part in *Doctor Who* was a big thing to have got, therefore he must be wonderful. Well, he wasn't. He was obnoxious. He was rude to people like wardrobe mistresses and make-up girls, and I can't be doing with that from anybody. I can't bear it. I mean, why do it? Especially when you're a new boy. . . . God knows he had no cause to behave that way, 'cause he couldn't act his way out of a cardboard box.

Bidmead didn't agree with JNT's insistence on including a very young man in the cast. He went along with the idea but said that he, JNT, and Letts all later agreed that the resulting character didn't satisfy them.

The E-space trilogy ended with "Warrior's Gate," an introspective tale on how different beings might view time's effects and power. The story's atmosphere of confusion reflected the disorganization and trouble behind the scenes. Originally, this final story of the trilogy was to be a Gallifreyan political thriller called "Sealed Orders," but writer Christopher Priest had trouble scripting his ideas into a format appropriate for television and for *Doctor Who* in particular. As a result, "Warrior's Gate," written by Stephen Gallagher, went into production instead. But as with some of the other new writers JNT had recruited, Gallagher wasn't used to writing for television and director Paul Joyce rewrote large portions of the script.

Then Joyce himself caused concern on set, and production assistant Graeme Harper, who had worked on several of the show's adventures, warned others that the man wasn't adequately prepared or skilled to direct. Joyce's arguments on set plus a carpenter's strike led to delays in filming and sacrificing parts of the story. Bidmead, having actively tried to salvage this adventure, decided soon after its completion not to remain as script editor for a second year.

In "Warrior's Gate" Romana meets people who would benefit greatly from having a Time Lord in their midst. As the Doctor runs back to the TARDIS in order to finally leave E-space, Romana announces she's going to stay and be useful rather than return to her native universe, where she will have to answer the summons of the Time Lords. The Doctor barely has time to say goodbye, giving her K-9 II as a parting gift. As he flies off, he proudly remarks that Romana shall be more than all right in her new home, "She'll be superb."

Lalla Ward protested that her ending was too abrupt and lacked the genuine emotion that should have informed a farewell between the Doctor and Romana, who had obviously developed a deep connection. She wanted Romana to acknowledge how her fellow Time Lord had changed her life. But Nathan-Turner insisted that doing so would make the show too much like a soap opera and that the departure of a companion was just a small part of the story. Since then, Ward has said in interviews that she doesn't mind her character's departure now and that the speed of it fits with the pace of the story's ending.

Before Romana's final adventure, Baker and Ward announced their engagement. Baker joked that the idea of not being able to argue with Ward on a regular basis was too much to bear. The two married in December 1980. Sixteen months later they divorced. Lalla Ward later reflected: "I loved and in many ways still love Tom very much. The trouble is, our careers came to be just as important as each other, and we grew apart."

Though they have said at various times that they hold no ill will toward each other and enjoyed their time on the program, Baker and Ward haven't kept in contact over the years. Douglas Adams later introduced Lalla to ethologist and evolutionary biologist Richard Dawkins, the man who gave us the word "meme" in his 1976 book *The Selfish Gene*. The two have been married since 1992, and she has illustrated several of his books.

Romana continued to fascinate fans after her departure. In the *Doctor Who* novels published by Virgin in the 1990s, Romana returned from E-space and became president of the High Council of Time Lords. Later novels published by BBC Books had her regenerate into a more ruthless incarnation. Ward reprised the role in several BBC audio dramas, though these productions didn't have rights to the character, meaning she could never be named directly.

Starting in 2000, Ward again reprised her role as Romana II for Big Finish audio dramas. These adventures adopted the idea that the character returned and became president, while ignoring the BBC Books stories that depicted a ruthless Romana III. In these audio dramas, Ward has appeared alongside several other Doctors as well as Baker's other female co-star, Louise Jameson, when the audio play *Zagreus* featured a meeting between Romana and Leela. Fans reacted positively to the pairing of two such different characters, both introduced alongside the Fourth Doctor, and it led to the *Gallifrey* audio series, featuring Romana and Leela working together to change Time Lord society for the better while dealing with political schemes and time terrorists. Both women had their respective K-9 units at their side.

According to Jameson, "Off-microphone, we have a fantastic relationship, Lalla and I, but we are quite opposite. She has such a scientific mind, and I do work more on instinct. . . . In many ways, it is a writer's dream, I would have thought, to have such polar opposites to work with. There was one story where we had to change character; Our [Leela's and Romana's] personalities were swapped. . . . Lalla loved it, I mean really loved it, and interpreted Leela's personality like some kind of hippy. I really struggled with the techno-babble and lack of instinct. I was very glad to get back into Leela's skin."

In the modern program, many fans have wondered if Romana can't return, believing that such a clever, driven woman might have found a way to survive the Last Great Time War. In *Doctor Who Annual 2006*, Russell T. Davies wrote that Romana was indeed President of the High Council of Time Lords when the Last Great Time War began. But years later, the two-part special "The End of Time" indicated that either she had been ousted from office before the end of the war or died and was replaced since a different president led the High Council during the final battles.

IT'S THE END

Following the E-space trilogy, the Doctor and Adric wind up on the peaceful planet Traken, befriending a scientist named Nyssa and her father, Tremas. The Master appears again and succeeds in extending his life beyond the twelve-regeneration limit, using powerful stolen energies to possess Tremas's body, killing the man's mind in the process. With his new lease on life, the Master displays a new twisted humor as well. When Nyssa confronts the villain about the murder of her father, the Master smiles and remarks, "But his body remains useful."

Peter Pratt and then Geoffrey Beevers—the latter the husband of Caroline John, who played Dr. Liz Shaw—had played the Master's final disfigured Time Lord form earlier during the Fourth Doctor's career. Having used his last regeneration, the character now survived through a combination of absorbed cosmic energy and sheer will, making him more monstrous. Anthony Ainley—who had appeared briefly in the James Bond film *You Only Live Twice* and whose brother had been Baker's roommate—played Tremas and then the new Master (notice that "Tremas" is just the villain's name with the letters mixed up).

Our hero already knew he was nearing the end of another life. Throughout the next "Logopolis," he saw a featureless figure stalking him. This "Watcher" turned out to be a projection of the Doctor's future self, his face blank because the Time Lord's new identity hadn't been forged yet. As Christopher Bidmead explained, this figure explored regeneration from a Time Lord's point of view. While humans might see it as a contained and sudden transformation, a Time Lord might perceive the glimmer of his next life as a Watcher who approaches and then fuses with him as regeneration begins. The Master's schemes had inadvertently weakened reality and causality, giving the Watcher physical form.

After the Master and the Doctor join forces to stabilize reality, the villain betrays the hero and tries to take the universe hostage. The Doctor destroys the Master's resources, suffering a fatal fall in the process. As he remembers the friends and enemies of his fourth life, the Doctor looks up at his new companions and smiles softly, whispering: "It's the end . . . but the moment has been prepared for." The Watcher and the Doctor merge, and the Fifth Doctor appears.

Baker initially didn't like the regeneration sequence. He felt that it wasn't terribly heroic to deliver his last lines while lying down, even if the hero's first and third regenerations had taken place lying down. He also questioned whether his farewell was too brief and quiet, proposing that, through the Doctor's attempt to prepare his companions, it be more emotional.

Later on, however, Baker admitted that the ending produced positive results. "People did say afterwards they found it very touching, the fact that I was unemotional." He also came to like the simplicity of those final lines rather than issuing a goodbye speech; it emphasized the sense of a change rather than ending. "I haven't really died, I've just been regenerated. You know, which is rather like a kind of Buddhist philosophy, isn't it? . . . 'Don't worry about me, I'm coming back as an otter.'"

When the crew met at a pub, Baker shared a drink with Peter Davison. According to Davison, Baker said something that he couldn't hear over the noise of others. Believing the older actor had offered him advice, Davison smiled and nodded politely. When asked about it, Baker said that he had probably suggested Davison purchase another round and would never dream of giving advice on the character. Each Doctor had to find his own path.

THE NEXT LIFE

"They ask me which other Doctor I admired. . . . I say, 'Other Doctor? OTHER DOCTOR?'"

—TOM BAKER, FROM THE DOCUMENTARY
ADVENTURES IN TIME AND SPACE (1999)

After leaving, Baker starred as Sherlock Holmes in a BBC miniseries adaptation of *The Hound of the Baskervilles*. He also appeared as the mad Captain Redbeard Rum in *Blackadder II* with Rowan Atkinson, Stephen Fry, and company. Years later, he portrayed Puddleglum in the BBC's adaptation of *The Silver Chair.* He also did a lot of voice work for television and video games, including the narration of the popular sketch comedy show *Little Britain,* starring Matt Lucas and David Walliams, the latter of whom is an outspoken Whovian.

Though he occasionally jokes that he is unaware of other Doctors, Baker has spoken out in support of all who have taken up the role, declaring that each made the hero his own. In *Doctor Who Magazine* #411, he generously said: "Looking back, nobody ever failed in the part."

In 1983, Baker declined to appear in "The Five Doctors," thinking the script didn't warrant his presence and believing it too soon for him to reappear after his departure. Until asked to record DVD commentaries, Baker had never watched his own adventures as the Doctor, fearing he would be too critical of his performance and what shots made it to the final edit. While other Doctors of the classic program were reprising their roles for audio dramas by Big Finish, Baker regularly turned down the opportunity.

He did, however, record many *Doctor Who* audio books, and twenty-eight years after leaving the role he finally agreed to record new audio plays released directly to CD by the BBC. The deciding factor for him had been the involvement of Nicholas Courtney, returning as the Brigadier. Unfortunately, Courtney's health prevented his involvement. Richard Franklin stepped in, reprising his role of Mike Yates. It was a skewed reunion since Yates had never met the Fourth Doctor. The first adventure was called *Hornets' Nest,* and four others followed before another series of direct-to-CD audio dramas called *The Demon's Quest.*

Louise Jameson later sent an e-mail to Tom Baker and spoke of her positive experiences with Big Finish Productions, swaying the reluctant actor to contact Big Finish and agree to star in new audio plays on a regular basis, revealing "untold" adventures of the Fourth Doctor.

Tom Baker has repeatedly expressed his delight at working with old friends again as he records new adventures of his old role. When asked if he finds the experience strange, he simply says that no actor who plays the heroic Time Lord ever leaves the part behind. As he said in an interview with *Doctor Who Magazine* in 2009, "I never did leave *Doctor Who.* And *Doctor Who* never left me."

14

The New Beginning

"That's the trouble with regeneration. You never quite know what you're going to get."

—THE FIFTH DOCTOR, FROM "CASTROVALVA" (1982)

Though the eighteenth season met with poor viewing figures, the BBC had been satisfied with the program's new stories and atmosphere. John Nathan-Turner officially became the show's producer, gaining the freedom to pursue his vision with a new Doctor.

In 1980, unlike Hartnell, Troughton, Pertwee, or Baker, actor Peter Davison had actually watched the show as a child, starting with the first adventure. When Davison's agent told him the BBC was looking for a new Doctor, the actor's reaction was, "Why are you telling me?" He thought it was ridiculous for him to be considered for the role, partly because he was too young. The Doctor was always a man in his forties or fifties, and Davison was only twenty-nine.

Peter Davison—born Peter Moffett—worked odd jobs, including as a mortuary attendant, before becoming an actor and assistant stage manager at the Nottingham Playhouse. He adopted his stage name to avoid confusion with director Peter Moffat. He appeared in the TV miniseries *The Hitchhiker's Guide to the Galaxy* and starred opposite Jeremy Irons in the *Love for Lydia* miniseries. By 1981, Davison wasn't the relative unknown that Baker had been more than seven years earlier. All of Britain knew him as the veterinarian Tristan Farnon in *All Creatures Great and Small*.

JNT had worked for a time as unit manager on that show and believed that Davison would bring a fresh new take on the Doctor. Christopher Bidmead also wisely pointed out that literal age wasn't important since the Doctor was more than several centuries older than anyone who could portray him. Why couldn't a being from another planet with a long lifespan and regenerative abilities look like a man in his late twenties? The important point was that the actor brought earnestness and gravitas to convince the audience he was the hero.

After careful consideration, Davison accepted the offer and signed a contract for three years. Following Baker's seven-year tenure as the Doctor, Davison found himself in a different fan atmosphere when the BBC announced his casting. Appearing on *Pebble Mill at One,* a popular daily talk show, the actor was presented with fan drawings and opinions of how his Doctor should look and behave, an experience the previous Time Lord heroes never had to endure. One mustachioed fan suggested Davison simply take Tristan and add a stronger quality of bravery, which the actor later joked is what he delivered in the end.

To his credit, Davison listened patiently to these suggestions, understanding the effect of Baker's tenure. He had, by this time, already discussed the role with Letts and Nathan-Turner, deciding that his Doctor would seem more human and occasionally unsure of himself, contrasting the confident alien nature of the fourth incarnation.

Davison later joked in interviews that he didn't find JNT as interested in discussing his character's nature as much as the costume. A cricket fan, Davison thought it might be fun to see the Fifth Doctor wear a casual cricketing outfit, then throw a long, dark coat over it. But JNT insisted on costume unity. "I would have preferred the Doctor to have gone into the changing room and just picked things off the shelf, mixed and matched," Davison remarked at Gallifrey One in 2011 during a Q & A session. "It was a bit too designed for my liking, but it was a very comfortable costume. . . . It really wasn't a Victorian cricketing outfit."

JNT wanted Davison to wear the question-mark shirt that Baker had worn in his final season, later adding that it would be good for the actor to have a unique ornament, just as Baker had his scarf. As Davison explained in an interview for this book, JNT "came to me after thinking about it for a couple of weeks, and he said, 'I've got it! Stick a celery on your lapel.' I said, 'Okay, as long as you explain it in the show. People are going to wonder.' He didn't have any explanation sorted out. He just wanted something weird to remind the audience that the Doctor is alien. So there I was, question marks and celery." Davison conceded to the vegetable—a prop, obviously, as a real one would have rotted during filming—but asked that they at least give a reason for its presence.

Sure enough, the Fifth Doctor finds a stick of celery during his first adventure, "Castrovalva," and then, with no explanation, attaches it to his lapel. His friends don't ask why, and the adventurers simply return to the TARDIS. It wasn't until Davison's final season that he reminded JNT to give the audience a valid reason for the vegetable's presence. In Davison's final story, fans learn that the Doctor's fifth incarnation is allergic to "certain gases in the praxis range." The celery acts as a warning system, turning purple in the presence of those gases.

It wasn't all that strange for the Doctor to have an allergy unique to one incarnation, as he had different physical attributes in different bodies. The Third Doctor liked wine, while the Eleventh Doctor was disgusted by it. The First Doctor needed glasses on occasion, but the Second Doctor had excellent eyesight. Davison still found the explanation of an allergy rather silly but was glad at least that it had been delivered before his departure.

As for his Doctor's personality, Davison described the initial ideas during the Gallifrey One convention in 2011, saying, "You start off using them [previous Doctors] as crutches for the first few stories. I took the irritability of William Hartnell and bits of Patrick Troughton. I made a choice not to act like Tom because he was too recent, and there was a sense that the Doctor had become like a superhero, so I was more vulnerable."

Along with this new vulnerability and less confrontational nature, Davison played the Doctor as if he were a little weary with age. He acted as an elder brother to Tegan, Nyssa, and Adric, almost paternal with them at times. During his earlier episodes, the Fifth Doctor occasionally wears glasses when studying a problem. In the 2007 mini-episode "Time Crash," the Tenth Doctor refers to them as "brainy-specs," revealing that his fifth incarnation hadn't needed them; he just wore them when he wanted to look clever.

THE NEW CREW

Sarah Sutton—a former ballet dancer and the youngest British actress to play the lead in *Alice in Wonderland* in live-action film or television—played

Nyssa, who echoed Vicki, another young scientific expert who joined the Doctor after the death of her father . . . and, in this case, her entire planet, thanks to the Master.

Nathan-Turner had decided that Adric and Nyssa weren't enough. For the first time since 1964, three people would join the Doctor. He approached Elisabeth Sladen about appearing in Baker's final story, serving as a familiar face to ease fans through the transition. Then she could remain as a companion for the Fifth Doctor. He believed fans would love seeing Baker and Sladen reunited and that they would more easily accept the new incarnation considering Sarah Jane's status as, in his words, "the most popular companion."

But Sladen declined the offer. She had left on a good note and didn't want to spoil it. She didn't want Sarah Jane to return to her old role with no serious change in her relationship to the Doctor and his world. As she later admitted, she was also somewhat scared to return to the old show and find that perhaps she didn't fit in anymore.

JNT also approached Louise Jameson about returning as Leela. She was happy to return for the regeneration story but didn't think she could commit to much more. As she explained, JNT "offered me Tom's last show and the following season. I only wanted to do two or maybe three stories. In retrospect, this is one of those 'Did I make the right decision?' moments. But maybe I wouldn't have been free to do *Tenko* had I accepted, and that would have been a tragedy."

Wishing to capitalize on new Australian interest in the program, Nathan-Turner suggested a new companion from Australia. Janet Fielding was cast in the role of Tegan Jovanka, a flight attendant trainee on her way to the airport when she stumbles across the Doctor and the Master during "Logopolis." After the Master kills her aunt, she helps the Doctor and witnesses his regeneration, then finds herself aboard the TARDIS with the Fifth Doctor who has trouble getting her home.

Along with having three companions on the TARDIS, it seems that Nathan-Turner also wanted to bring back the first-season theme of at least one crew member not wanting to be there. Like Barbara and Ian, Tegan couldn't wait to get back to the life and home she knew, constantly put out by the Doctor's inability to pilot, annoyed that he kept running into monsters and deadly situations.

JNT wanted the audience to relate to the characters more than with previous companions, believing people couldn't really connect to Romana or Leela. But in assembling these new characters, he created a TARDIS crew consisting of a flight attendant trainee and three alien geniuses. The more typical science fiction spaceship team posed a long-tailed irony: Sydney Newman had said decades earlier that having three scientific experts as your main characters wouldn't make for interesting dialogue or drama that children could enjoy.

Along with the new crew, Nathan-Turner made one more major alteration to the program. While he certainly didn't use it in every adventure, fans knew that the Doctor could rely on his trusty sonic screwdriver to extricate himself from a variety of dungeons and jail cells or to mess with computer systems and signal transmissions. Christopher Bidmead considered the sonic screwdriver a "plot-killer," thinking it a bad idea to give the hero a generic tool to solve various dramatic situations. JNT agreed, calling the screwdriver a magic wand. In the TV story "The Visitation," the device was destroyed, and the Fifth Doctor remarked that it was like losing an old friend.

As the year went on, the crew gelled. Nyssa was a capable scientist rather than a traumatized girl. Tegan griped a lot, but also assisted in several fights against evil. The Doctor developed a stronger mentor relationship with Adric, perhaps seeing something of himself in the boy.

Just as the crew was seemingly becoming a family, the penultimate story of the season shocked many when Adric died trying to save Earth. Rather than ending on its usual music, the episode's credits ran silently over a still-frame image of the mathematics badge the young genius had always worn. A companion hadn't died since "The Daleks' Master Plan," and Tegan and Nyssa ask why the Doctor can't use the TARDIS to go back in time and prevent the death. Angry and defensive, the hero explains that such an action is too dangerous to risk and demands they never ask him to alter events in his own timeline again. The season ended with Tegan leaving the TARDIS, although she returned during the next year.

ROTATING STAFF

Behind the scenes, problems regarding the scripts were still occurring. With Bidmead gone, Antony Root became interim script editor. On his first day,

Nathan-Turner handed him a stack of scripts and treatments, telling Root to go through them and to produce the one he'd already selected. "By the way," Nathan-Turner added, "I'm off to the US for a *Doctor Who* convention." JNT wouldn't return for a full week.

Root knew production was waiting for him to release the first script, but felt obligated to read it first. Concluding it wasn't ready for production or good enough to launch the season, Root took his concerns to Letts, who agreed and brought back Bidmead to dash off a new introduction adventure for the Fifth Doctor. When JNT returned to find that the script he'd selected wasn't in production, he argued with Letts, who criticized him for placing such a task in the hands of an interim editor and then leaving for a week when time was of the essence.

To avoid another damaging Saturday night rivalry with ITV, the BBC now aired *Doctor Who* twice weekly. Root decided to leave after a few months, and Eric Saward, who had written "The Visitation," became the new script editor. Saward happily accepted but found it difficult to organize the scripts into a cohesive season. That each story also had four regular characters rather than two also proved a challenge.

Despite these hardships, the nineteenth season became a great success. Ratings nearly doubled, and many were excited about the show again after having grown accustomed to its previous style. Some in the media had dismissed this new, younger Doctor—referring to him as "Dr. Whozat" and "The Wet Vet" (referencing his previous role as Tristan)—but Davison's portrayal was changing minds, as were the stories. Fans felt this more human Doctor seemed heroic because of, rather than despite, his increased self-doubt.

Sadly, tensions rose yet again behind the scenes. JNT decided that each story of the twentieth year would feature the return of an enemy from the show's past. He also had the casting department look for well-known stars to appear in episodes and decided to dress the female characters in outfits that showed off their legs and skin to attract more viewers.

In the "The Arc of Infinity," the Doctor returns to Gallifrey and encounters a tough, by-the-book Commander of the Chancellory Guard who winds up shooting him. Commander Maxil was played by Colin Baker, happy to join a program he had watched as a child. But Colin Baker

Peter Davison (foreground) and his companions Janet
Fielding (Tegan Jovanka), Mark Strickson (Vislor
Turlough), and Sarah Sutton (Nyssa)
Photograph courtesy of Big Finish Productions

feared that taking the role very likely meant he wouldn't ever play the
Doctor.

This season featured the Black Guardian trilogy, in which the cosmic
villain who had chased after the Key to Time came back for revenge, recruiting a young student named Vislor Turlough to kill the Doctor. The boy failed
but joined the TARDIS, the Black Guardian forcing him to try again. By the
end of the trilogy, the Doctor realized the truth and that the young man
had been coerced. The hero offered him forgiveness and Turlough remained
on the TARDIS while Nyssa found a new life as a physician in Earth's future.
Though the idea of a hidden enemy aboard the TARDIS was appealing initially, many felt that extending this sub-plot for weeks and weeks greatly
diminished the threat. Even Mark Strickson, who played the role, later said
that the plot didn't sustain well across such a large portion of the season.

Davison was also growing more impatient with the filming of the show.
He believed that the TARDIS crew members were being written as charac-
teristics rather than fully realized characters. Rehearsal time tightened,
and the directors sometimes rushed through filming. In one case, Davison
recalled a time when they skipped rehearsal for one scene altogether, and

he was filmed walking into an area without properly arranged lighting, leaving him quite literally in the dark.

Season nineteen also had budget concerns, sacrificing two episodes to fund *K-9 and Company,* a spin-off pilot JNT hoped would become its own show. Starring Elisabeth Sladen and John Leeson, the story featured Sarah Jane now having strange adventures on her own. At her side was K-9 Mark III, sent to her special delivery from the Doctor. The pilot failed to generate interest and Sladen often joked later that the end result was a little embarrassing.

Eric Saward also had difficulty with JNT. The script editor wanted to bring back a little of the old humor and suggested recruiting Robert Holmes, as he had written some of the most famous stories and had established much of the Time Lord mythos. But JNT resisted both ideas, feeling they would regress the program rather than push it forward.

Figures dropped again. Some viewers were confused by the many references to events depicted on the show years ago. Omega hadn't been seen or even mentioned in almost a decade, so his sudden return didn't seem all that dramatic to viewers under ten. (Although reruns were now broadcast, this was still when people caught them by chance and couldn't call up episodes via a streaming service.) A grim tip of the hat occurs in the season finale story "The King's Daemons," when the Doctor remarks that the Master isn't performing up to his usual standards.

Perhaps the biggest proof of how odd the program had become was the introduction of a new character in "The King's Daemons": the shape-shifting android Kamelion. First seen as a tool of the Master's, Kamelion was freed from the villain's control and joined the TARDIS. While JNT thought K-9 was silly, an android was perfectly acceptable.

Behind the scenes, Kamelion wasn't an actor in a suit. It was a real mechanical device that John Nathan-Turner had decided to use in the show. Unfortunately, the production team had a difficult time controlling the robot's movements and making sure his mouth moved in sync with recorded dialogue from actor Gerald Flood. For this reason, it was said that Kamelion preferred to stay on board the TARDIS. After his first appearance, he wasn't seen again until the Fifth Doctor's second to last adventure "Planet of Fire," when the Master takes control of him once again, leading to the android's destruction. Peter Davison was happy to be rid of the prop, even though he hadn't had to work with it often.

THE ANNIVERSARY

JNT had to sacrifice part of the next season's budget in order to air a twentieth anniversary TV special. He convinced the BBC to broadcast the special in the anniversary month of November, putting it in between the twentieth and twenty-first season. He then negotiated with the Australian Broadcasting Commission to help fund it.

Saward once again approached Nathan-Turner about bringing back Robert Holmes, this time to write the anniversary special. After some discussion, JNT agreed to meet with the writer. Holmes, however, had his own reservations, not eager to reference too much past continuity that he himself hadn't established. He accepted the task, nonetheless, and began writing a script he entitled "The Six Doctors." The title was a nod to an intended plot reveal that the First Doctor (played by Richard Hurndall) is actually a cyborg infiltrator sent by the Cybermen, a joke on the fact that viewers knew this wasn't the deceased William Hartnell.

But Holmes was having difficulty with the script and informed Saward that he didn't think it would work. The script editor understood and thanked Holmes for informing them ahead of time, suggesting that the writer might return to pen a different tale in the subsequent season. Saward then commissioned a new script from Terrance Dicks, who agreed on the condition that the story include neither Daleks nor a K-9. After Dicks began writing the script, JNT had him include a single Dalek and a cameo for K-9 Mark III.

Both Troughton and Pertwee agreed to return, though some negotiation took place with the latter actor, who wanted more money. Tom Baker refused to commit fully until he had read the script. Terrance Dicks gave the Fourth Doctor the strongest part on the justification that, while Peter Davison was the current Doctor, Baker was still the most popular. But Tom Baker finally declined. Rather than relay his decision by phone or mail, the actor met with Nathan-Turner in person to explain his reasons and wish the project well.

JNT had hoped that Colin Baker would return to reprise his role of Commander Maxil, but a schedule conflict prevented him. If the casting had gone according to plan, some wonder if JNT would have decided not to cast Colin Baker as the Sixth Doctor later, the actor becoming fixed in viewers' eyes as a different Time Lord. Carole Ann Ford reprised the role of Susan for the first time in nineteen years. Ford and Davison hoped to address the emotions of the Doctor reuniting with his granddaughter after so long, both of them now very different people. But JNT nixed the story point, saying it was too much like a soap opera rather than a science fiction story, and fearing the familiarity between Davison and Ford could be mistaken for romance.

Filming didn't go smoothly, and the Doctors found it disappointing not to have more scenes together. JNT believed warring egos would cause problems and kept each Doctor separate for the most part. Davison later observed the silliness of this fear: "We're each our own Doctor."

"The Five Doctors" was delayed by two days to air in cooperation with that year's charity broadcast of Children in Need. This didn't affect the broadcast schedule at PBS in Chicago, though, which aired the special on the actual anniversary date, November 23, 1983. As a result, "The Five Doctors" became the first of two *Doctor Who* adventures to air outside Britain first. (The other is the 1996 TV movie.)

Soon after accepting the role of the Fifth Doctor, Davison had run into Patrick Troughton, who advised him not to remain more than three years. After the experiences of the twentieth season, even the relative success of "The Five Doctors" didn't seem enough. Davison took Troughton's advice and didn't renew his contract. The next season would be his last.

DARKER DAYS

"Oh, marvelous. You're going to kill me. What a finely tuned response to the situation."

—FIFTH DOCTOR, FROM "FRONTIOS" (1984)

In the twenty-first season, JNT went for darker stories to increase viewer interest. "Resurrection of the Daleks" by Eric Saward depicted civilians gunned down in the streets by policemen and had a higher body count than several action movies. To this day it retains the highest number of on-screen deaths for a *Doctor Who* adventure. Fittingly, the Doctor became more sarcastic over the course of this year.

The story has the Daleks' chief scientist, Davros, attempt to create a new Dalek race, a plot by the Dalek Supreme to infiltrate Gallifrey, yet another precursor to the Last Great Time War. At the story's climax, Tegan acknowledges the darker direction of the show, leaving the TARDIS because traveling with the Doctor is no longer fun and involves too much death.

After leaving the show, Janet Fielding became a theatrical agent and represented Paul McGann when he became the Eighth Doctor. She became an outspoken advocate of stronger women in television and film and criticized *Doctor Who*. After declining to participate in audio dramas for years, she had a change of mind in 2006 and has participated in multiple Big Finish adventures, reprising her role as Tegan.

After "Resurrection of the Daleks," the next story, "Planet of Fire," features Turlough's departure as he reunites with his father's people and finds a new home. The same adventure introduces Perpugilliam "Peri" Brown, an American college student studying botany. Played by Nicola Bryant, Peri was John Nathan-Turner's attempt to appeal to Americans just as he'd hoped Tegan appealed to Australian viewers—though in this case, the actor was actually British. Going for sex appeal, the show introduced Peri in a swimsuit and she sported various formfitting costumes for her adventures. Bryant was happy to take the role, her first professional part on television. She got along well with Davison, joking later that he was indeed an old soul like his Doctor and that he reminded her of her father.

Peri's first outing as an official companion came in "The Caves of Androzani" in 1984, Davison's final regular appearance as the Doctor. Along with the return of Robert Holmes as a scriptwriter, this story debuted former production assistant Graeme Harper as a director. To this day, fans speak glowingly of "The Caves of Androzani." It had superb direction, a well-paced story, sharp dialogue, and a heroic sacrifice in the end. Harper's much more hands-on approach and Holmes's writing impressed Davison instantly, and the show's lead said later that he would have happily stayed another year if this was how episodes were filmed.

As happy as he was with his final adventure, Peter Davison has often pointed out (with laughter) that the camera angle during his final moments meant that one of his favorite performances was upstaged by Nicola Bryant's cleavage.

KEEPING BUSY

"I still do that, the voice thing, I got that from you. . . . 'Cos you know what, Doctor? You were my Doctor."

—THE TENTH DOCTOR TO THE FIFTH,
FROM THE MINI-EPISODE "TIME-CRASH" (2007)

Davison continued to appear in various television shows and stage productions and joined the show's thirtieth anniversary charity special, "Dimensions in Time." In 2007, he played King Arthur in the London production of *Spamalot* and starred alongside his daughter, Georgia Moffett, in *Fear, Stress, and Anger*. In 2007, he also returned to *Doctor Who* in the mini-episode "Time Crash."

"It was a very cleverly written piece," Davison said. "It was about the Tenth Doctor remembering being the Fifth Doctor but also about David Tennant remembering watching me on TV. . . . A funny thing about 'Time Crash' was that David was surprised at some of what [writer] Steven [Moffat] pointed out in it. He joked that he hadn't realized he sometimes resembled me with some of his behavior and the 'brainy-specs' we both wear. I was just happy to fit into the old suit—I'm larger now. David's foolish for buttoning his jacket up all the time. When he comes back years from now to meet a future Doctor and he's larger, he'll regret that. . . . I'd be happy to show up for the fiftieth anniversary as well, if they'll have me."

15

A Volcanic Experience

"Change, my dear, and it seems not a moment too soon."
—THE SIXTH DOCTOR TO PERI,
FROM "THE CAVES OF ANDROZANI" (1984)

Born in London during World War II, Colin Baker studied to be a lawyer but changed course at twenty-three, enrolling at the London Academy of Music and Dramatic Art—despite his father's disapproval of the profession. Throughout the '70s and early '80s, he made regular TV appearances, including an episode of Terry Nation's *Blake's 7*. Following his regular role on *The Brothers,* he found TV jobs lacking and went back to theatre. He said in an interview for *Timeless* #3, "That's the trouble with TV series: They tend to restrict your future employment. So I did a lot of touring. . . . I was pretty constantly employed, I'm pleased to say."

Colin Baker had considered asking his agent to try getting him the role of the Fourth Doctor when he'd heard Jon Pertwee was leaving but decided against it. When Tom Baker was leaving the role seven years later, Peter Davison was announced before anything could be done.

He had been quite excited to join "Arc of Infinity," later telling *Timeless*:

> I've never been one to regard a small part as a small part. So this guy Maxil struck me as the most important person in the show . . . and at the end of it, John Nathan-Turner said to me . . . 'This isn't about Maxil the guard, it's about the Doctor. . . . Could you tone down the reactions, please, and the acting in the background?' Ha ha! But because of that, when Peter Davison said a few months later that he was going to leave, JNT thought of me for the part of the Doctor. So it paid off in the end!

Colin Baker became the first, and thus far only, actor cast as the Doctor who had already appeared on the show in a different role. Also unlike the previous Doctors, he was a dedicated science fiction fan, counting Ursula le Guin, Anne McCaffrey, and Frank Herbert among his favorite authors. In 1984, he told *Doctor Who Bulletin,* "After the recording [of 'The Caves of Androzani'], I went home, got out of my car, opened my front door, walked in to where my wife was sitting watching television, and stood there and said, 'I am the Doctor.' She looked at me and said, 'Oh, yes? Could you take the rubbish out, please?'"

As is often the case in *Doctor Who,* he was told to keep his casting a secret until the announcement went out. During our chat at New York Comic-Con, Colin Baker said, "John Nathan-Turner and I were at a pub, and Peter Davison showed up purely by chance. JNT was so determined to keep me a surprise, I needed to pretend we hadn't been talking about *Doctor Who.* I had to make up some story instead of saying, 'Yes, I'm the next Doctor.'"

When Davison did find out that Colin Baker was taking the role, he played a joke by warning Nicola Bryant to be wary. On meeting Baker, Bryant proceeded with caution at first but quickly realized that the man was friendlier than his Doctor would be.

BUILDING THE SIXTH DOCTOR

"Oh, Doctor. If that coat is an example of their top-of-the-range raiment, I'm not surprised they're exclusive. I imagine you are their only customer."

—EVELYN SMYTHE TO THE SIXTH DOCTOR,
FROM THE AUDIO DRAMA *REAL TIME* (2002)

Not surprisingly, John Nathan-Turner first wanted to establish how the Sixth Doctor would dress. Colin Baker didn't wish to appear native to a specific period of Earth's history nor some imagined future. Initially, he suggested something in black, more akin to the Master or the First Doctor. JNT suggested instead that the Sixth Doctor wear a costume in "very bad taste." Colin Baker agreed, imagining several items thrown together without a care if they clashed.

Initially costume designer Pat Godfrey came back with what Colin Baker later described as an interesting and "exquisitely tasteful design of lots of apparently clashing colors." But JNT deemed it "too good," so she was asked to redesign it, resulting in a patchwork, multicolored coat that she personally found appalling. Along with this, the Sixth Doctor wore bright yellow trousers, a bright waistcoat, a long floppy polka-dotted bow tie, and the now-familiar question mark shirt. Colin Baker often commented later that the costume kept him warm in cold locations at least, and wearing it meant he didn't have to look at it himself.

Some have remarked the Sixth Doctor's costume accurately reflected pop culture of the time. As Russell T. Davies said in the documentary *Doctor Who: A New Dimension*, "If you go back and see photographs of yourself in the '80s, they're absolutely terrible, and we all look shocking. And there's Colin Baker in the loudest, most colorful, most 1980s fashion you could have." In a 1987 interview with Michael Sibley, Colin Baker said, "I did keep saying that I wanted to change the costume, but it's a large expense, unfortunately. John liked it as it was and so was not prepared to waste money, as he saw it. They did let me have new waistcoats and ties, just in order to make the timescale clear. I had a different tie and cat button in each of the different time zones."

The cat button on his lapel, which the Sixth Doctor occasionally touched for luck, was Colin Baker's personal addition. As he explained in an interview for this book, "There's that work by Rudyard Kipling, 'The Cat That Walked by Himself,' and there's a repeated line, 'I am the Cat who walks by himself, and all places are alike to me.' I thought, *Well, that's rather like the Doctor, isn't it?* I still like that bit because it hints at the Doctor's nature. The rest of the costume doesn't; it gives you the wrong message about what kind of man he is and what kind of program it is.

"I wanted the Doctor to be alien and complicated," he added. "He'll fight for good and the weak, but he won't always react as we think a typical hero would. If he acts too human, why bother making the character a Time Lord with a mysterious past? He's irascible, argumentative, and impatient with people. He doesn't think to take an extra moment to be polite. 'Don't bother me with social graces, I have evil to fight.' But he can be disturbed by certain types of destruction and loss. . . . I was contracted for three years initially, and, since I mentioned it would be nice to peel layers of the character, John Nathan-Turner agreed and thought I should start off very unpredictable, rather like William Hartnell, and slowly over many stories my Doctor would become more heroic, maybe more mellow. That suggestion of unpredictability wound up turning into this idea that I would have moments of madness during my very first story."

Rather than have the Sixth Doctor's debut adventure begin the next season, Nathan-Turner decided to air his first story immediately after Davison's departure. He feared that the nine months before the twenty-second season began was too long for viewers to wait and they might not care enough to come back to the show. JNT put out the word that he and Eric Saward were accepting submissions for the Sixth Doctor's first adventure. The accepted script was from Anthony Steven, who had previously written episodes for *All Creatures Great and Small, The Prime of Miss Jean Brodie,* and TV adaptations of classic literature.

Colin Baker revealed his Doctor's new costume to the press in January 1984. Production for his first full adventure, "The Twin Dilemma," began weeks afterward and later than intended, due to a labor dispute. Though he enthused for the shoot and the press, Colin Baker was dealing with a personal tragedy. A month earlier, his two-month-old son, Jack, had died of sudden infant death syndrome.

STRANGE BEGINNING

The Fifth Doctor had suffered mental complications and bursts of amnesia in the hours following his regeneration. Nathan-Turner suggested doing this again for the Sixth Doctor but in a more extreme way. In "The Twin Dilemma," the Doctor is pleased with his new form and persona. Peri protests that the previous incarnation had been sweet, which the Doctor finds annoying, saying that he never cared for that version of himself.

Despite a brief anxiety attack, the Doctor seems well enough. But suddenly he attacks Peri, convinced she's an enemy, then backs away in fear at the sight of his own reflection. The Time Lord burst into laughter and then forgets the whole event moments later.

JNT believed the Sixth Doctor's fits of madness would sharply contrast his regeneration with the Fifth Doctor's, who seemed lost and frightened at first. But in the case of "Castrovalva," fans not keen on the timid, amnesiac Fifth Doctor only had to wait until the end of the story to see him grow into a more stable and assertive character. That wasn't the case for Colin Baker, who was still abrasive and possibly unstable by story's end. This, along with his bad attitude toward his companion and the fact that he had mocked the Fifth Doctor only a week after the heroic sacrifice in "The Caves of Androzani," left many viewers with a bad first impression that they would be stuck with for nine months. Insult further compounded injury when, right before the credits rolled, the Sixth Doctor declared: "Whatever else happens, I am the Doctor—whether you like it or not."

Even if they didn't harshly criticize the new Doctor, many simply found "The Twin Dilemma" an uninteresting adventure. Some blamed this fault on writer Anthony Steven not having experience in science fiction, prompting Peter Moffat to request rewrites by Saward when he complained that parts of the story didn't make sense. Others look toward the many disagreements between Saward and Nathan-Turner over the direction. In any event, the damage was done and the next season already seemed shaky.

OFF AND RUNNING

When the twenty-third season began, the Doctor was still suffering gaps in his memory. He was no longer violent with Peri, but still often impatient and insensitive.

The season continued the previous year's higher level of violence. In "Attack of the Cybermen," the villains crush a man's hands, forcing him screaming to his knees as blood pours. The Doctor later uses a Cyberman gun to shoot the villains. These scenes shocked some, while others pointed out that Cybermen were meant to be vicious and the Doctor only grabbed the gun in self-defense when he had no means of escape.

In "Vengeance on Varos," the TARDIS lands on a planet where reality TV forces people into deadly situations, the audience often voting on whether they live or die. The commentary on television violence and viewer desensitization invited quite a lot of criticism, particularly when a person who attacked the Doctor falls into a pool of acid and the hero glibly says, "You'll forgive me if I don't join you." Colin Baker defended that violence had always been a part of the show and that the Doctor had often caused the destruction of his enemies, even if he usually did it indirectly. The Third had used martial arts, while the Fourth used blow guns ("The Deadly Assassin"), took an enemy hostage with a bomb ("Destiny of the Daleks"), and even brandished a gun on rare occasions.

During this season, the format also changed so that stories now ran in two episodes of forty-five minutes rather than four episodes of twenty-five minutes. This changed the familiar pacing and allowed for only one cliffhanger in each story. The show's Saturday evening time slot also pitted it against ITV's broadcast of *The A-Team*. Along with this ratings competition, the system of measuring viewership also came into question. People now had access to VCR technology and could watch at their convenience rather than during fixed time slots.

The season continued with fights against Davros, the Daleks, the Master, and a Time Lord called the Rani, a woman with no scruples about using living subjects for her biological experiments. Meanwhile, the Doctor's relationship with Peri was shifting slowly, making them friends who bickered and teased each other. It may have been a shaky season for viewers, but Colin Baker considered it an incredible time in his life, confident that his hero would continue to develop nicely. He told several people that he intended to remain longer than Tom Baker.

THE DARK TIMES BEGIN

"We could very well be stuck in a limbo of space and time."
—THE SIXTH DOCTOR, FROM "VENGEANCE ON VAROS" (1985)

The BBC supported the show less and less as the 1980s progressed. The UK economy suffered from inflation, but the BBC didn't adjust the program's budget accordingly. During the late 1970s and early '80s, America had been releasing more and more science fiction shows and films with respectable budgets and production values. According to many, there was a growing feeling at the BBC that science fiction was becoming an American genre, something their sensibility and their budgets couldn't match.

According to Colin Baker, "During the 1980s, not just at the BBC but also in much of Britain, there was an increasing embarrassment towards science fiction, that it was popular drama rather than legitimate drama. It's a ridiculous attitude since science fiction lets you explore any topic, social commentary, any aspect of humanity. . . . People were especially embarrassed by *Doctor Who* since on top of being science fiction it was really meant for kids. But that makes it important because children benefit greatly seeing a hero who wants to investigate and looks beyond the obvious. . . . My stories had violence absolutely, but many children's stories and fairy tales are scary, too. It makes the danger real and the hero important."

The show also fell victim to Michael Grade, who became controller of BBC One in 1984, a position he held for roughly two years. He quickly caused controversy when he canceled broadcasts of the hugely popular US series *Dallas*. Some felt that he had done so to show that he was helming the ship now. The numerous and immediate protests from viewers prompted him to change his decision, however. But he said he still had to cancel a program to save money for production of a new drama. Many already knew that Grade didn't care for *Doctor Who,* and during an interview he referred to it as a terrible, tired old format past its prime and laughable when compared to science fiction stories such as *Star Wars* and *E.T.* Grade announced to John Nathan-Turner that *Doctor Who* was leaving the airwaves.

Jonathan Powell was head of Series and Serials at the time and called it an understandable decision since the BBC wasn't really supporting the show any longer, and the writing and direction were suffering from a "lack of inspiration." Colin Baker for his part feared that people would point to his performance as the Doctor as the cause for cancellation. "'We want to do new things, and the only way we can do that is by canceling some of the old things,'" Colin Baker said to *Fantasy Empire* of Grade's decision. "That was his [Grade's] logic."

JNT leaked the news of the cancellation to the press. Although Grade also ended a few other programs, it was *Doctor Who* that got the country's attention. Thousands of letters of protest poured in from British viewers, then even more when American and Australian fans got wind of the news.

Several newspapers reported on the shocking announcement, while political cartoons depicted Daleks storming into the BBC ONE offices to exterminate Michael Grade. Several fans even threatened to protest outside the House of Commons armed with Daleks.

According to Powell, a meeting ensued at which he was told that there had to be new *Doctor Who* episodes. Grade announced that the show wasn't canceled but merely suspended for eighteen months. Then he went on vacation. In later interviews, Grade continued to speak of how silly the show was, intimating that the thousands of protest letters were written by just three desperate fans. Jonathan Powell admitted later that they had considered replacing JNT but they simply couldn't find anyone to take on the job of producer.

During this hiatus, Nicola Bryant and Colin Baker recorded a *Doctor Who* radio play called *Slipback,* providing a new adventure for fans while they waited to see whether the show would return. The Sixth Doctor still appeared in the comic strips of *Doctor Who Magazine,* where he and Peri were joined by the strange character Frobisher, a member of a race of shape-shifters called Whifferdills. Frobisher initially appeared as a self-styled, street-smart detective with a featureless cartoony face and glasses. He later adopted the form of a penguin that became less realistic and more cartoonish as time went on.

Perhaps the strangest result of the year and a half suspension was the release of a song called "Doctor in Distress," written and performed by Ian Levine and Fiachra Trench, who had collaborated on the theme song for *K-9 and Company*. Since Grade had said that he'd dismissed *Doctor Who* to save money, the pop song was meant to raise enough funds to overcome that problem. After the song's production was announced, rumors circulated that Elton John—a known *Doctor Who* fan—would be involved. The rumors proved false. A group of twenty-five performers assembled, along with Colin Baker, Nicola Bryant, Nicholas Courtney, and Anthony Ainley. The now legendary film composer Hans Zimmer played the music. Unfortunately, the single lacked in quality, and many stations, including BBC Radio, didn't broadcast it. Considered a failure, what proceeds it did raise went to cancer research.

But while "Doctor in Distress" didn't change matters, the ongoing and ever-increasing protests from fans evidently wore down Michael Grade. He agreed to let *Doctor Who* return in late 1986 but with fourteen episodes each twenty-five minutes in length, making it the shortest season in the program's history to date. The production office was told to relaunch the show's style completely. The next season would determine whether *Doctor Who* continued.

SOME TIME LATER

"Matter disperses, coalesces, forms into other patterns, other worlds. Nothing can be eternal."
> —THE SIXTH DOCTOR, FROM "THE MYSTERIOUS PLANET" (1986)

Eric Saward met with Robert Holmes, and the two decided that the new fourteen-episode season would involve one long sub-plot: three adventures of four episodes each, framed by another story that came into focus for the final two episodes. Saward and Holmes took inspiration from *A Christmas Carol*, setting up a tale in which the Doctor would confront his past, his present, and his future. As the program itself was on trial, the same would hold true for the Doctor.

The season, called "Trial of a Time Lord," features the Sixth Doctor possibly years after we'd last seen him. The hero has been spirited away by the Time Lords from his most recent adventure with Peri, his memory of what he was doing now clouded. A man called the Valeyard accuses the Doctor of acts unbecoming a Time Lord, and will show three examples to prove it.

Two of these adventures feature an older and more mature Peri. The Sixth Doctor acts much more nicely toward her, and the two interact like trusted friends. The program had fast-forwarded the Sixth Doctor's development to show the hero he was meant to become. Nicola Bryant not surprisingly had decided that this would be her last season and requested of Nathan-Turner that, whatever Peri's fate, it should be dramatic and not an abrupt goodbye. JNT told writer Philip Martin to kill Peri in the second main story of the season. When asked for more detail, JNT said he didn't care how it happened, just as long as she died.

In the second adventure of "The Trial of a Time Lord" (officially titled "Mindwarp" later), Peri is chosen to be the host body for a malicious entity.

The Doctor and his new ally, King Yrcanos (played by Brian Blessed), head to the lab where she is being held, hoping to rescue her. Before they can reach it, though, the Time Lords spirit the Doctor away to his trial and freeze Yrcanos in time, waiting to see if this dangerous mental transfer device works. Peri is fully possessed, her mind erased to make way for its new inhabitant. To ensure this technology is never used again, the Time Lords release Yrcanos, who flies into a rage, killing Peri while also destroying the machines.

Nicola Bryant quite liked the story. It was a dramatic and unique end for a companion. The next story in the trial (later officially titled "Terror of the Vervoids") depicts a future adventure with a companion whom the Doctor hadn't met yet: Melanie Bush, a computer programmer from Pease Pottage, West Sussex, at the turn of the twenty-first century.

According to Eric Saward, John Nathan-Turner told him one morning: "I was driving home last night . . . and I thought we need a redheaded companion." On this reasoning, JNT immediately suggested Bonnie Langford, a child star and ballet dancer who had performed in the 1974 Broadway revival of *Gypsy* with Angela Lansbury and had made regular appearances on the children's program *Junior Showtime*. Langford was known for being able to deliver a powerful scream, which some say was a factor in casting her since JNT wanted the companion to deliver such a cry when confronted by monsters. Langford played Mel as an effervescent, optimistic, but not naive young woman. Along with a photographic memory and a fine grasp of technology, Mel had an abiding concern with health and fitness, forcing the Sixth Doctor onto an exercise bike and insisting he drink more carrot juice.

Langford immediately came under criticism. Some didn't want such a well-known television personality cast as the companion. Others felt that Mel was too perky to work well with the occasionally gruff and sarcastic Sixth Doctor. But others enjoyed the relationship between the two, and Colin Baker has said that any criticism about Mel is really about certain scenes with her rather than Bonnie Langford herself.

But Langford wasn't the only one being criticized. Fans expressed their discontent with the new season, not seeing enough improvement since before the hiatus. An increasing number believed that John Nathan-Turner was the problem. Eric Saward credited some of the season's failings to several writers, some having dropped out or written scripts deemed unacceptable. Jonathan Powell very openly found the season's initial story by Robert Holmes uninteresting.

Rather than showcasing an exciting new direction for the show, the shortened twenty-third season was floundering.

ALTERED ENDINGS

Another problem concerned Robert Holmes. After writing the opening four-part adventure of the season (unofficially titled "The Mysterious Planet"), he was supposed to write the final framework story with Saward but fell terribly ill. Having grown close to Holmes, Saward worked on the last part with him.

Holmes, Saward, and JNT had agreed at the start that the season finale would reveal the Master as the hidden villain. Referencing "The Final Problem" in which Sherlock Holmes and Professor Moriarty seemingly die by falling over the Riechenbach Falls together, this story would end with the Master and the Doctor locked in battle as they fell through a time vent, their final fate unknown. Either the time vent transports them elsewhere, or (in the event the BBC didn't renew *Doctor Who*) it marks their mutual end.

Although too ill to stay with the production, Holmes agreed to finish the script for the finale. He wrote the penultimate episode and outlined the final one before being admitted to the hospital. He died days later.

Deeply upset, Saward went to work finishing the script. He became angry when Nathan-Turner suggested changes, believing that they should leave the story alone out of respect for Holmes and because they had agreed to this course at the beginning of the season. He finally did concede on one point, though—that the Valeyard rather than the Master be the main villain and fall through the time vent with the Doctor.

In the new version, the Master would actually be an uneasy ally, refusing to kill the Doctor when the High Council orders him to do so. The Master also reveals the truth behind the trial: It's all part of an elaborate scheme by the Valeyard, who is in fact the Thirteenth Doctor, corrupted by events yet to come and motivated by a desperate need to live past his final incarnation by somehow stealing life from his young self. The Vale-yard had blackmailed the High Council into arranging the trial and helping this scheme by materializing his TARDIS around a time vent in the Matrix, which will inevitably unleash chaos across all reality if left open. Now revealed, the Valeyard opens the time vent, but the Doctor then grabs him and pushes them both through the crack in space and time. The Master shuts the vent, ending the threat but possibly trapping the Doctor and the Valeyard in eternal combat in limbo.

The ending satisfied Saward, but JNT later decided that ending on a cliffhanger was a bad idea. It didn't, in his mind, resolve the trial and the BBC could use the possibility of the hero's death as final justifica-tion to end *Doctor Who*. He also didn't care for the Valeyard being the Doctor's future self. After more arguments, Saward left the program and threatened legal action if his script for the final episode was plagiarized in any way.

This meant that John Nathan-Turner had to have a new script written from scratch. He gave the task to Pip and Jane Baker (no relation to Tom or Colin), who had written Mel's introduction adventure. Now, the finale (unofficially titled "The Ultimate Foe") indicated that the Valeyard was a physical manifestation of the Doctor's dark desires and impulses, created in the hero's future during his regeneration into his thirteenth self. The Vale-yard has traveled back into the Sixth Doctor's life and arranged this trial in order to steal his remaining regenerations and become more powerful. The villain seemingly meets his end, but then viewers see that he has replaced the Keeper of the Matrix.

Nathan-Turner decided that it had been a mistake to kill Peri, so in "The Ultimate Foe" the Doctor learns that the Valeyard had faked the images of her death. Peri survived the adventure, despite the Doctor's absence, and now serves as a warrior queen alongside Yrcanos. Happy that his friend is enjoying a new life, the Doctor resumes his adventures. This abrupt shuffle took Nicola Bryant aback; she didn't believe such a sudden romance would be Peri's fate.

THE VERDICT

"I shall beat it into submission. With my charm."
—THE SIXTH DOCTOR, FROM "ATTACK OF THE CYBERMEN" (1985)

Before the season ended, Michael Grade had decided to renew the program for another year, but he still believed the show needed a very different atmosphere. He consulted Sydney Newman.

Newman suggested several ideas on the condition that he produce *Doctor Who* again. Among them was that the Doctor become more akin to Patrick Troughton, a cosmic hobo who is wise but also innocent and scatterbrained. He also believed it would be interesting if, after twenty-two years of running from his people, the Doctor had a firm reason to return to his home planet but couldn't because the TARDIS would now be unpredictable again. He suggested sibling companions, a homesick twelve-year-old girl and her reckless brother of eighteen. Newman also proposed that after a few adventures with the children, just as they were getting used to him, the Doctor regenerate into a woman.

Grade wasn't sure about these suggestions. Jonathan Powell met with Newman and decided that his ideas for a relaunch would cost more than the BBC wanted to spend, particularly when there was a growing feeling that the show wasn't wanted. Grade informed Nathan-Turner that *Doctor Who* would return for another year but that Colin Baker would not, saying the Sixth Doctor had been on long enough in his estimation and hadn't brought in the ratings they'd wanted. Grade also considered that Baker had fulfilled his contract of three years—even if one of those years hadn't involved production of a show. JNT then expressed a desire to leave the program himself, having produced it for six seasons now. He was told he could, but he still had to break the bad news to Colin Baker.

As Colin Baker shared in *The Story of Doctor Who,* "I had a phone call from John Nathan-Turner, by that time a good friend, saying, 'I've got bad news and good news. . . . Well, the program is coming back next year.' What's the bad news? 'Well, Michael Grade just said we have to find a new Doctor.'" Colin Baker considered it a "body blow." In an interview with *Radio Wammo* in 2011, Colin Baker remarked, "Do you remember *Monty*

Python's Flying Circus? Do you remember that large foot that comes out the sky and stomps people? Well, when you say, 'I'd like to beat Tom Baker's record,' boy, you climb to the mountain top for the foot to arrive and stomp on you. That was ill judged and a little naive."

Former *Doctor Who* production manager Gary Downie later suggested that Grade had personally targeted Baker because the controller was close friends with Liza Goddard, who had bitterly divorced Baker some time before and then married rock musician Alvin Stardust in 1986. In 2004, Downie told *Doctor Who Magazine,* "Michael Grade was determined. He did not want Colin working for the BBC."

Adding to the defeat, Eric Saward gave an interview in which he spoke critically against John Nathan-Turner as producer and Colin Baker as the Doctor, saying he didn't think the latter's performance was good and never believed the actor was appropriate for the role. Years later, in the documentary *Trials and Tribulations,* Saward maintained this position: "He lacks that quality that I think the part demands. Troughton had it. Tom Baker certainly had it in bucket loads. Peter didn't really have it, but Peter was a good actor, and he brought a certain something to the part. Colin is a fair character actor but not really a leading man, not for something as big as that."

The BBC asked Colin Baker to do a four-part story opening the next season, at the end of which his Doctor would regenerate. He refused. Afterward, Jonathan Powell told him that his refusal to return was inconvenient for the BBC. Baker countered that it was inconvenient for his acting career to be put on hold for months because he still had contractual obligations to *Doctor Who.* He remained firm in his decision and didn't appear in the regeneration scene.

When the next season started, viewers saw the TARDIS, mid-flight, suddenly shot down and forced to crash land. The Sixth Doctor and Mel lie on the floor, unconscious. The Rani enters and the Doctor is glowing, suddenly becoming a new man.

To cover for Colin Baker's absence, the production team had Seventh Doctor Sylvester McCoy put on the Sixth Doctor's costume and a blond wig. McCoy has joked that, because of this, he is the only actor officially to play two Doctors. Many fans wondered what exactly caused this regeneration.

Had something happened just before the TARDIS was shot down, some unknown adventure?

Later tie-in media explained that the Doctor smashed his head into the console during the crash, prompting the change. The Sixth Doctor's fate was expanded in the novel *Spiral Scratch,* published in 2005, when the past Doctor novels were ending to make way for the modern day program's tie-in books. Gary Russell wrote that the Sixth Doctor saved the multiverse in his final adventure, but this drained his body of chronal energies. When the Rani forces his ship to crash, the impact is too great for the greatly weakened Doctor, and the regeneration begins.

Before he goes, the Sixth Doctor comforts his companion in a scene that finally gave the incarnation a chance to bid farewell to fans. He says, "Don't cry, Mel. It was my time. Well, maybe not, but it was my time to give. To donate. I've had a good innings, you know, seen and done a lot. Can't complain this time. Don't feel cheated."

ANOTHER CHANCE

Though soured by events surrounding his departure, Colin Baker remained positive about the actual experience of being the Doctor. In 1989, when Jon Pertwee had health issues, Baker resumed the role of the Doctor for the stage production *Doctor Who: The Ultimate Adventure* (the script slightly altered to better fit his incarnation). He also wrote *Doctor Who* stories and

Sylvester McCoy, Peter Davison, and Colin Baker take a break from recording "Sirens of Time" (1999) *Photograph courtesy of Big Finish Productions*

comic strips, and provided dialogue for the 1997 video game *Destiny of the Doctors.*

Colin Baker began recording new audio dramas with Big Finish Productions in 1999. Taking place sometime after his trial, the Sixth Doctor's first solo adventure, *The Marian Conspiracy,* introduces a new companion, a middle-aged history teacher named Dr. Evelyn Smythe, played by Maggie Stables. With sharp stories, new enemies, and fine performances, the Sixth Doctor audio dramas quickly became a success, and they continue to this day. The Sixth Doctor has risen in popularity with fans who've now heard what kind of hero he could have been, given the proper stories and the chance to grow.

It was just a matter of time.

16

High Camp and Time's Champion

"Doctor, are you sure you're well?"

"Of course. Fit as a trombone."

—THE RANI AND THE SEVENTH DOCTOR,

FROM "TIME AND THE RANI" (1987)

While Colin Baker was being forced off the show, JNT resented being forced to stay. First BBC executives told him that he could produce another program, but then they couldn't find another person to take the reins, so he had to remain. JNT had to make up for lost time since he hadn't put any effort into commissioning stories or finding a new script editor, thinking he was leaving.

Pip and Jane Baker came back to pen the opening story, featuring the Rani since actor Kate O'Mara had recently returned to England after appearing as a regular in *Dynasty*. They wrote the adventure, originally called "Strange Matter," to serve as Colin Baker's finale, since JNT had told them that the actor would change his mind and return to give his Doctor a send-off. The script ends with the Sixth Doctor destroying the Rani's lair, only to be caught in the explosion. Mel then finds the newly regenerated Seventh Doctor lying in the rubble.

JNT then brought in new script editor Andrew Cartmel, who wanted to do a very different *Doctor Who*. Influenced by critically acclaimed writer Alan Moore's recent work on comics such as *Swamp Thing*, *Watchmen*, and *V for Vendetta*, Cartmel wanted to deconstruct the Doctor's nature and adventures. He requested changes to "Strange Matter," which was retitled "Time and the Rani." And of course, with Colin Baker still refusing to return, this meant the story needed to be rewritten for a Doctor yet to be cast.

ENTER: MCCOY

Sylvester McCoy was born Percy Kent-Smith in Dunoon, Scotland, to an Irish mother. His father, an Englishman, had died during World War II before the child's birth. Kent-Smith initially studied to become a priest, but then worked in the insurance industry before taking a job at the box office of The Roundhouse in Chalk Farm, North London. He performed comedy on stage there, his most popular act being the portrayal of a stuntman named Sylveste McCoy. A reviewer didn't realize it was a scripted comedy and referred to Kent-Smith as if he were the character. Thus it became his stage name, eventually evolving into Sylvester McCoy.

When Colin Baker left, McCoy was playing the Pied Piper at the National Theatre. After years of comedy, portraying a dangerous hero appealed to him. He also liked the prospect of having Bonnie Langford as his companion, having worked with her a few years before in *The Pirates of Penzance* at Theatre Royal Drury Lane (along with Tim Curry).

Sylvester McCoy's agent called Nathan-Turner and then, according to McCoy, the producer received another call minutes later from children's program producer Clive Droig, who also recommended him for the role. "It was just kismet," McCoy said in an interview for this book at Gallifrey One 2013. "John figured, 'Well, he's playing the Pied Piper right now. I may as well go see if he can act.' Thank goodness he did!"

Seeing McCoy's performance as the Pied Piper, JNT believed him the right man for the job and informed his superiors. But after two years of low ratings, his casting was questioned for the first time. Jonathan Powell suggested he formally audition other potentials just to be sure.

Sylvester McCoy did screen tests for the role, along with Irish actor Dermot Crowley (*Return of the Jedi, Father Ted, Luther*) and the mustachioed David Fielder (*Superman III, Inspector Morse, The Bill*). JNT engineered the auditions deliberately for these other two actors because, while he regarded them as good, he didn't think either right for the role. This way, he could show Powell that video-taped proof that McCoy was the strongest choice. For the tests, Janet Fielding read opposite the three men.

JNT told McCoy he wanted to return to a Troughton-style Doctor. Despite initially wanting to go darker, the actor conceded and took inspiration from

Charlie Chaplin. Since the Sixth Doctor had often quoted philosophers and writers, Nathan-Turner decided the Seventh would mix up clichés: "A poor workman blames his fools," and "Time and tide melts the snowman." Pip and Jane Baker disliked this wackiness, saying it was forced. That JNT insisted on including a bit in which the Seventh Doctor played the spoons took them aback even further.

As McCoy tells it, "We were out to dinner, and I was playing the spoons as a gag. John says, 'That's great. We need to include that in *Doctor Who.*' I thought he was joking!" He later agreed that the campy comedy went too far in his debut story. "I can see that stuff as a mistake now, even though we were having fun on set. People wanted to know what the new Doctor was like, and they wanted to see him fight evil."

Originally, the Bakers wrote the Seventh Doctor as existing already. But Nathan-Turner thought this a mistake, leading to the hastily added regeneration scene. In later interviews, Andrew Cartmel admitted that he shouldn't have interfered with the story and should have seen it as a learning experience before delving into his job. "Time and the Rani" aired in September 1987, nine months after Colin Baker's final adventure. It wasn't well received.

The rest of the Seventh Doctor's first season proved just as short as Colin Baker's final year, with four stories divided across fourteen episodes that continued to present a lighthearted, clownish hero. Verity Lambert counted herself among those who criticized these adventures, saying, "I'd watch it and think, *Nobody's really believing what they're doing here. They just think it's all rather funny and they're rather smart and clever.*"

Some also criticized Mel for doing little more than asking plot questions and screaming in fear. On this point, McCoy said, "Bonnie is a fine actress and a professional. She had a magnificent scream, and JNT wanted to use that, and she was doing her job. . . . I loved working with her, but she wasn't always given the best chance to shine in those early stories. Nor was my Doctor, really. I was becoming too clownish."

The creative team dropped Mel at the end of the season in a story called "Dragonfire." The same story introduced a space station waitress named Dorothy, aka Ace. Played by Sophie Aldred, Ace was a teenager from the late twentieth century who had been caught in a time storm, catapulting her into the future (echoing Dorothy Gale from *The Wizard of Oz*). She was assertive, sassy, and made a hobby of creating homemade explosives called Nitro-9.

Aldred quickly developed a natural chemistry with McCoy, and Ace formed an interesting contrast to Mel. By the end of the adventure, JNT and Cartmel decided that Ace would be the Doctor's next companion. "We were keen to move on not from Bonnie so much as the character she was portraying," Cartmel said. "We wanted to bring on a character who was much tougher, much more street level, much more streetwise."

"There was no resentment about the decision for Mel to leave," McCoy said of this casting change, in an interview for this book. "Now I'd have a companion who was my own and didn't know any Doctor before me. I did object to how she left, though. Originally, it was even more abrupt, and I said there should be more of a goodbye between us. John didn't want an emotional goodbye. He said, 'She's only been with you for a few adventures.' I said, 'But she's actually been with the Doctor much longer. Colin and I are the same character!' . . . They listened. . . . We used a bit I liked from my audition scene. I was already thinking by then that I wanted to explore how strangely the Doctor must view the universe with the senses of a Time Lord."

> **MEL:** "I'm going now."
> **THE DOCTOR:** "Yes, that's right, you're going. You've been gone for ages. You're already gone. You're still here. You've just arrived. I haven't even met you yet. It all depends on who you are and how you look at it."

Along with Mel's departure and Ace's introduction, "Dragonfire" remains famous for two considerations: First, a villain's face melts off in one scene, prompting an outcry and many letters; and second, it featured perhaps the most loathed cliffhanger for a *Doctor Who* episode. At the end of the first episode, writer Ian Briggs (no relation to Nicholas) has the Doctor walking alongside a path on the side of an ice cliff that abruptly comes to an end. He decides to climb the steep cliff, slipping and barely catching himself. With the sudden risk of a fatal fall, it was a literal cliffhanger.

Cartmel and the cast thought the script's events clear and effective. But in director Chris Clough's hands, the scene came off quite differently. As shot, the Doctor is walking on a path with a railing alongside a cliff. He looks over the railing and sees a sheer drop down. Then, *for no reason,* he climbs over the railing and hangs from it, exacerbating the situation by holding on via his umbrella rather than simply climbing back up. At this point, the episode ends.

As the twenty-fourth year closed, a different atmosphere for *Doctor Who* was on the way.

THE MASTER PLANNER

McCoy decided it was time to give the hero a darker, more mysterious nature. As he explained to me, "I spoke with Andrew Cartmel, and he and I were very much thinking the same thing. We'd said in 'Time and the Rani' that the Doctor was . . . 953 years old. Over nine hundred years he's walked and so much of that time was spent fighting. He must have so many parts he doesn't reveal. He must understand things in ways we can't quite imagine. He must feel so disconnected at times, too. . . . My grandmother died after one hundred years and three months, and she was sad about all the people who'd gone before her. But in those last months, she'd realized she'd never had a drink, so she went about getting drunk and laughing until she simply went to bed one night, and that was that. I wanted to bring that weight to the role."

Along with McCoy's new direction, Cartmel and JNT decided to involve more references and connections to *Doctor Who* stories of the past, which were now more readily available to the public thanks to VHS releases. The next season opened with "Remembrance of the Daleks" and even featured a return to I. M. Foreman's scrap yard at 76 Totter's Lane. Ace finds herself wandering through Coal Hill School and comes across Susan's abandoned copy of *The French Revolution* from "An Unearthly Child." The adventure has the Doctor work alongside the British military—not UNIT but close—and reveals more of Time Lord history.

The Doctor had definitely changed. More introspective now, he lamented the risks of time travel even as he manipulated friends and enemies alike into fulfilling a master plan. He spoke darkly of the human capacity for ignorance and violence. He orchestrated the destruction of an enemy planet and talked a Dalek into destroying itself. Because of this, in the novelization of "Remembrance of the Daleks," the villains of Skaro label the Doctor Ka Faraq Gatri, which translates loosely to "bringer of darkness" and "destroyer of worlds."

In later stories, the Seventh Doctor showed a more pragmatic attitude in the use of his mental abilities. Like the Master, he was not above using hypnosis to make his life easier. He even displayed the ability to cause mental pain by touching another's head. But along with this darkness came a mentor role. "It was important that Ace not just be a sidekick who asked the questions," McCoy said to me. "I wanted [a partnership] more like Steed and Peel [from the TV show *The Avengers*] . . . she was growing into a hero who could have her own adventures. Wouldn't it be wonderful if we could have a show like *Doctor Who* with a young lady as the hero in charge? She [Ace] was already more fully formed than other companions . . . . We even visited her home, which was never done before [with a *Doctor Who* companion]. . . . I thought science fiction needed another strong woman or five. It still does."

McCoy also wanted to remodel the TARDIS interior to have a steampunk-style. The actor was a fan of Jules Verne's work and liked the idea of the ship's technology being as paradoxical as the Doctor himself. But the idea was deemed unnecessary and expensive.

Writer Kevin Clarke wanted to script a story for this season and was told that the only open slot was for the twenty-fifth anniversary story in November. Clarke agreed, saying he already had an excellent story in his pocket to celebrate the occasion. The creative team asked him to explain it the next morning. But Clarke had lied—and had no idea what to do when he arrived at the meeting. He bought time by saying that the anniversary story should address the question "Doctor *who*?" reminding the audience that twenty-five years later they still didn't know his name or true origins. Nathan-Turner called it a good start, but what was the answer?

"He's God," Clarke said suddenly. He proposed that the Doctor was taking care of Earth because he had unleashed forces on it long ago that had escaped his control. The villain of the story would be Nemesis, the

Devil. JNT considered this and told Clarke to write the story but not to make direct reference to God or the Devil. He also insisted that the Cybermen appear since they were silver, and twenty-five years marks a silver anniversary.

The story went through a few rewrites and became "Silver Nemesis," striking many as one of the show's stranger tales. The Doctor has imprisoned a statue of living metal named Nemesis into an asteroid that circled Earth, compelling dark events to happen every twenty-five years. A witch who knew the Doctor's secret past was after Nemesis, hoping to use its power to rule the world. Also seeking the living statue was a group of neo-Nazis and the Cybermen.

The story led to many questions from fans. Who was this witch, and how did she know the Doctor? If the hero knew the asteroid was causing trouble on Earth, why not simply stop its orbit at an earlier date or hide it somewhere else in the universe that wasn't inhabited?

Clarke wanted to reveal the Doctor's identity, but JNT didn't want to destroy the character's mystery. Further complicating the situation, Clarke wasn't familiar with the Cybermen and was later criticized for his treatment of the characters.

David Banks, who reprised the part of the CyberLeader, told *Doctor Who Magazine,* "The writer didn't really understand the Cybermen," he said, "so he used them as a kind of metaphor for Nazis. . . . Nazi ideology is not logical, it's emotional."

"Silver Nemesis" came only weeks after "Remembrance of the Daleks," and many fans noted that it felt recycled. Both adventures had monsters teaming up with Nazis of some sort. Both involved groups searching for a great item of power that the Doctor had hidden. Both ended when the Doctor seemingly turned this weapon over to the villains, only to turn the tables on them. Not helping matters, Ace herself even remarked in "Silver Nemesis" that the Doctor's victory over the CyberFleet mirrored his recent victory over the Daleks.

Despite this story, Ace was gaining a strong fan base, and viewers found this new take on the Doctor intriguing. The program would continue for another year.

THE OTHER

"Do you feel like arguing with a can of deodorant that registers 9 on the Richter scale?"

—ACE, FROM "DRAGONFIRE" (1987)

Clarke's pitch—asking the question "Doctor *who*?"—helped seed what became known to fans as the Cartmel Masterplan, though the script editor himself said it wasn't so much a plan as a "mood and direction." Cartmel wanted to remind people of the mystery that surrounded the Doctor, believing that ratings had fallen because the character was now taken for granted. He liked the idea that the hero was more powerful than anyone suspected.

Along with remarks in "Silver Nemesis" that the Doctor was more than simply a renegade Time Lord, a scene in "Remembrance of the Daleks" implied that he had been present during his people's original time travel experiments. Previous stories indicated that Gallifrey had barriers safeguarding its past from observation or alteration. How then could the Doctor have been there, even with a time machine at his disposal?

Cartmel envisioned that Time Lord society had been founded by three figures: Rassilon, Omega, and the Other, whose name was lost to the ages. The Doctor would turn out to be a reincarnation of the Other. Along with this, Cartmel considered that the Doctor was preparing to send Ace to Gallifrey, where she would train to become the first human Time Lord, bringing a new point of view to a society that prided itself on never changing. Cartmel then proposed that Ace's true mission and the Doctor's identity as the Other would be revealed in a twenty-sixth season adventure called "Lungbarrow," written by Marc Platt. In the 1970s Robert Holmes had rejected an earlier draft of the script, called "Fires of the Starmind." Cartmel worked with Platt to incorporate his own ideas. The story takes the Doctor to his childhood home, the House of Lungbarrow on Gallifrey. The Doctor's family is introduced, all cousins, and it's revealed that Gallifreyans have been sterile for centuries, using biological looms to procreate. There the Doctor would face some of his greatest fears from his past.

JNT thought the story revealed too much and didn't care for some of the concepts. "Lungbarrow" was reworked into the story "Ghost Light," now with Ace confronting her past in a large house on Earth. It involved a group of aliens obsessed with cataloging life, and an angelic being named Light. Many viewers found the adventure bizarre and vague.

Older fans were quite pleased, however, that the twenty-sixth season featured the return of retired Brigadier Lethbridge-Stewart and UNIT. In "Battlefield," the Brig and the Doctor join forces against Morgaine le Fey and Mordred. Morgaine and many of the other characters recognize the Time Lord as Merlin—though they remark that he is wearing a different face. The Doctor tells Ace that he has never been Merlin but perhaps he will be one day.

"Battlefield" was meant to end the Brigadier's career, the old soldier sacrificing his life to stop a demonic entity. Nicholas Courtney endorsed this plotline, believing the show wouldn't last much longer due to low ratings and lack of BBC support. But after several rewrites, the creative team decided that the Brigadier's death didn't work. Instead, the Doctor finds his friend lying on the ground and cries out, "You're supposed to die in bed!" The Brigadier then smiles as he opens his eyes. This ending allowed Courtney to reprise Lethbridge-Stewart in Big Finish audio dramas with the Sixth and Eighth Doctors—having adventured with neither in on-screen episodes—and to appear in *The Sarah Jane Adventures*, by which point he'd been knighted.

In the 2012 episode "The Wedding of River Song," the Eleventh Doctor calls up a nursing home facility, possibly operated by UNIT, and asks a staff member to wake his old friend. But he is told that Sir Alistair has recently died in his sleep. This sad moment reflected Nicholas Courtney's own passing months earlier.

Nicholas Courtney (Brigadier Alistair Gordon Lethbridge-Stewart)
Photograph courtesy of Big Finish Productions

EVERYTHING ENDS

Star Trek: The Next Generation began airing in the US in 1987. Within two years, its fan base had increased significantly and was about to grow even more, thanks in part to a dramatic third-season finale episode involving its own race of cyborgs villains. By comparison, though, *Doctor Who* seemed childish with its lesser special-effects budget and stories that relied more and more on supernatural beings. While the *Star Trek* franchise was gaining acclaim for political and social allegories, *Doctor Who*'s story "The Happiness Patrol," intended to mock the politics of Margaret Thatcher, featured a robot villain made of candy. John Nathan-Turner still wanted to move on and the BBC still couldn't find anyone in house to take over.

In the meantime, BBC moved *Doctor Who* from its slot on Saturday evenings and placed it opposite *Coronation Street,* a highly successful drama on ITV. Many saw it as a sign that the BBC had lost faith and was setting the program up to fail in order to justify cancellation. Slumping ratings indeed led to the announcement that the Doctor wasn't returning for a new season. The last story broadcast was "Survival," and a voiceover by McCoy was added over the ending scene, giving a sense that while the Doctor and Ace were leaving television, they would still have many adventures across space and time.

In the documentary *The Story of Doctor Who,* McCoy said: "We were not advertised at all when we came back for that season. I think there was a desire to get rid of it then. . . . We were kind of ignorant of that because, you know, you've got to be an optimist. . . . So it was a bit of a surprise when I was told it wasn't carrying on."

Sophie Aldred agreed that the move was unfortunate. Had there been a twenty-seventh season, her character would have gone to Gallifrey to begin Time Lord training. The next adventure would have involved the Doctor meeting a skilled thief named Raine Creevy. There was also talk of a new interior for the TARDIS, the time rotor connecting to the ceiling and suspending the control console above the ground, and possibly another regeneration. But all of this was not to be, and *Doctor Who* ceased production after twenty-six seasons.

NEVER SAY DIE

"I just do the best I can. I fight monsters. I win."
—THE SEVENTH DOCTOR, FROM THE AUDIO DRAMA *LOVE AND WAR*

The adventures of the Seventh Doctor and Ace continued in comic strips in *Doctor Who Magazine*. In 1989, two years after the show's cancellation, Virgin Publishing purchased Target Books. Rather than continue the Target tradition of novelizing TV stories, editor Peter Darvill-Evans got licensing rights from the BBC. Virgin published original material that took place after the events of "Survival," calling the series *Doctor Who: The New Adventures*. Since these books directly followed the path set forth for the Seventh Doctor in the program, writer John Peel coordinated with several of the television writers, including Andrew Cartmel, to create consistent themes and background information. Known *Doctor Who* writers wrote the first three books in the Timewyrm saga, a four novel mini-series that started the *New Adventures* line. But a new author, Paul Cornell, wrote the final part. A fan since

Chase Masterson, who voices several characters in the audio dramas, and Sylvester McCoy
Photograph courtesy of Big Finish Productions

childhood, Cornell had won a writing competition in 1990, and the BBC produced his entry, "Kingdom Come" for TV broadcast.

As Paul Cornell explained it, "the *New Adventures* worked on the principle of an author introducing some new element and the following authors reacting to it, rather than them being editorial-led or with group discussions. I still have never met John Peel, that I recall."

According to writer Dan Abnett, "The Sylvester/Sophie partnership was an extremely important one in *Doctor Who* because they became the gatekeepers. They were the last Doctor and companion we saw on television. It gave them a life in the comics and novels that was much longer than they would have had if they'd stayed on the air for another year, with Ace being replaced and then the Doctor regenerating a year or so later. . . . I think only Sarah Jane Smith has had more impact than Ace."

Along with the novels, McCoy and Aldred have reprised their roles of the Seventh Doctor and Ace for many Big Finish audio dramas, showing how their characters were meant to evolve. Eventually, the "lost stories" of Andrew Cartmel were adapted into audio, meaning the Seventh Doctor finally met Raine Creevy, as played by Beth Chalmers. Since it wasn't established just how much time passed between "Survival" and the TV movie where the Seventh Doctor met his end, there's very little limit on how far they can take McCoy's incarnation. And we never did find out for sure just what happened to Ace in the end. Accounts vary.

Benny and Canon

"Every great decision creates ripples, like a huge boulder dropping in a lake. The ripples merge and rebound off the banks in unforeseeable ways."

—THE SEVENTH DOCTOR,
FROM "REMEMBRANCE OF THE DALEKS" (1988)

In 1992, Virgin's *Doctor Who: The New Adventures* series intended to have Ace leave the Doctor in favor of a new companion created by one of the authors. Different writers came up with different interesting characters, including Kadiatu, great-great-granddaughter of Lethbridge-Stewart. But the one who had that extra-special quality was Paul Cornell's Bernice Surprise Summerfield, who called herself a professor even if technically she hadn't earned the title.

An adventurous, flirtatious, hard-drinking archaeologist who recorded her experiences in a journal, Benny came from Earth's future, a child of the Second Dalek War. Behind the scenes, her character was described as "Indiana Jones in space." She balanced midway between the educated, aloof nature of the Doctor and the passionate, occasionally reckless Ace. As a thirty-year-old—fairly old as far as companions go— and used to following her own path, Benny intentionally didn't fall into the "sidekick" category.

Peter Darvill-Evans described Benny to *Doctor Who Magazine*, "The Doctor's intellectual equal, an adult character, somewhat spiky, but who could also supply a certain amount of sex appeal, as well as being able to handle a heavy weapon. That kind of character was always in the back of my mind. Paul Cornell came up with the rounded character, however."

Benny arrested the attention of many fans, bringing to the stories a sense of irony and wit that sometimes had been lacking. Although she left his side in the novel *Happy Endings*, she made more appearances afterward, appearing in forty-four *Doctor Who* novels. When the *Doctor Who* license reverted back to the BBC in 1997, editors Peter Darvill-Evans and Rebecca Levene decided to continue the series with Benny

Lisa Bowerman (Bernice Summerfield, companion of the Seventh Doctor)

as their lead character. *Doctor Who: The New Adventures* became *The New Adventures,* and Benny stepped into the spotlight, the first companion to have her own spin-off series. Now officially a professor of archaeology at St. Oscar's College, Summerfield starred in twenty-three novels.

After these books, Big Finish secured the license to produce Benny stories. They have continued publishing various novels and short stories featuring her and in 1999 started producing audio dramas for the character. These have starred actor, director, and photographer Lisa Bowerman, who appeared in the final *Doctor Who* TV story "Survival."

Bowerman reflected on Summerfield's enduring appeal: "This heroic woman archaeologist with a journal existed years before Lara Croft and certainly before River Song, yet she's more grounded than both, which I find more interesting. She's completely human, and she's not the best athlete. She's very fallible, though she does grow from her experiences. I'd argue that Ace was sort of the embryonic state of Benny, but Ace was a girl, whereas we met Benny as a woman, and over time she's been married and has even been a mother . . . and you almost never see that for an action hero who's a woman. . . . That combination of someone who's completely in charge of her own world and just gets on with things is so refreshing. . . . She's not shouting every few minutes that she's a strong woman; she lets that speak for itself. It's obvious."

That Benny Summerfield worked so well independently from the Doctor opened the door to other spin-off audio series. *Gallifrey* followed. Jago and Litefoot, two characters the Fourth Doctor met in "The Talons of Weng-Chiang" got their own series. Iris Wildthyme, a hard-drinking woman claiming to be a Time Lord, first appeared in the novels and now features in different audio dramas starring Katy Manning. Even the military characters whom the Seventh Doctor met in "Remembrance of the Daleks" have their own audio dramas under the title *Countermeasures*. Collectively, these stories have created a fictional universe with many different aspects that don't necessarily reference each other.

Some have argued that these spin-offs and their influence shouldn't be taken too seriously; after all, they're not official or canon. But *Doctor Who* TV episodes have mentioned details from the tie-in media, such as 2005's "Boom Town" in which Rose mentions a place she visited in one of the tie-in novels. Russell T. Davies had the Ninth Doctor use the phrase "The Last Great Time War" because *Doctor Who* novels such as *The Infinity Doctors* had spoken of two previous Time Wars in Gallifrey's past. Many of the TV writers have also written comics, audio dramas, and novels for the overall story, so some fans have adopted the attitude that everything is official except works that clearly don't square with later revelations made on-screen.

According to Paul Cornell, *Doctor Who* continuity is never fixed. At the 2009 Phoenix Convention in Dublin, Ireland (affectionately known as P-Con), he said: "There is nobody in the *Doctor Who* production office who has ever declared anything about canon. . . . I think this has given us a remarkable plasticity and power as a show. . . . The Time Wars rewrote an awful lot of *Doctor Who* history, so in many ways you can say that all the *Doctor Who* in all the different media did happen at some point and then may have unhappened, including bits of the TV show. . . . Because of time travel, the show rewrites its own continuity."

17

The Wilderness Years

"Only the madman can see the way clearly through the tangled forest."

—THE SEVENTH DOCTOR, FROM "GHOST LIGHT" (1989)

Many classic *Doctor Who* fans referred to the period after the program's cancellation as the Wilderness Years, in which they groped through metaphorical forests for any sign that the Doctor would return.

Before the cancellation, Disney considered making an offer to purchase the franchise in the early 1980s, but this never went far. Starting in 1987, the BBC was negotiating a *Doctor Who* movie deal with a consortium of investors working through the Daltenreys company, founded by George Dugdale, John Humphreys, and Peter Litton. Daltenreys created a smaller production company called Coast to Coast, later renamed Green Light, that would film the movie and, if it proved successful, two sequels.

Similar to the 1965 Peter Cushing movies, the theatrical release would exist outside the TV program's continuity. Mark Ezra wrote the screenplay, which Johnny Byrne, who had written television stories for the Fourth and Fifth Doctors, edited.

In 1989, three weeks before the *Doctor Who* TV program filmed its final studio scene, Philip Segal at Columbia Pictures, contacted the BBC. Born in Essex, Segal was a longtime fan of the show and wanted to develop a new US television version. BBC Worldwide feared a new TV show could draw attention away from their upcoming movie, particularly if not handled properly. In 1992, the BBC told Segal that it was too soon to bring back the program.

Moving to Amblin Entertainment, Segal got permission from Steven Spielberg to pursue relaunching *Doctor Who*. With Spielberg's name attached, negotiations with the BBC began. Segal recruited help from Peter Wagg, producer of the successful TV series *Max Headroom*.

MOVIES THAT MIGHT HAVE BEEN

Several discussions covered who might play the Doctor in the Green Light film, including John Cleese, Tim Curry, Rutger Hauer, Dudley Moore, Alan Rickman, and Donald Sutherland. The initial script has the Doctor in an asylum, suffering from amnesia. He befriends a seventeen-year-old girl named Millie who helps him escape. The Doctor returns to his TARDIS, which gets stuck in the shape of a police box. Entering the ship, he regains his memories of Gallifrey, ruled by Time Lords and their agents, temporal heroes known as Time Rangers. A villain named Varnax has attacked Gallifrey with an army, leaving the Doctor the only apparent survivor.

Byrne overhauled the story, now called *Doctor Who: Last of the Time Lords*. Millie became Lotte Wellins, the asylum slid back into the nineteenth century, and now the Doctor was on a quest to find his father. Later rewrites renamed the Time Rangers as the Time Battalion and introduced a Time Lady named Zilla, a former lover of the hero. Lotte was later changed to a human-Gallifreyan hybrid who fell in love with the Doctor. Different versions of the script also involved Pog, a hairy Latin-speaking creature that inhabited the TARDIS's interior garden. (Yes, you read that correctly.)

None of the stories generated much interest, so Byrne presented a new outline under the title *Doctor Who: The Movie*. He wrote a couple of versions, each featuring the Doctor as an old man who teams up with a young version of himself (named "Theo" in one script) to defeat a great evil. The two versions of the Doctor would meet a young woman who would be attracted to both of them, creating a strange romantic triangle that was only resolved when she met a third version of the hero.

As before, Byrne's story didn't generate enough interest to pursue.

DIMENSIONS IN TIME

The BBC started running reruns of *Doctor Who* on BBC Two in 1992 thanks to Alan Yentob, station controller since 1987. While BBC One is aimed at mainstream audiences, BBC Two is styled to deliver slightly more highbrow and niche entertainment, and BBC Three aims for edgier, "innovative" entertainment.

A supporter of science fiction programming, Yentob wanted the BBC to take more pride in the series rather than treating it as something to forget. "I was always an enthusiast of the early [*Doctor Who*] and believed that it did have potential," Yentob explained in the documentary *The Seven Year Hitch*. He said he received "almost daily correspondence" from fans hoping he could help bring back the show.

When Yentob later took over as BBC One controller in 1993, he spoke freely to reporters and fans that he was open to new *Doctor Who* productions, though he had no plans yet. That same year, BBC Worldwide began production of a feature-length thirtieth anniversary special to be released directly to video.

Originally called *Lost in the Dark Dimension,* the special was set to feature Tom Baker as the lead Doctor, since he had been the most popular, with the Brigadier and Ace at this side. In the story, Ace has no memory of her time with the Doctor and it's discovered that a villain has changed history, preventing the hero's regeneration into his fifth self. After meeting the notably older version of the Fourth Doctor who inhabits this new timeline, Lethbridge-Stewart and Ace travel through time and space to restore the timeline. Although they win, Alex Stewart, the Brig's son and Ace's lover, sadly dies.

Set to direct was Graeme Harper, still praised for his work on the Fifth Doctor's swan song "The Caves of Androzani." The character Professor Hawkspur was to be played by Brian Blessed or David Bowie. Yentob developed an interest in *Lost in the Dark Dimension* and arranged for the film to have a bigger budget than planned. He also intended to air the special on BBC One rather than sending it straight to video.

The BBC gave Philip Segal a copy of the script, asking if he would have a problem with the release. Segal insisted that the special would mire the property in the past rather than allowing his own new take on the series to take flight. "I read the script, and it was awful," Segal said during *The Seven Year Hitch*. "It was going to muddy the waters and confuse people especially because we were so close to delivering our [series] bible and our script."

Although Graeme Harper defended it as a "superb story," others shared Segal's opinion. According to several, the script relied too heavily on Tom

Baker's Doctor as the lead, making the other Doctors seem inconsequential. To continue negotiations with Segal, the BBC shut down *Lost in the Dark Dimension*. Instead, the thirtieth anniversary was celebrated with a fifteen-minute adventure divided into two mini-episodes called "Dimensions in Time," released as segments of the Children in Need charity broadcast. Part One ran on November 26, 1993, with Part Two transmitted the next day. The simplistic story had the Fourth Doctor summoning his other incarnations and several companions to hunt down the Rani.

Some still defend "Dimensions in Time" as a fun, simple romp not to be taken seriously. Others criticize it as a lost opportunity to do something really special. Although none of the Doctors occupy the same scene, "Dimensions in Time" so far remains the only instance in which Tom Baker and Sylvester McCoy participated in an on-screen multi-Doctor team-up (not counting pre-recorded footage of them being used) and is the one time the Brigadier Lethbridge-Stewart and the Sixth Doctor appear on-screen together.

THINGS FALL APART

Meanwhile, Green Light was having difficulty making progress and the rights reverted to BBC Worldwide. A new contract was written that stipulated a progress deadline of April 6, 1994. To make sure they didn't lose the project again, Green Light joined forces with Lumiere Productions, a French-owned company with interests in Britain. The deal cost $31 million.

In 1993, some confused Amblin Entertainment's proposed TV series with the Green Light film and reported that Spielberg was directing a theatrical *Doctor Who* movie. According to Daltenreys founder John Humphreys, these reports spawned fear that Spielberg's efforts for a new series would undermine viewer interest in their film. Lumiere Productions left the project.

Green Light pushed forward, commissioning a new script from screenwriter Denny Martin Flinn, who, along with Nicholas Meyer, wrote the screenplay for *Star Trek VI: The Undiscovered Country*. An avid *Doctor Who* fan, Flinn took inspiration from "The Five Doctors" and the Key to Time season. He wanted to use the Master as the main villain, but the BBC asked him not to do so.

Flinn's story involves the Doctor, a Time Lord adventurer who learned sword fighting from Zorro. After saving Shakespeare from being killed by a bearded man in a pub, the Doctor is in his TARDIS with K-9 (mute in this story). The Doctor later recruits Aman, a man from Egypt in 2500 BC, and Amelia Earhart, called "Amy" throughout most of the story. Twice in the story, the Doctor and Amy must kiss to thwart their enemy's schemes.

As the adventure continues, the Doctor crosses paths with a former friend who is now an enemy, a Time Lord called the Mandrake, known on Earth as Vlad the Impaler. With his army of headless henchmen, the Mandrake wishes to collect the hidden segments of the Key to Time, the final piece of which lies hidden at a 1960s concert performance of British rock group The Who.

The story also included a cameo by Tom Baker as a past incarnation and a scene where the Doctor and his friends become incapacitated after drinking wine laced with LSD. After Amy dies, the Doctor goes back to the fight with Shakespeare, and the bearded man (the Mandrake) dies in the pub fight by falling on his own knife, negating everything that happened afterward.

With the exception of the Doctor taking LSD, the BBC approved of the bizarre story. But Green Light wanted to start shooting scenes of the film's version of the First Doctor in advance and asked Flinn to expand the flashbacks of his life. Several rewrites followed, with one version calling for Tom Baker to play himself, now running a shop in San Francisco that sold "Crystals and Other Spiritual Paraphernalia."

With a completed script, Green Light secured Leonard Nimoy as director, fewer than two months before the BBC deadline. Segal still saw the Green Light film as an obstacle in his negotiations with the BBC, though, and believed that hiring Nimoy amounted to a publicity stunt. In later interviews, Segal revealed that he called Nimoy himself and shared this belief, prompting the director to opt out of the project soon afterward.

On April 6, 1994, the deadline passed, and film rights reverted back to BBC Worldwide. According to Daltenreys, the affair cost the company $775,000. The *Otago Daily Times* quoted John Illsley, bassist of British rock group Dire Straits and an investor in Daltenreys, as saying, "When they started talking to Spielberg, it totally pulled the rug out from under us."

Despite his efforts, Segal's deal with the BBC fell through. He went on to work on Amblin's TV series *SeaQuest DSV,* which aired from 1993 to 1996. During this time, Alan Yentob and others from the BBC arrived on the set of *SeaQuest DSV* and requested a tour. Segal acted as Yentob's personal tour guide, taking the opportunity to plead his case to helm a new *Doctor Who* series. In 1994, Segal and Yentob made a deal to develop a new BBC–Amblin Entertainment coproduction of a show that would reimagine the character.

THE REBOOT DOCTOR

Universal Television funded the US side of this coproduction and had Segal hire writer John Leekley to develop the series bible, a reference document establishing details on character, background, location, series premise, and so on. Leekley was familiar with *Doctor Who* and keenly wanted to delve into Time Lord society and history. Michael Wearing, head of Serials at the BBC, assigned executive producer Jo Wright to the project.

Wright explained to *The Seven Year Hitch:* "One of the reasons they put me on it was to be the keeper of the keys, as far as the BBC was concerned. . . . Are they going to want an American Doctor? Are they going to change everything?"

Segal didn't care for Jo Wright checking his work, so she mostly communicated with Alan Yentob, who saw her as "a real champion of the project." Segal later remarked that Jo Wright was indeed a "consummate professional" and admitted he had been difficult with her. With Segal's aid, Leekley outlined a two-hour pilot followed by thirteen self-contained hour-long episodes. Leekley wrote the series bible as if it were the personal journal of Cardinal Borusa. Like the movie scripts, the vision for the new show, to be titled *The Chronicles of Doctor Who?* or simply *Doctor Who?,* underwent a few revisions.

According to the bible, the Doctor is an adventurous and occasionally reckless Time Lord who is raised alongside the Master by the villain's grandfather Cardinal Borusa, a descendant of the great Time Lord Rassilon.

After the Master is made the royal leader of Gallifrey, the Doctor is revealed to be his half-brother, the product of a union between the lost Time Lord Ulysses and a woman from the planet Earth. Seeing the Doctor as a threat to his power, the Master sends forth his deadly minions the Daleks (now with metal casings that expand into spider-like legs). Escaping with his life and hoping to find his father, the Doctor steals an old TARDIS, but he isn't going to travel alone. The recently deceased Borusa transfers his spirit into the time rotor's power crystals. The TARDIS is now a living ship, and Borusa can appear before the Doctor as a hologram. They launch forth through space and time.

The series bible then describes the Doctor's subsequent adventures. It describes the hero as a ruggedly handsome man who smokes cigars and wears a long duster with many pockets and buckles. A later version of the pilot script makes mention of his piercing blue eyes, a sign of his human heritage since all Gallifreyans have dark eyes. This detail riffs on the fact that all the actors who'd played the Doctor had blue eyes (until David Tennant). Though glad to fight evil where he finds it, the Doctor is mainly searching for clues leading to his father.

Several of the adventures reimagine classic *Doctor Who* stories. Whereas the adventure "The Talons of Weng-Chiang" took place in 1889 London, this version has a similar adventure in present-day New York City. "The Daemons" now takes place in Salem, Massachusetts. "Tomb of the Cybermen" becomes "Tomb of the Cybs," with the emotionless cyborgs reworked into vain villains. Romana and the Celestial Toymaker appear, and it's revealed that the Doctor's father, Ulysses, was known on Earth as the famous pirate Blackbeard.

The series bible also revised the TARDIS, designating only five main areas in the ship: Captain's Quarters, Lab, Engineering, Cosmos, and Cloister Room. A later version gives the sections as: TransMat Bay, Engineering, Lab, Cloister Room, and Living Quarters.

Segal pitched all of this to Robert Greenblatt, head of Series at Fox. Greenblatt was happy to take on *Doctor Who?* as a TV movie but had no interest in a series. After discussing it more with Segal, Greenblatt agreed that they would make the movie as a backdoor pilot. It would stand on its own, but, if the ratings held up, it would launch a series to follow.

However, Fox and Spielberg didn't care for the pilot script, so it needed work before production could begin. It was revised several times, first by the original screenwriter, John Leekley, and then by Robert DeLaurentis, who had worked with Segal on the series *Earth 2*. New versions introduced Winston, a bulldog the Doctor picks up in WW II England. In one script, the Daleks could disguise themselves as humans, while another draft renamed them "Zenons." A couple of drafts partnered the Doctor with a companion named Gog, described as a pumpkin-shaped alien creature with a horn.

Meanwhile, there were ongoing discussions concerning the casting. Peter Wagg outlined a list of possible Doctors: Rowan Atkinson, Billy Connolly, Michael Crawford, Liam Cunningham, Tim Curry, Eric Idle, Jonathan Pryce, and others. Paul McGann later auditioned for the role, unaware that his brother Mark had done so earlier. Sean Pertwee, Jon Pertwee's son, was also considered. Wagg settled on Liam Cunningham, Jeff Goldblum, and John Slattery as his three favorite candidates for the lead, though he later expanded this list and included Michael Bean, Matt Frewer, Rutger Hauer, Chris Isaak, Hugh Laurie, Kyle MacLachlan, Gary Sinise, and David Strathairn.

Segal discussed the script with Tim Curry but then decided Paul McGann was his choice, seeing his Doctor as a cross between Patrick Troughton and Tom Baker. McGann wasn't sure that he was the right choice for the Doctor, but his friend Sylvester McCoy encouraged him and he accepted the role. The actor signed a contract agreeing that, if the TV movie led to a fully realized series, he would remain as Eighth Doctor for at least six years.

A CONTINUATION

Meanwhile, Spielberg still didn't like the pilot scripts, thinking them too heavy on continuity and too similar in places to what he already had done in the Indiana Jones films. Amblin Entertainment pulled out of the deal. By his own admission, Segal didn't inform anyone at the BBC about this rather significant development until he had renegotiated certain points with Fox.

Segal suggested that rather than reimagine the mythology, the story should continue the classic TV program's continuity. It would begin with the Seventh Doctor pursuing the Master, regenerating into the new Eighth Doctor, played by Paul McGann.

Fox agreed to the new plan and casting. The BBC hesitated to ask Sylvester McCoy to return, however, arguing that he hadn't been a popular enough Doctor to save the classic program cancellation. Jo Wright asked if Tom Baker could play the role of the "Old Doctor" instead, but Segal argued against it. The BBC agreed that McCoy could appear as long as he didn't have many lines or scenes. Wright also stressed that this story should mark a whole new era rather than feel like the next episode after "Survival."

Fox had concerns of its own, too. First, the network wanted more physical action, aiming to avoid *Star Trek*'s style of solving dangerous situations through a discussion of science fiction concepts. Second, the Master would be played by an American. Executives worried that having both a British villain and hero, neither actor well known in America, would deter US viewers. Fox provided Segal with a list of acceptable actors to play the Master; all of them had work contracts with the studio already, and their salaries fit with the budget. Fox also suggested that the Doctor not fight any strange monsters, only human-looking villains that the audience could take seriously.

Segal conceded to these points, casting Eric Roberts as the Master. He did, however, object to composer John Debney's request to write a new *Doctor Who* theme, insisting he base it on Ron Grainer and Delia Derbyshire's arrangement. In 1995, at Fox's suggestion, Segal met with Matthew Jacobs, a screenwriter for the series *The Young Indiana Jones Chronicles.* By coincidence, Jacobs's father, Anthony, had portrayed Doc Holliday in the First Doctor TV story "The Gunfighters." Segal hired Matthew Jacobs to write a new script from scratch, but retaining the idea that the Doctor was half human to justify his love of Earth.

In this new story, the Master, seemingly dying, transforms into a slug-like creature. He and the Doctor wind up on Earth, either in New Orleans or San Francisco, on Halloween. The villain mortally wounds the hero and a surgeon named Dr. Kelly Grace attempts to save the hero, but doesn't understand his anatomy. Regeneration occurs and the Eighth Doctor emerges while the Master uses his new powers to raise an army of animated corpses. After saving the day, Kelly and the Doctor sail off into new adventures.

After some discussion, more rewrites happened. A young character named Jack became Lee, the story shifted to New Year's Eve in San Francisco, the zombie army was eliminated, and Kelly Grace became Grace Halloway. The Doctor would also now leave without a companion at the end of the story.

At last, the script was approved. UK film and TV director Geoffrey Sax had been working in the US for some time and was hired to direct the TV movie. With McCoy, McGann, and Roberts ready to go, the cast was rounded out with Daphne Ashbrook as Grace and Yee Jee Tso as Lee. Fox provided $2.5 million to the budget, with BBC Worldwide and Universal Television providing $2.2 million. BBC Television gave $300,000, making the movie's budget $5 million. As 1996 approached, production was ready to begin in Vancouver, British Columbia.

18

The Many Lives of the Eighth Doctor

"I can't make your dreams come true forever, but I can make them come true today."
—THE EIGHTH DOCTOR, FROM THE TV MOVIE *DOCTOR WHO* (1996)

Paul McGann's parents encouraged him and his brothers to pursue and develop their talents from a young age. After training at the Royal Academy of Dramatic Arts, he embarked on a career in television and film, gaining widespread attention in 1986 when he starred alongside Richard E. Grant in the cult classic comedy *Withnail and I*. After his other film appearances, including a role in *Empire of the Sun* and brief appearances in *Alien 3* and Disney's *The Three Musketeers*, commentators grouped McGann with Colin Firth, Bruce Payne, Gary Oldman, and Tim Roth into "the Brit Pack."

Once the TV movie was definitely happening, Sylvester McCoy happily joined the project, believing that his involvement in a regeneration scene would cement McGann's legitimacy as the Eighth Doctor. "We're old mates, Paul and I," McCoy explained, "and what a chance to really do a proper regeneration. No lying on the floor with a wig. We got to do it proper and with new special effects now. It was fun and weird, with lightning all around, and then you get very sad as my Doctor goes away and the not-as-handsome new Doctor arrives."

McGann discussed with Segal what kind of Doctor he wanted to bring to the screen. Remembering Hartnell's incarnation, McGann wanted a mysterious figure but one different from McCoy. Not a master manipulator, this Doctor could be more impulsive and a bit rougher around the edges, enjoying his travels but also slightly guarded and cynical from all his experiences. McGann suggested emphasizing this visually, ditching the anti-fashion style of the previous Doctors for a more modern look of short hair and a black leather jacket. The actor actually had much shorter hair when he showed up on set than he had in rehearsal, having cut it to play British Special Forces operative Chris Ryan in the recent movie *The One That Got Away* for ITV, where he starred alongside David Morrissey.

"They panicked because they'd loved my long hair and thought it was very Doctor-like," McGann explained at Gallifrey One 2012 in an interview. "I told them, 'No, it's fine; don't you see? . . . I'll be a new Doctor for a new era. That's what we want, right? He can still be fun, but he's got baggage, you can see that.' But no, they insisted that a man with short hair and a black leather jacket wasn't Doctor Who. No one would accept that. . . . They also wanted to bring back Tom Baker's scarf in some way. I said, 'Then have me find it and toss it aside because my Doctor wouldn't wear that.'"

McGann was given a wig to make his hair longer again. His costume was a romantic Edwardian look, which matched the new Jules Verne style TARDIS interior. The console room became a huge area with different mini-sections. The console itself, now wooden and brass, had not only a scanner screen but a holographic ceiling as well.

"I loved that TARDIS," McCoy said, smiling. "I absolutely am in love with steampunk, though it wasn't called that when I was young. Some of the Victorian style of science fiction, like when I saw Disney's *20,000 Leagues under the Sea,* I loved that kind of thing. When I walked onto that TARDIS, I was so happy. This was finally exactly what I'd wanted. Then I died, and this bloody new boy from Liverpool stole it from me, and everyone calls it the Eighth Doctor's TARDIS. It's not! It's my TARDIS! He inherited it from *me*. I hate him, I hate him, I hate him! Three hates make twenty-four!"

Production went smoothly for the most part, though reports indicated that Eric Roberts was difficult at times, demanding better accommodations as soon as he arrived. The story now involved the Master, in his sluglike state, once again extending his life by inhabiting the corpse of a human being he had killed. His next plan was to steal the Doctor's remaining five lives.

Fox continued to worry that the piece lacked enough action and excitement. Studio representatives apparently asked on occasion why the Doctor, an alien with advanced technology, couldn't carry some form of ray gun. Despite these hiccups, production concluded, and the TV movie was ready for the public.

THE CURTAIN RISES

"He's back! And it's about time!" the commercials declared.

The TV movie *Doctor Who* aired in Canada on May 12, 1996, the US on May 14, and the UK on May 27. Reactions and results were mixed. Some rejoiced. Some asked why it featured a new Doctor rather than continuing the adventures of the seventh incarnation. Some immediately dismissed the idea of an American production, despite that director Geoffrey Sax, writer Matthew Jacobs, and executive producers Philip Segal and Jo Wright were all British and the film was shot in Canada.

The movie kept the idea that the Doctor would die on an operating table. Caught in the crossfire of a gang fight while pursuing the Master, the hero would have recovered from the bullet wounds but the well-intentioned actions of Dr. Grace Halloway, confused by Time Lord biology, ensured that a regeneration would occur.

"It's a startling how dark and violent it is, and there's even visible blood on the Doctor," says Nicholas Briggs. "The movie was playing toward an older audience, but I don't think modern *Doctor Who* would do a death like that. They're still targeting younger viewers, and I think they'd be afraid to upset anyone." Gary Russell, who novelized the film, held a different view: "It's definitely a violent death, but it works, and it's a very American kind of regeneration scene. Besides, it's a lot better than saying he regenerated because his ship was shot down and he hit his head."

As Sylvester McCoy sees it, "In America, *Doctor Who* was something college kids and older adults watched rather than in Britain where it was meant for children but was good enough that their parents and older siblings would enjoy it as well. Americans tend not to think of it as a family show or don't always realize just how much is intended for children. So it made sense to me that this was more adult, more violent, because this was American *Doctor Who*, meant for American viewers."

His body pumped with anesthetics, three hours pass between the Doctor's apparent death and when his next regeneration finally kicks in, the only one to occur without the TARDIS or another Time Lord present. It's a difficult change, leaving the Eighth Doctor amnesiac as he stumbles through the hospital, wrapped in a Christ-like shroud, humming *Madame Butterfly* (which played on a stereo while he was operated on). He finds Grace and befriends her, convincing the surgeon that he is the same man who "died" on her table.

We're meant to see this new Doctor through Grace's eyes. He's effervescent, excited by simple pleasures, a thrill seeker, mischievous, a master of sleight of hand, and a slightly arrogant name-dropper. This is a man who will take himself hostage to get what he needs and who will pause during a chase to activate a fire alarm, simply because he wants to "liven things up." He has youthful energy but an old soul, occasionally stopping to guide people to fates they don't suspect.

When the Doctor finally remembers who he is, he kisses Grace in celebration. The kiss caused quite a stir for many fans, who believed that the Doctor wasn't meant to be romantic. McGann didn't know that the Doctor had never kissed anyone on-screen before and rightly assumed that the character had some romantic quality since he'd had a granddaughter from the beginning. At the same time, he consciously chose to keep the kiss somewhat innocent by making it closed mouth.

The Doctor and the Master have a final showdown in the TARDIS Cloister Room, and the villain seems to meet his final end, his essence scattered across space and time. The Doctor asks Grace to travel with him, but she declines. He then takes off, settling down with a cup of tea before realizing a piece of the TARDIS is malfunctioning. Again.

REACTIONS

While some criticized the story and direction as too American, McGann's performance received broad praise. In the UK, the TV film did extremely well, garnering a viewership of 9.1 million. But Fox was more concerned with the US audience. Only 5.6 million viewers tuned in, not enough to prompt a regular series. Part of the lower-than-hoped ratings might have derived from competing against ABC, which was airing new episodes of *Roseanne, Ellen,* and *Home Improvement,* while NBC was broadcasting new episodes of *Third Rock from the Sun, Wings,* and *Frasier*—all hugely popular sitcoms at the time. *Roseanne* in particular attracted many viewers that night with its "Heart and Soul" episode, a follow-up to one of the main characters suffering a heart attack the previous week.

With no new series on the horizon, McGann was naturally disappointed, pointing out that he had only been the Doctor for six weeks and considering himself the franchise's equivalent to George Lazenby, who portrayed James Bond only once, in *On Her Majesty's Secret Service*. Daphne Ashbrook felt much the same, telling me: "I had a great time doing it, and I loved getting to be part of the *Doctor Who* history, but I do feel a bit like I was part of an anomaly."

CONTINUITY

Sylvester McCoy criticized that his Doctor may have had too much screen time in the movie. As he sees it, "it was a mistake to start with me and not bring in Paul until almost half an hour into it. If you're new to the story, you're wondering about my Doctor, and then he's gone, and you have to go wondering about who this new person is. . . . I think it should have begun with the Eighth Doctor waking up confused, figuring out who he was . . . and then when he does remember, you could have a flashback to see how I'd met my end. Or if we'd been confirmed as a series, we wouldn't need me in the first episode at all. Paul's Doctor just immediately runs onto screen, fully formed. And then a few episodes in, he explains how he'd recently regenerated, and then we'd finally see what happened to me. It was supposed to be his show, not mine, but you wait half an hour just to see him, and then it's yet another twenty minutes or so before his memory's back, and he starts acting like the new Doctor."

Other aspects of the TV movie weren't easy to grasp if you'd never watched or read about the show before. Nicholas Briggs has described speaking to American viewers who saw the opening shot of the Seventh Doctor in his console room but didn't realize that they were seeing the interior of the flying police box depicted moments earlier. Seeing no sign of movement and not knowing that this blue box was a ship that was larger on the inside, they assumed that the story had cut to a different scene. Likewise, some new viewers didn't understand whether the new Doctor was a newborn person unaware of what the previous Doctor had done or the same person with a new appearance.

Even experienced fans found themselves confused on a few points, though the novelization and tie-in media gave explanations and fixes for several things.

Despite the confusion and continuity contradictions, many fans wanted to see more of this Eighth Doctor, even if it wasn't on television.

SEPARATE LIVES

The ratings for the TV movie in England, and the media attention surrounding it, proved that the thirty-three-year-old franchise still could gather new fans and explore new areas.

After spending years telling new untold stories of different Doctors and what happened after "Survival," *Doctor Who Magazine* now published the Eighth's Doctor's adventures following the TV movie. The comic strips gave a new take on a companion: a science fiction fan. Izzy Sinclair is a *Star Trek* and comic book geek unsure of her place in the world, often preferring to be called "Izzy Somebody" or simply "Izzy S." She quotes classic science fiction films when she encounters strange enemies and criticizes the Doctor's ship for having neither transporter units nor a holodeck. Eventually the comic strips revealed that she is gay, making her the hero's first openly homosexual companion. (Russell T. Davies wrote to the magazine and praised this move.)

In 1997, the Virgin Publishing license to use characters in the Whoniverse reverted back to BBC Books, which issued the novelization of the TV movie as its first new tie-in in the 1990s. BBC Books soon began publishing new tie-in novels, creating two series: *Eighth Doctor Adventures* (EDA) and *Past Doctor Adventures* (PDA). The EDA books offered a continuous, linear succession of tales featuring McGann's incarnation (in a separate timeline from the comic strips), while the PDA series consisted of stand-alone novels that could feature any of the previous seven Doctors. The BBC also published three anthologies entitled *Short Trips,* featuring short tales of various Doctors and other characters in the Whoniverse. The first *Short Trips* book introduced the character Iris Wildthyme, whom writer Paul Magrs had used (in different form) in the book *Marked for Life.*

The final Virgin novel featuring the Seventh Doctor, *Lungbarrow,* brought forth most of the Cartmel Masterplan, the Doctor experiencing memories of having once been the ancient Time Lord known as the Other. The BBC Books for the most part didn't reference this storyline particularly because the EDA stories tended to follow the idea that the hero was half human, which didn't gel with the revelations of *Lungbarrow.*

The EDA series contains seventy-three books featuring the Doctor's eighth incarnation—literally thousands of pages of corollary narrative. The Doctor teams up with a young woman named Sam Jones and later recruits a young man named Fitzgerald Michael Kreiner or "Fitz." Later still, he travels alongside companions named Anji Kapoor and Beatrix "Trix" MacMillan, the latter a con artist (and possibly former prostitute) who stowed away on the TARDIS. A woman named Compassion, who joins the Doctor for several books, began as a member of Faction Paradox, a group of guerrilla time travelers who enjoy anomalies and use rituals similar to voodoo in direct opposition to Time Lord practice and philosophy. The Faction's founder, Grandfather Paradox, turns out to be a future version of the Doctor. The hero eliminates this future version and all the paradoxes that he and his group have caused, restoring the proper timeline. As a result, though, Gallifrey is destroyed. Faction Paradox creator Lawrence Miles criticized this last development (not his, obviously) and continued the Faction into its own franchise that now includes its own comic books, novels, and audio dramas. Spin-offs beget spin-offs.

The EDA series met with mixed reactions. Some enjoyed its high-concept science fiction plots and strange developments. Other criticized it for lacking the same fun and morality of *Doctor Who.* Even those who consider themselves fans have remarked that certain plots and ideas seemed to be forced retroactive explanations and unwanted twists; Romana regenerating from friend into ruthless adversary, and the Eighth Doctor suffering from amnesia twice more, the second time having it last for several books.

With the arrival of the modern-day TV program, the EDA series ended in June 2005 to make way for novels featuring the new on-screen Doctor. *The Gallifrey Chronicles,* the final EDA book, had an open ending: Readers received three potential versions of the Ninth Doctor yet to come—a joke since by this time audiences had seen Christopher Eccleston, Richard E.

Grant, and Rowan Atkinson all play the role in some form (as we'll soon discuss). While Gallifrey is destroyed in the novel, the Eighth Doctor possesses all its knowledge and information in his mind and can apparently restore it.

The novels and comic strips generally didn't consider each other's continuity. The Big Finish audio drama *Zagreus* later implied, helpfully, that they were actually two parallel timelines. Big Finish also acquired the license to publish new *Short Trips* anthologies featuring tales of the first eight Doctors. The *Repercussions* collection implied that time paradoxes and shifts sometimes removed events and even companions from the Doctor's life. Since it's apparently the Eighth Doctor who later fought in the Last Great Time War imagined by Russell T. Davies, some fans have assumed that the Eighth Doctor's multiple continuities are a side effect of the massive temporal chaos unleashed by the conflict. But one version of the Eighth Doctor has the added support of including the direct participation and approval of Paul McGann himself.

CALLBACK

In 1999, impressed with their work on the Bernice Summerfield audio dramas, the BBC granted Big Finish Productions the license to make new *Doctor Who* adventures featuring the past Doctors. After a year of new audio plays featuring the Fifth, Sixth, and Seventh Doctors, Big Finish approached Paul McGann about reprising his role. They worried initially that he might not wish to return to the part, but the actor happily joined in.

In January 2001, Big Finish released the audio drama *Storm Warning,* written by Alan Barnes, who also wrote many of the Eighth Doctor's comic strip adventures. An undefined amount of time following the events of the TV movie has passed, and the Eighth Doctor finds himself aboard the R101, the famous airship that crashed in 1930. There he meets Charlotte "Charley" Pollard, a young woman who claims the title of "Edwardian adventuress." Although he knows that history recorded Charley's death aboard the R101, the Doctor, taken with the young woman, recruits her. India Fisher, who made her voice work debut in the Fifth Doctor audio drama *Winter for the Adept,* played Charley.

The two characters become fast friends, hurtling from one adventure to another, teaming up with Lethbridge-Stewart, exploring a haunted house where it's always Christmas and there's a murder every hour, and stopping the Daleks from wiping Shakespeare from history. Old and new fans praised McGann's reprise, finally seeing what kind of Doctor he could have been. By the fortieth anniversary story, *Zagreus,* it was clear that the Eighth Doctor was changing. Defeats hardened his attitude and made him more cautious. As seasons rolled forward, he felt an ongoing disappointment in the universe. Whereas once the Time Lords had exiled him, now he chose full exile rather than stay in a society where half the people were crazy and the other half were boring.

Years after she first brought Charley to life in the audio dramas, India Fisher had an e-mail conversation with show runner Russell T. Davies about the new program. Fisher said that Russell loved the character of Charley Pollard and even told her, "without her as a vanguard, Rose Tyler would never have been written." Following Charley's departure, BBC7 produced further adventures of the Eighth Doctor, now joined by the acerbic and occasionally reckless Lucie Miller, played by Sheridan Smith. Lucie's sarcasm, humor, and occasional impatience with the Doctor made her a fan favorite who stayed for several seasons.

Julie Cox (Mary Shelley in the audio dramas)
Photograph courtesy of Big Finish Productions

Big Finish released other audio dramas of the Doctor from before he met Lucie or Charley, revealing adventures he'd shared with novelist Mary Shelley. In November 2012, the company released the mini-series called *Dark Eyes,* taking place after Lucie's departure and introducing new companion Molly O'Sullivan, an Irish World War I nursing assistant played by Ruth Bradley. As the *Dark Eyes* stories begin, the Eighth Doctor, emotionally damaged by recent experiences, now sports the short

Ruth Bradley (Molly in the audio dramas)
and Paul McGann
Photograph courtesy of Big Finish Productions

hair and dark leather coat that Paul McGann always wanted. He even has a new sonic screwdriver, one with a wooden handle that matches his TARDIS console and utilizes a blue crystal similar to the ones seen in models used by the Ninth and Tenth Doctors. When McGann modeled his new costume at a convention, some wondered whether the design heralded the Eighth Doctor's return to TV.

Nicholas Briggs couldn't be happier with how the Eighth Doctor continues to gather new fans almost twenty years after the TV movie. "We really got something quite special with Paul," he said. "I sometimes get nervous he'll decide, 'Well, that was nice, but enough's enough.' But each year, he's willing to do more. I think he really came to appreciate how much people love his Doctor and what a large world *Doctor Who* really is."

Paul McGann himself said at Gallifrey One: "You'd think people would be bored with me, but I guess you can't play the part just once. . . . And that's the beauty of it—this is a story that can do anything. There's time travel and regeneration, and each Doctor can grow and change on his own. You never have to stop."

Half Human?

When the 1996 TV movie aired, something made many Whovians scratch their heads: The Master notices the Doctor's retinal pattern and concludes that our hero is actually half human. Later in the film, the Doctor is trying to charm a scientist and remarks, "I'm half human—on my mother's side." He then reveals to his friend Grace that this remark was just a distraction while he pilfered the scientist's ID badge.

Some fans accept that the Doctor is half human. Others argue that the Master or another Time Lord should have realized this earlier if it was simply a matter of looking into the hero's eyes. In the 2008 episode "Journey's End," it is confirmed that the Doctor is not part human when he is surprised to meet a version of himself who is. Another point against the Doctor having a human mother comes in the two-part special "The End of Time," in which a character appears in visions, a Time Lord whom the credits identify as The Woman. Many wondered if this Time Lord was supposed to be the Doctor's mother. Writer Russell T. Davies later revealed that he did intend this, but he also didn't specify it in the dialogue to give later storytellers the option of revealing her as someone else.

Many fans who don't accept the Doctor as half human have chosen to assume that the Master made an error in his conclusion, a result of his increasing mental instability. Seen another way, the Eighth Doctor's joke was just that: a remark meant to distract the listener that happened to match up with the Master's conclusion.

As time has gone on, more and more fans are adopting the idea that, although the Doctor doesn't have a human parent, his eighth incarnation did leave him with human traits during that life. In "Destiny of the Daleks," Romana showed she could regenerate into a seemingly non-human/Gallifreyan form if she wanted. The Eighth Doctor also told Grace that Time Lords could change species (or seem to) when regenerating. The Big Finish audio play *Circular Time* features a story in which a Time Lord directs his regeneration so that his next incarnation will adopt traits of the dominant native life form, seemingly becoming a hybrid.

Perhaps the Doctor recognized that his eighth body had human features, which prompted his joke.

Some fans have also hypothesized that the Doctor's final thoughts and regrets before regeneration may influence his next incarnation's behavior. The First Doctor knew he was irascible and bad tempered, so he changed into a more jovial, outgoing person. Thus was born the Second Doctor. As Professor Langley puts it: "Each new Doctor seems to be a reaction to the last one. . . . As he's looking back on his last life just before regeneration, thinking about how he could've been different, it could be like a person focusing on something just before sleep and then having that idea become an influence in their dreams."

The Seventh Doctor often seemed disturbed by his actions and how aloof he had to be for his plans to work. In the 2006 audio drama *Time Works*, the Eighth Doctor remarks that his previous incarnation realized in later years how much he regretted becoming a master planner, more of a Time Lord, when what he really wanted deep down was to be more human. Perhaps his regeneration into his eighth form, a difficult one altered by drugs, temporarily granted his wish in a strange way.

19

The Last of the Time Lords

"It won't be quiet, it won't be safe, and it won't be calm. But I'll tell you what it will be: The trip of a lifetime!"
—THE NINTH DOCTOR, FROM BBC COMMERCIALS (2005)

It's the first day of shooting for Christopher Eccleston. He's running down a hallway—practically a *Doctor Who* trademark—chasing a pig in a space suit while nearby military men look up in confusion. The role he accepted months ago has become very tangible. The cameras are rolling. Now and for the rest of his life he is the Ninth Doctor.

The journey began a couple of years earlier. The BBC couldn't ignore that every year letters and phone calls still poured in, asking about *Doctor Who* returning to the air. Polls in magazines and online forums showed a strong desire for the program's return.

Russell T. Davies, a writer and executive producer often referred to as RTD, had impressed many at the BBC. His acclaimed series *Queer as Folk* had inspired a US version and he had gained a good reputation with colleague and crew. RTD, a known *Doctor Who* fan, had written for the tie-in media. By now, new blood was coursing through the BBC, and those in charge had fond memories of *Doctor Who* from their own childhoods.

But although the BBC was interested in discussing a new version of the program with Davies, there was a problem with the rights. Between the film deals and the TV movie, only tie-in media seemed able to tell new Doctor stories and BBC Worldwide wanted to look into a theatrical film again. Davies knew of these issues, so he dismissed these early calls from the BBC, thinking any *Doctor Who* deal would stall at the development stage.

Despite this hassle, bits of *Doctor Who* did still appear on-screen. For 1999's Red Nose Day—a British charity telethon event—Steven Moffat wrote a comedy short that included the Master and the Daleks. "The Curse of Fatal Death" opened with Rowan Atkinson as the Ninth Doctor, who regenerated several times in the story, becoming Richard E. Grant, Jim Broadbent, and Hugh Grant. When the Doctor's thirteenth life ended, the Doctor impossibly regenerated again into the Fourteenth Doctor, played by Joanna Lumley. "The Curse of Fatal Death" played for laughs, but Moffat seriously loved *Doctor Who*. In his hit series *Coupling,* one character, a die-hard Whovian, constantly refers to the show.

Meanwhile, BBCi (the BBC's network of websites that is now once again called BBC Online), experimented with continuing the show as an animated "webcast" (a web-based broadcast). Sylvester McCoy appeared in *Death Comes to Time* in 2001, an adventure that strangely ended with the hero's death, negating the TV movie and anything that came afterward. The 2002 webcast *Real Time* featured the Sixth Doctor and his Big Finish companion Evelyn Smythe and was largely recorded, as the title suggests, in real time. Using scripts of the unfinished Fourth Doctor story, Paul McGann and Lalla Ward performed in the *Shada* webcast in 2003.

These webcasts engendered new hope for a full-blown TV program. Some still claimed the show wouldn't work for a modern audience, that it was either too old-fashioned or that the larger effects budget that a new science fiction audience demanded would ruin the show's charms. But various new media were approaching familiar tropes with a postmodern take, so the BBC considered restoring the property with a fresh approach.

In 2003, BBCi released an animated *Doctor Who* webcast written by Paul Cornell and featuring Richard E. Grant. *Scream of the Shalka* was intended to be the first in a series of webcasts officially continuing the franchise. The BBC, still unsure whether a live-action program would happen any time soon, recognized Grant's animated incarnation as the official Ninth Doctor, a cynical and sarcastic man, whom the actor described as Sherlock Holmes from outer space. At his side (and voiced by Sir Derek Jacobi) stood the Master, forced to atone for his past by helping our hero, his essence trapped in a robot body that couldn't leave the TARDIS.

But then on September 26, 2003, everything changed. BBC One controller Lorraine Heggessey had determined to get the program back on the air, with Davies at the helm, and she no longer cared about BBC Worldwide's plans for a film. On the audio documentary *Project: WHO,* Heggessey recounts, "I just said, 'Enough! We have to do it, we have to do it now. I don't care what the situation is, get it sorted. And BBC One should now take priority because we've been waiting for this movie that hasn't yet appeared.'"

That September morning, she announced that it was happening, and it wouldn't be a reboot, as some expected, but a continuation of the old program. Over the years, others had pitched ways of reimagining the franchise from scratch—ignoring that the point of the show was that it rebooted itself internally—often with a darker, cynical edge and using a TARDIS with a working chameleon circuit. Davies didn't want to obey every single bit of continuity established by the original program, nor did he want to ignore it. Repeats of classic adventures had been airing on television for years following cancellation, and the parents of many children watching the new show would recall watching previous actors in the role. It had to be a continuation, and it had to be the Ninth Doctor, not a new First Doctor.

Some asked why RTD didn't recruit Paul McGann. Davies answered that it was important to approach this as a completely new show. The audience would meet the new Doctor and not need to know anything about him. Older fans wouldn't be telling newer fans of past stories featuring the hero seen on-screen. They'd discover the character together.

While Davies acknowledged the legitimacy of Paul McGann's Doctor and praised it, he didn't consider *Scream of the Shalka* in line with his vision of the character and didn't find its depiction of the Time Lord particularly impressive. In statements to the press, he made it clear that the new Doctor would be the official Ninth Doctor and he wasn't worrying about the webcast. Richard E. Grant's incarnation became known as the Shalka Doctor to fans, a parallel universe version featured again only in one other prose story, "The Feast of the Stone."

BUILDING THE SHOW

Initially, the plan called for a season of six episodes, a standard in the UK for many dramas, and the BBC suggested multi-episode arcs relying on cliffhangers. It was a classic *Doctor Who* formula, but Davies countered that modern audiences were used to what he called the American model: standalone episodes that formed a larger saga but also worked on their own.

Davies suggested that new *Doctor Who* episodes have a cold open, allowing a mini-cliffhanger before the theme music began. When he later realized his episodes tended to end shorter than what was needed, he added previews for the subsequent adventure at the end.

The BBC agreed and then increased the number of episodes from six to thirteen. Davies needed more writers and now had to reconsider the general character arc. Converting six of the episodes into three two-part stories (a formula that RTD generally followed for the next few years) allowed for more nail-biting storytelling. As this was now a mainstream Saturday evening drama with a respectable budget, it was a very different atmosphere from previous *Doctor Who* eras. Months were spent filming, with episodes going through weeks of post-production work before they would be ready to air.

As producer Phil Collinson saw it, while the new program wouldn't be beholden to the original, it was still important to keep the atmosphere and inspiration consistent. Along these lines, executive producer Julie Gardner expressed that the creative team had no desire to alter the character significantly. He would still be a centuries-old Time Lord with two hearts who enjoyed traveling in a stolen and unreliable time ship that looked like a police box.

Russell T. Davies did want to tap into some of the sensibility of the Paul McGann TV movie, particularly that the Doctor could appeal romantically to someone who traveled with him even if he didn't (or wouldn't) return those feelings. He also took influence from *Smallville* and *Buffy the Vampire Slayer,* wanting characters to make similar comments and comparisons to classic science fiction television, echoing the thoughts of the audience.

Davies also decided to focus on Earth-bound stories, believing that going to a planet with a society unlike Earth's to protect people unlike humans might prove difficult for some audiences to embrace. Seeing humanity in different time periods gave a stronger connection. Even if the Doctor did take Rose to another planet or a space station, humans were walking about. Likewise, RTD didn't want the companion to come from another planet or time. To keep the Doctor a mystery, the companion needed to become the focus, someone whom the audience could relate to and who wouldn't regenerate if faced with certain death.

Rose Tyler was a working class girl who'd dropped out of school and lived with her widowed mother, occasionally hanging with her on-again, off-again boyfriend, Mickey Smith. She was making a living but not living her life.

Rose and the Doctor meet in the series premiere episode, the hero grabbing her hand and yelling at her to run from a horde of Autons, living mannequins not seen since the 1970s. The style of this introduction for the Ninth Doctor, played by Christopher Eccleston, met with some debate. RTD explains:

> Jane Tranter, who was the control of Drama, wasn't happy with the Doctor's first appearance [when he says, "Run!"] . . . that's exactly how it was written. When you look at it now, you sort of think, *Actually the door should have flung open, and there should be back lighting and smoke and, you know, this . . . terrifically powerful man should've gone, "Run!"* . . . I'm glad we never reshot it because in my heart . . . it's meant to be quite low-key. . . . Because this whole thing is from Rose's point of view. So to her, he's just a stranger that pops up and says, "Run!" and she's running. . . . It's a hard one, isn't it? It's tricky.

MEET THE DOCTOR

"Nice to meet you, Rose. Run for your life!"
—THE NINTH DOCTOR, FROM "ROSE" (2005)

Christopher Eccleston trained at the Central School of Speech and Drama. Appearing in various film and television roles throughout the 1990s, he became well known as a regular cast member of the series *Cracker* and then *Our Friends in the North*. He played the lead in *Second Coming*, an ITV miniseries written and produced by Russell T. Davies that the BBC had turned down. Broadcast in February 2003, *Second Coming* had ratings of more than six million, a pleasant surprise for a station criticized for presenting unchallenging drama at that time.

Months later, Eccleston heard the announcement that Davies was bringing back *Doctor Who* to the BBC. He wanted in. Eccleston admittedly had never followed the classic program as a dedicated fan. He'd watched several episodes casually and always made sure to see certain Dalek episodes and the Doctor's regenerations. But even as a child, the idea of a man who could alter his body and mind fascinated him. Now he wanted to play the hero himself. In many interviews, when asked why he developed such an interest in portraying the Doctor, Eccleston's go-to answer was: "Because Russell T. Davies was writing it."

In *Doctor Who Magazine* #343, Eccleston said that the more he thought about the role, the more he fixated on the strange hero.

> I remember thinking, *He's always moving through time. He's never at home.* That struck me as quite sad, really, and quite resonant for our times—somebody who feels out of place, but also seems to care about human life. I thought about that quite a lot, that melancholy side to him. And then, that night, I happened to watch *Blade Runner* for the first time in my life. Although I'd seen the film, I never properly watched it, and I was very, very affected by it. The whole thing you get with [Roy Batty] longing to be human, and all the stuff about whether [Rick Deckard] is human or not. I thought that was very moving, and in some ways it complemented what I'd been thinking about the life of a Time Lord. So I e-mailed Russell with my thoughts about it. Afterwards I felt quite pretentious about sending it, as I do now talking about it. I put a P.S.—just on instinct, really—saying, 'If you're auditioning for *Doctor Who,* can you put me on the list?' He never replied to say whether or not he thought the e-mail was pretentious, but he did say, 'Of course, I'll consider you.' That was the end of 2003.

Eccleston met with Davies and discussed more ideas about the Doctor's nature. The actor wanted to emphasize that the Doctor would lose patience with humans who were not patient themselves, that he found closed minds frustrating, but would also care about people to a fault, sometimes taking on too much responsibility. Eccleston once mused: "He has two hearts. Does that mean he cares twice as much?"

After Eccleston secured the role, the next step of course was wardrobe. What do you wear to portray a centuries-old alien whose technology makes him seem magical? Davies didn't want to give him a costume as Nathan-Turner had, nor did he want the Doctor of the twenty-first century to look like someone who belonged to the nineteenth. "The Doctor is already eccentric," Davies said. "He doesn't need to dress eccentrically." According to Julie Gardner, "We met lots of costume designers and production designers who had brilliant ideas, but they were thinking in a sci-fi way . . . the color of the costume changing every time he's in oxygen—nonsense things that you really didn't need."

The job of costume design eventually fell to Lucinda Wright. In the book *Doctor Who: The Inside Story,* she explains her take on the man.

> I thought about Christopher Eccleston, and what you get with him is that he's rather raw, isn't he? . . . He's slim, tall, and angular. Because I wanted him to be a Doctor with a silhouette you could instantly recognize. . . . We must have gone through hundreds of jackets. . . . I really wanted Chris to have input because he needed to be comfortable, able to run in it and also have something he could throw off. We decided the jacket needed to look as though it had been lived in for a long time.

Wright also gave the Ninth Doctor shirts in muted colors so he would never distract from the various aliens or strange settings he encountered. Eccleston commented that the outfit wasn't something he personally would wear, but he believed it perfect for his Doctor. This design, matched with Eccleston's closely shaved hair, reflected what McGann had wanted for his own Doctor. At the Armageddon convention in Auckland, New Zealand, in 2010, McGann joked that seeing Eccleston get away with such a costume and haircut made him "hugely bitter," adding, "I was first, I wanted to do it first!"

Because Davies wanted fans both old and new to enter the show on a level playing field, he didn't ask the previous Doctor to return to film a regeneration scene. It was clear for older fans, however, that Eccleston's incarnation was experiencing the first hours of his life. When he enters Rose Tyler's apartment, he sees his reflection in a mirror. Surprised by his own face, he remarks, "Ah, could've been worse. Look at the ears." Though not angry about the situation, Paul McGann did tell *Digital Spy* in 2009 that he felt "short-changed" at not having the opportunity to do an official regeneration scene. Still, the episode "Rose" seems to sneak in a reference to the Eighth Doctor when the Ninth plays with a deck of cards to see if he possesses his previous incarnation's skill at sleight of hand. To his disappointment, he doesn't.

To balance this strange hero, the companion Rose Tyler was played by Billie Piper—known for years in the UK as a musical pop star. Some worried that her casting meant the show wasn't taking itself seriously and wanted to court younger viewers with famous faces. But Piper had already received positive reviews for her role in *The Canterbury Tales,* and approached the role seriously, finding Rose an interesting character, heroic but also quite childish and selfish.

In *Doctor Who Annual 2006,* Davies revealed further background information about Rose. She'd turned her back on school, her boyfriend Mickey (played by actor and writer Noel Clarke), and her mother (played by Camille Coduri) when she'd fallen in love with a young musician named Jimmy Stone (mentioned in the premiere episode, "Rose"). To live with Jimmy, Rose even stole money from her mother. But the musician's eye wandered, and Rose returned to her mother and the forgiving Mickey. She took a job in a clothing store to make back the money she'd stolen and earn her keep. As she later described it, she had no purpose or joy in life and was going through the motions. Until the Doctor came along.

When we first meet him, the Doctor isn't terribly concerned with how blowing up a building may affect others as long as no one's inside. He knows Rose's boyfriend has been kidnapped, but it doesn't occur to him to figure out if Mickey is still alive. When he invites Rose to join him and she initially refuses, his face shows an instant sadness. Yet there's still a bit of fun in this Doctor, who cracks jokes, shouts "Fantastic" when he's excited, and gives ridiculous answers to annoying questions.

In the commentary for "The Space Museum," Maureen O'Brien said, "For me, Christopher Eccleston is the closest to [William Hartnell's Doctor] because he has such danger. . . . He has a dangerous personality, and he has a love of danger, which is what makes him want to go and explore."

"Christopher Eccleston was, in a word, fantastic," according to Sylvester McCoy. "His Doctor was alien. Dangerous. I was a huge fan of his. Even when he was being comedic, his Doctor seemed uncomfortable with the humorous part of him. You can feel he has secrets and guilt. So interesting."

POST-TRAUMATIC STRESS DOCTOR

Davies's relaunch operated on the premise that the Doctor was now the last of his kind, traveling in the last living TARDIS in the universe. RTD spoke of a Third and Last Great Time War, which ended with the Doctor making a final play that wiped out both sides.

Many on the staff found this notion surprising. It drastically departed from the old show's atmosphere, in which Time Lords could drop in at any moment to force the hero into a new mission or act as obstacles. But Davies argued that it simplified matters. The Doctor would be alone in the universe, and if things got really bad you couldn't wonder *Why doesn't he swallow his pride and call the Time Lords for help?* It also made situations more dangerous and history more unstable. In "The Long Game," the Doctor finds humanity's future altered and can't truly explain why. In "The Unquiet Dead," he reveals that history can alter in a snap. The Time Lords can't tidy up all the paradoxes and ripple effects now. The Eye of Harmony on Gallifrey was said to ensure things neither fluxed nor withered—what if it had acted as an anchor for reality itself, and now that anchor was gone with the planet's destruction?

RTD felt this simplified continuity and baggage. We now have an alien meeting a human, two individuals. In a BBC interview, he explained, "He's not bringing his whole civilization with him. She's bringing hers because we understand hers. But actually they are alone in the universe together." Julie Gardner adds: "It also strengthens the relationship with Rose the companion. If you're the last Time Lord traveling through time and space, you need someone. You may not acknowledge that, you may not even really know it. . . And it becomes a much more intense and more dramatic experience and relationship, I think."

The Ninth Doctor definitely had a more dramatic relationship with his companion than previous incarnations had. Their combination hit a chord, as did their adventures, blending humor and an embrace of absurdity with serious discussion on morality. As writer Simon Guerrier said, "This was truly universal programming. Kids were actually planning their nights around being able to watch *Doctor Who,* and parents were watching with them."

The day the new *Doctor Who* premiered, Eccleston did an interview on *BBC Breakfast.* He said: "Hopefully, it's going to be a program that the family will watch together, like all the best television. I would like eight- to twelve-year-olds to take me into their heart. I don't think I've got much of a chance with Tom Baker and Jon Pertwee fans, and I respect that fidelity, really. I have it myself to Sean Connery as James Bond. But I'm hoping that eight- to twelve-year-old children will—I'll be their first Doctor, and they'll love me the way people love Baker."

On *BBC Breakfast,* Eccleston was directly asked if he might stay on the show for as long as Tom Baker. "I can't answer that," he replied. "It's impossible. If you think about it, thirteen forty-five-minute episodes in the old days is two series . . . forty-five minutes, not half hours. I've done two series already."

Soon after the transmission of the second episode, "The End of the World," reports leaked that Eccleston was leaving at the end the first season and it was later confirmed. Eccleston was reportedly quite angry that the news had leaked, spoiling the drama of the Ninth Doctor's upcoming regeneration.

ONLY 900 YEARS OLD?

"I'm called the Doctor. Date of birth . . . Difficult to remember. Sometime soon, I should think."
—FOURTH DOCTOR, FROM "NIGHTMARE OF EDEN" (1979)

The Doctor's age was a matter of debate during Hartnell's years. Newman settled on the hero being between 600 to 650 years old, but others in the production staff believed he was centuries older or younger. On-screen, the Doctor finally mentions his age for the first time in the 1967 Second Doctor story "Tomb of the Cybermen," the hero saying he is roughly 450 by Earth standards.

In "Planet of the Spiders" in 1974, the Third Doctor was said to be 748 years old. In the 1978 story "The Ribos Operation," the Doctor said he was now 756, but was then informed that he'd lost count and was actually 759. The next story "The Pirate Planet" established that the Doctor had been traveling in the TARDIS for 523 years, which would mean he had been 236 on the day he stole the TARDIS. Since the person making this claim was Romana, it seems likely she measured in Gallifreyan years, and it's uncertain how that translates to Earth years.

Years later, the Sixth Doctor claimed he was 900 years old, though later amended that this was a rough estimation. Hours after his regeneration, the Seventh Doctor mentioned in the 1987 story "Time and the Rani" that he was now 953.

The age became a topic of debate again when the modern day program began. Christopher Eccleston's Ninth Doctor said he was 900 years old, a creative decision by Russell T. Davies. Throughout the modern day program, the age was now referenced again and again and it's become a marker of linear time passing for the hero even in a show about time travel.

The Eleventh Doctor said he was 907, but then spent several periods traveling alone in between his adventures. In the sixth season opener "The Impossible Astronaut," he said he was 909. During the last episode of the season, he said he was now 1103. By the 2012 episode "A Town Called Mercy," he claimed to be about 1200.

Steven Moffat had evidently tried to write in an explanation for why the Ninth Doctor's age contradicted what was said in the classic program. In the 2005 episode "The Empty Child," the Doctor said he had been *traveling* for 900 years, implying he was now counting his age from the day he'd left Gallifrey. On the other hand, the 2011 episode "The Doctor's Wife" said he had only been traveling for roughly 700 years.

Fourth Doctor Tom Baker said in different interviews that he imagined the Doctor lost track of his age often due to absentmindedness and how relative time became when you lived in the TARDIS. In the 2009 Big Finish audio drama *Orbis,* the Eighth Doctor admits he not only loses track of his age often, but also sometimes changes the system of dating he's using. When asked about the age contradictions, Steven Moffat has repeatedly suggested that the Doctor simply has no clue how old he is and is constantly lying.

THE WAR CONTINUES

The sixth episode of the first new season marked a halfway point, and Davies treated it as a second pilot. The Doctor and Rose would appear without making much mention of the previous five episodes and their dialogue would summarize who they were for any viewers discovering the program that week. The sixth episode "Dalek" also acted as a major link to the past by referencing not one but three archenemies. Finding himself in a museum of alien technology and biology, the Doctor sees a Cyberman head and is then confronted by a living Dalek. When asked about Davros, the hero simply describes the scientist as a madman.

For a while though, it looked as if the Daleks wouldn't return in the modern program. The Terry Nation estate and the BBC argued about creative control regarding the stories and episode writer Robert Shearman was advised that he might need to write an alternate version introducing a new enemy, a race powerful enough to engage in a Time War with Gallifrey and evoke the same sense of dread in the Doctor that the monsters from Skaro had once done. Fortunately the pieces fell into place. "Thank God we got the Daleks back. It would have been a poorer series without them," Davies later told *Doctor Who Magazine*.

Robert Shearman loosely adapted parts of the episode "Dalek" from a successful audio drama he'd written for Big Finish entitled *Jubilee*. Knowing that people mocked the Daleks' resemblance to pepper shakers and their seeming inability to traverse stairs (despite evidence to the contrary), Shearman emphasized their danger, particularly their single-minded purpose.

The Dalek's height was increased so the monster could stare Rose Tyler in the eye. RTD also wanted to add a sense of weight, so the casing was made to look like brass and decorated by rivets. Originally, bullets bounced harmlessly off the Dalek shell, but the production team quickly realized it would cost too much to animate a spark for each ricochet. To save money, it was established that Daleks now had a force field that disintegrated bullets before they made contact. While the Seventh Doctor story "Remembrance of the Daleks" showed a Dalek with limited hovering capability, this new version would be able to truly fly.

Although an operator still sat inside the Dalek prop, another person now moved the head piece by remote control. These two coordinated their moves with Nicholas Briggs, who provided the voice from another position on set. (Briggs couldn't provide the voice and control the head piece at the same time since the ring modulator's signal interfered with the radio control.)

When the Doctor told Rose that his people had died fighting the Last Great Time War with a powerful enemy, many classic series fans assumed he meant the Daleks. Shearman's episode confirmed this and added that the Doctor had brought the war to an end. "Ten million ships on fire. The entire Dalek race wiped out in one second. . . . I watched it happen. I *made* it happen!"

When asked about the Time Lords, the Doctor said that his people had "burned" alongside the Daleks. He didn't survive the event by choice, either because he didn't expect to regenerate or because something else happened. No wonder he seemed so scarred and guilty now, driven to anger when others didn't hold up his expectations. He was still angry at himself, not only for having to destroy his own people but perhaps for not having destroyed the Dalek race when he'd been present at its genesis.

As always with *Doctor Who,* some wondered if episodes like "Dalek" would frighten children more than was necessary. In his *BBC Breakfast* interview, Christopher Eccleston said: "It's the psychology that's frightening, particularly for instance when the Doctor confronts the Daleks. . . . Is the Doctor actually as bad as the Daleks because he's prepared to exterminate them willy-nilly? So the psychology's very well-drawn, and the children will listen to that as well as look, you know? If you make good television for children, the adults will come. That's the way I think about it."

NEW COMPANIONS

"Dalek" included Rose recommending a new traveling companion, a young genius named Adam Mitchell, played by Bruno Langley. Rose is drawn to

Adam, perhaps because of similarities he shares with the Doctor, but the young man proves too reckless with time travel, and his attempts to profit from the future have disastrous consequences. In "The Long Game," Adam Mitchell becomes the first companion actually kicked off the TARDIS.

Rose also attempts to profit from time travel, but in her case it is to regain her lost father. "Father's Day" showed just how dangerous paradoxes could be if too many accrued in the same arc of space and time. The Time Lords could have fixed such matters in the past, but not so now. But the heart of the story was the understandably selfish wish many of us might make if we found ourselves in a time machine, to bring back a loved one we'd lost. In Rose's case, it was also a chance to really meet the father she'd never known. "Father's Day," written by Paul Cornell, attracted more than eight million viewers and was nominated for the 2006 Hugo Award for best dramatic presentation. It lost to another *Doctor Who* story that year.

Not counting his comedy sketch for Red Nose Day, Steven Moffat finally got the chance to write an on-screen *Doctor Who* adventure with a two-part tale in the episodes "The Empty Child" and "The Doctor Dances." For the first time in years the Doctor references having been a grandfather, and finally adds that he was a parent, too. He also later implies that he had indeed known romance, with Moffat deliberately using the word "dance" as a euphemism.

The novel *Lungbarrow* had established that Time Lords were produced asexually. But Moffat and Davies agreed that this actually made the Doctor *less* interesting. It was more intriguing, Moffat argued, to give the Doctor the capacity and even the desire for romance but then choose not to engage in it for reasons the audience could debate.

Moffat's story also brought back the Time Agency, first mentioned in the Fourth Doctor TV story "The Talons of Weng-Chiang," and introduced actor John Barrowman as Captain Jack Harkness, named after the Marvel Comics character Agatha Harkness (often seen in *Avengers* and *Fantastic Four* comics). Jack hailed from the fifty-first century, a rogue Time Agent who couldn't remember two years of his life. RTD wanted Jack to start as a coward who didn't consider the consequences of his actions and be molded into a hero by the influence of Rose and the Doctor. Davies also needed Jack to arm troops and rally them into an army for the season finale, which

RTD didn't want the Doctor to do directly. He was a counterpart to the Doctor; overtly sexual, shallow, and reliant on typical science fiction gadgets.

But what really brought people to attention was Jack's omnisexuality. By the fifty-first century, labels of sexual orientation evidently had become passé. RTD thought it was high time that bisexuals enter mainstream television and liked that Jack made for a heroic figure whom both men and women could admire instead of just serving as the butt of a few jokes. Rather than immediately broadcasting Jack's sexuality and possibly imply that he was a token character, it was a full episode and a half before the revelation was made, letting viewers decide beforehand whether or not they liked him. After writing Jack's introduction, Moffat commented that the character's sexuality seemed perfectly natural, adding that Jack was just a James Bond of the fifty-first century, one willing to "bed anyone."

EXPANDING WHONIVERSE

When his first season of *Doctor Who* went into production, Davies contacted *Doctor Who Magazine* and offered it the chance to show the official regeneration scene, leading into the episode "Rose." Though initially excited, the staff worried that the scene wouldn't work. In the Eighth Doctor comic strips, the hero had recently recruited a new companion named Destrii, a young woman with a somewhat corrupt idea of the universe and morality. The Doctor hoped to change her through their adventures together.

Three possibilities presented themselves as to what to do before the comic strip shifted to the Ninth Doctor and Rose: Destrii could die just before the Doctor's regeneration, which seemed unnecessary and a waste; Destrii could leave the Doctor's side before he regenerated, which again seemed a loss of potential; or the final story could show the Eighth Doctor and Destrii walking into the sunset, implying that they had many adventures before the Doctor began his ninth life. The magazine went with this final option, thanking RTD for the offer.

This wasn't the only time the modern program reached out to the tie-in materials. In *Doctor Who Annual 2006,* Russell T. Davies wrote about the events leading up to the Time War and referenced not only TV stories such as "Genesis of the Daleks" and the TV movie, but also the Big Finish audio drama *The Apocalypse Element*. In the episode "Boom Town," Rose Tyler mentions an alien pyramid that she encountered in one of the BBC Books tie-in novels.

"HAVE A GOOD LIFE"

The Ninth Doctor grew over his single year on-screen. He learned to be more patient, more careful, and to let his guard down just a little. In his second episode, he coldly watched as an enemy died in front of him. By his last few stories, he no longer seemed to be the kind of man who would do that. Rose, Jack, Mickey and others had reminded him who he had been before the Time War.

The thirteenth and final episode of the season, "The Parting of the Ways," has the Doctor face the same choice he'd had during the war: to end things by wiping out both sides. But this time, he chooses to accept defeat if he has to rather than kill allies and innocents to ensure victory. It provides closure to the Last Great Time War (for the moment anyway), making it a fitting end to the incarnation characterized as a damaged war survivor. After the battle, Rose is in danger and in saving her the Doctor forces his own regeneration. But he has enough time to say goodbye, telling Rose that she was fantastic . . . and so was he.

Eccleston's role on the program won him the SFX Award for Best TV Actor, the TV Quick Award for Best Actor, and the National Television Award for Most Popular Actor. Billie Piper won the SFX Award for Best TV Actress and the National Television Award for Most Popular Actress. Both were nominated for BAFTA Cymru Awards, and, though it didn't win, the first season did win the BAFTA TV Audience Award and the BAFTA TV Award for Best Drama Series.

Christopher Eccleston made his decision to leave prior to the season airing. With several episodes left to film, Russell T. Davies had enough time to properly write a regeneration scene into the season finale, and it bore some resemblance to the Eighth Doctor's finale comic strip adventure in *Doctor Who Magazine*. RTD also had enough time to properly cast the next Doctor. But many fans wondered, why did Eccleston leave after one year?

When asked, the actor pointed out, as he did before, that his one year of *Doctor Who* was similar to two years of other UK dramas and he'd thought he'd had a good run. He also mentioned that he often disliked staying in a role for too long, not wishing to repeat the same basic steps over and over again. In her own interviews, Billie Piper touched on this same point, saying how frustrating the role of the Doctor could be for an actor as it didn't allow for much dramatic growth or change because of the nature of the franchise and the need to keep the hero alien and mysterious.

After leaving, Eccleston said in interviews that he had no interest in his Doctor returning to the show either in flashback or for a team-up, joking it was not a good idea to "bathe in the same river twice." In more recent interviews, however, he implied that he wouldn't be averse to returning under the right circumstances.

In discussing the modern program with *Doctor Who Magazine* in 2009, Tom Baker said: "I was amazed that they didn't have Christopher Eccleston—who's a very powerful actor—on a contract for two seasons because he was such a hit!"

On July 20, 2011, Eccleston spoke at an acting master class at the Theatre Royal Haymarket and *Doctor Who* came up. The podcast BadWilf later provided a transcript of his response.

> I left *Doctor Who* because I could not get along with the senior people. I left because of politics. I did not see eye-to-eye with them . . . So I left, I felt, over a principle. I thought to remain, which would have made me a lot of money and given me huge visibility, the price I would have had to pay was to eat a lot of shit. I'm not being funny about that. I didn't want to do that and it comes to the art of it, in a way . . .
>
> We are vulnerable as actors and we are constantly humiliating ourselves auditioning. But if you allow that to go on, on a grand scale you will lose whatever it is about you and it will be present in your work . . .
>
> My face didn't fit and I'm sure they were glad to see the back of me. The important thing is that I succeeded. It was a great part. I loved playing him. I loved connecting with that audience. Because I've always acted for adults and then suddenly you're

acting for children, who are far more tasteful . . . It's either good, or it's bad.

Even during his final weeks of filming, the actor had felt that the experience was worthwhile. In the TV special *A New Dimension,* aired just before his first episode premiered, Christopher Eccleston said: "I've loved playing him [the Doctor], and I love taking part in the basic essence and message of the series, which is: It's a short life. Seize it, and live it as fully as you can; care for others; be respectful of all other life forms, regardless of color or creed. And to be part of that has been . . . fantastic."

New TARDIS, New Screwdriver

"Who looks at a screwdriver and thinks: 'Ooh, this could be a little more sonic'?"

—JACK HARKNESS, FROM "THE DOCTOR DANCES" (2005)

One morning at 3:30, Chistopher Eccleston was on a London street with Billie Piper. It was the first day that the two were shooting with the TARDIS, in a scene in which the Ninth Doctor and Rose Tyler had traced the alien Nestene Consciousness to a spot near the Eye of London. "I came round this corner, and I just glanced around to my left, and there was the TARDIS," Eccleston told *Doctor Who Confidential*. "That's when it dawned on me kind of what I was doing, and I also realized how much the TARDIS is part of our cultural lives. I didn't say 'police telephone box,' which is basically what it is. I thought, *TARDIS. There's the TARDIS.*"

With the exception of Tom Baker's alternate control room and the TV movie console room, the TARDIS interior had remained largely unchanged since 1963. But the modern-day production team wanted to give the old girl a complete makeover. The idea was to embrace a more obviously alien atmosphere, with pillars that seemed to grow between the ceiling and the floor. As the Doctor revealed in "The Impossible Planet," TARDISes aren't built, they're grown, with equipment installed later. The 2013 episode "Journey to the Heart of the TARDIS" also revealed the ship had a tree within that grew new technology.

Production designer Edward Thomas explained to *Doctor Who Confidential,* "We looked mostly to nature, to organic structures. Things like coral were quite a nice idea. . . . We've got some Gallifreyan text [on the scanner screen] which spells out all the different information that's relevant for flying the TARDIS."

The Gallifreyan text and symbols created for the scanner screen have become a staple of the program, the one language that the TARDIS doesn't translate for travelers. With no set formula, the language has inspired many fans to create their own Gallifreyan translations online.

Some even have the Time Lord equivalents of their names tattooed on their bodies.

The console itself changed as well. Although the controls remained divided into six sections, the shape of the console went from hexagon to circle. From the classic buttons and clean switches that had adorned previous models, the TARDIS had become a mix of alien tech, loose cords, and recovered items, including a bicycle pump, bell, hand brake, and many knobs and levers added on haphazardly. A mallet on a string stood at the ready for whenever the Doctor needed to perform "percussive maintenance." The idea was that, due to the Time War, the Doctor now had limited resources. Even before the destruction of Gallifrey, he had relied on found parts to make repairs. Another reflection that this was the last living TARDIS.

Davies also at last confirmed what many fans believed, and had been said in different tie-in media: A crew of six was meant to pilot the TARDIS, hence the hexagonal controls. It also explains why the Doctor often has such a hard time with the ship.

The reworking of the ship led to a new design for the sonic screwdriver, which now resembled part of the console itself. In the early 1980s, producer John Nathan-Turner and writer Christopher Bidmead agreed that the sonic screwdriver was a "plot-killer" and cure-all that had to go, hence its destruction, after which it was not seen again in the classic series.

The TV movie brought the sonic screwdriver back, however, and the Eighth Doctor used it in his audio dramas for Big Finish and in the comic strip adventures for *Doctor Who Magazine*. Davies could have dismissed this detail, having the Doctor lose the device during the Time War, but he liked it. RTD wanted kids to be able to play with their own sonic screwdrivers at home, whether a licensed toy or a pen accompanied by a *whrrr* sound. If the Doctor was, at his core, a bit of a wizard (as Hartnell had often said), it made sense for him to have a magic wand.

Davies also thought the sonic screwdriver now made sense as a multipurpose device. If humans in the twenty-first century had progressed enough that they carried mobile technology that could access the Internet, transmit messages, record video, play music, and more, then surely the advanced science of the Time Lords could come up with an equivalent device with more practical applications for the Doctor's adventures. Furthermore, with the Doctor's adventures now averaging just under fifty minutes, rather than roughly two hours, the sonic screwdriver cut through certain scenes in which our hero would have had to find equipment, pick a lock, or cobble together a scanner.

We also first see psychic paper, which the Doctor used to get past guards and other wary people by reflecting their own ideas of impressive identification back at them. In the novel *World Game,* it was revealed that psychic paper was an invention of Gallifrey's Celestial Intervention Agency.

While some criticize these items as cure-alls for many problems, it's important to note that the Doctor still finds himself in situations where his tools don't help. "School Reunion" revealed that a device known as a "deadlock seal" blocks the effects of a sonic screwdriver, as do certain substances such as wood. Psychic paper doesn't fool highly intelligent people or those with proper training. In one case, the Doctor's attempt at using psychic paper failed because the lie he wanted it to tell was too big—namely that he was a "responsible adult."

The sonic screwdriver has become more symbolic of the Doctor himself in the new show. That the time traveler River Song possesses one is strange and significant, despite that the Doctor gave Romana one during the classic series and had entrusted Sarah Jane with "sonic lipstick" (as revealed in the pilot of *The Sarah Jane Adventures*).

In 2010, the Eleventh Doctor's regeneration forced his TARDIS to rebuild itself. Under Steven Moffat's direction, the control room became a brighter place with multiple halls and stairwells leading in different directions, implying just how vast the ship is. Moffat stuck with the idea that the controls would include parts and devices from different sources, but otherwise the console differed significantly, regaining its old hexagonal design. The TARDIS control panels now each dealt with a specific area of operation (mapped out for Matt Smith to learn so he could operate the ship consistently on-screen).

In the "Amy's Choice" episode, viewers with fast eyes or thumbs spotted an interesting inscription on the tool box housed beneath the control console. It reads: "TARDIS. Time And Relative Dimension In Space. Build Site: Gallifrey Blackhole Shipyard. Type 40. Build date: 1963. Authorised for use by qualified Time Lords only by the Shadow Proclamation. Misuse or theft of any TARDIS will result in extreme penalties and permanent exile."

In the 2012 Christmas special, "The Snowmen," the Doctor unveils a new TARDIS interior. Although it incorporates some of the modern cobbled-together bits and the modern Gallifreyan text, the general style resembles the classic TARDIS interiors. A fitting design considering that the show's fiftieth anniversary year began less than a week later.

20
The Renaissance

"All those planets and creatures and horizons! I haven't seen them
yet, not with these eyes. And it is gonna be . . . fantastic!"
—TENTH DOCTOR, FROM "THE CHRISTMAS INVASION" (2005)

Not only was the show a success, it was regaining the kind of mainstream popularity it hadn't held since the 1970s. Including recordings, the final viewing figures for the opening episode, "Rose," hit 10.5 million, making it the #7 watched show across UK television. Both viewership and critical reception were so high that on March 30, only four days after "Rose" aired, BBC Head of Drama Jane Tranter announced that the new show would have a second season in 2006 as well as a Christmas special beforehand.

Puzzlingly, however, despite high ratings, wide-scale praise, and numerous awards, US networks had little interest in licensing the show, believing Americans either wouldn't be interested or would remember it as a strange cult show from the past with no production budget. The Sci-Fi Channel (now SyFy) aired the first season a year later, after cutting lines and shortening scenes to accommodate the longer commercial breaks of US television.

But back in the UK, no one had any doubts that the new program was a massive hit, earning both the respect and support that the classic program never fully attained. Over the next few years, the BBC hosted promotional events and concerts, a museum about the show opened, and tons of press for all things *Doctor Who* followed. An asset once considered a barely tolerable silliness had become a prized possession. Many critics, journalists, and TV historians suggested that this recognition stemmed from the Doctor having evolved from simply a TV character to a quintessential British hero on the level of James Bond and Sherlock Holmes.

Of course, there were still critics who recognized the show's success but didn't believe that it was truly a continuation of the classic series. Some argued that the special effects budget alone made it a different show, along with the constant pop culture references in the dialogue. Others thought it had more to do with the sudden presence of sexual innuendo and romantic possibility, making the program less innocent.

As time went on, some critics changed their position. What seemed fresh during Eccleston's season may have become predictable for them by Tennant's third year. Or they didn't care for the program at first, but warmed up to it once they got used to certain new aspects. And some chose just to appreciate it, even if it wasn't something they were interested in following. In 2010, two years before he played a robot on *Doctor Who*, comedian David Mitchell spoke of the new show on his webcast *David Mitchell's Soapbox*. "I used to be a big fan of *Doctor Who* . . . And I watched the new version at first, until I found myself irritated by the undermining of what I felt to be its core principles . . . But really, so what? These so-called core principles of mine were simply my remembrance of feelings I'd had towards the show as a child. And the sign that the new show is doing the job it's supposed to is that children love it."

At New York Comic-Con 2012, Peter Davison shared his thoughts on the program's new status:

Now *Doctor Who* is one of the BBC's premier prestige programs. It really wasn't in those days. It was very successful, and it sold to many countries and made the BBC lots of money, but it was never considered a premier drama series. So the people who wrote for *Doctor Who* quite often were people who wrote for a detective series one week, *Doctor Who* one week, and then maybe a hospital drama the week after. They weren't really driven by their love of science fiction. . . . [the new] *Doctor Who* is written by people with a passion for what they're doing. A comfort for me about that, and the other classic Doctors, is these people were all sitting out there as kids in the audience and watching *us* do *Doctor Who*; they're all fantastic fans.

However some people felt about it, success had arrived for *Doctor Who*. Now the program needed to stay on the course despite recasting its hero after only one year.

THE TENTH DOCTOR

Although Jack Harkness was a quick hit with fans, Davies had a practical reason for removing him from the TARDIS moments before the Doctor regenerated. RTD wanted to emphasize the frightening and strange experience of Rose witnessing her trusted friend physically transforming, echoing how he thought some of the younger viewers would feel who perhaps hadn't been prepared for such a change. As a Time Agent, Jack would have known about regeneration and would have tried to explain it in a way that would calm her down.

When asked to participate in the 2005 Children in Need charity Christmas event, RTD took advantage of the situation to explain regeneration and provide a peek at the new Doctor. In an untitled mini-episode for the charity special, the Tenth Doctor tells Rose that he's the same person as before, not some replacement. Rose understandably has difficulty absorbing this information and then asks what no companion ever had: "Can you change back?"

The answer of course was no and the episode ended with the Tenth Doctor having a fit of temporary madness. Until "The Christmas Invasion" finally aired, viewers wondered what kind of man this new hero would be. That had certainly been the topic of many discussions behind the scenes once David Tennant had been cast.

Born in Bathgate, Scotland, to a Presbyterian minister, David McDonald was an avid fan of *Doctor Who*, regularly watching the adventures of Tom Baker and then Peter Davison. At the tender age of three, he told his parents that he wanted to become an actor because of *Doctor Who*. He entered the Royal Scottish Academy of Music and Drama at seventeen, one of the youngest students ever to pass the audition. Learning that another David McDonald had registered with the Equity union already, he took the stage name "Tennant" from Neil Tennant, singer of electronic pop band Pet Shop Boys.

Tennant joined the Royal Shakespeare Company and impressed many with his work. Still making occasional appearances in TV and on film, he played opposite Christopher Eccleston in the 1996 movie *Jude*. Starting in 2004, Tennant appeared more regularly on television, including as a singing detective in the miniseries *Blackpool,* in which he played opposite David Morrissey (who later played the titular character of the 2009 TV special "The Next Doctor"). In March 2005, while the new *Doctor Who* was making its debut, BBC Three aired the miniseries *Casanova,* created by Russell T. Davies and featuring Tennant and Peter O'Toole as the Italian protagonist at different times in his life.

Before 2005, David Tennant had been doing voice work for Big Finish, appearing in *Doctor Who* audio plays. He still had a strong affection for the character and was excited to see how Russell T. Davies would modernize it for a new audience. Tennant even provided the voiceover narration for the documentary *Doctor Who: A New Dimension.*

When RTD and Julie Gardner discussed finding a new Doctor to succeed Eccleston, David Tennant's name quickly arose. Impressed with the actor's work and aware that some were predicting he was "the next big thing" in television, Gardner offered him the role. Tennant was at first surprised, then ecstatic, proclaiming, "I want a long coat!"

There were plenty of Eccleston episodes left to air, so Tennant was asked to keep his casting a secret. Unfortunately, news of Eccleston's departure leaked, which annoyed both RTD and the Ninth Doctor actor since it robbed them of being able to make a big announcement. Curious about the fan response, Tennant visited the message boards of the *Doctor Who* fan website Outpost Gallifrey. He told *Doctor Who Magazine*:

> I went on there, and the first comment I read was very nice, and the next comment was terribly flattering, and then the next comment said something like, 'I can't bear the sight of him!' And the one after that said, 'Who?' The one after that said, 'I'd rather have David Morrissey.' The one after that said, 'That's it! The dream is finished! Someone who looks like a weasel could never play the Doctor! It's over!' And then I thought to myself that maybe it's best not to read this sort of thing too much.

Tennant pushed forward on constructing his version of the Time Lord. He and costume designer Louise Page discussed a military look, dismissed in favor of a suit. Tennant wanted his Doctor to look like a proper student or young teacher, similar to what Jamie Oliver had worn on the show *Parkinson*. He wanted "geek chic" but also a suit comfortable to run and leap around in. For similar reasons, he elected to wear casual running shoes. He found a pair of brown trousers with blue pinstripes that he liked. There was no matching jacket, so Page bought several more pairs of the same trousers and made jackets from the material.

Page told *Doctor Who Magazine*, "The jacket shape was based on a 1930s period suit. . . . The long coat started off much more theatrical and period-looking, with bigger lapels, but Russell asked me to pare it down to make it narrower. I said, 'He's going to end up looking like a pencil.' Russell said, 'I like that idea!'"

Tennant grew up with the Fourth and Fifth Doctors, and we can see their influence on him. The Tenth Doctor has a vulnerability and occasional indecisiveness reminiscent of Peter Davison's portrayal, yet he also possesses a wild, childish energy and bouts of righteous anger that bring the Fourth Doctor to mind. While danger excited the Ninth, the Tenth thrills at the unknown, human creativity, and enduring hope in spite of the odds. This Doctor doesn't lose his temper and call people "stupid apes" all the time. He seems practically in love with *Homo sapiens*. Billie Piper told *Doctor Who Magazine*, "Chris would go away in between breaks and save his energy for the performance—whereas, with David, we'll kind of chat, we'll have a laugh, but then, as soon as he needs to focus, he'll find his own way of doing that. David dances with it more. He's a bit more like—I don't know—a baby deer. He's my little Bambi!"

At the same time, there was a darkness to this Doctor, a remaining glimmer of the ninth incarnation. Soon after his regeneration, the Tenth Doctor witnessed Prime Minister Harriet Jones destroy alien invaders who had surrendered and were leaving. In the past, the Doctor would sometimes walk away in such a scenario, unwilling to fully impose his values on a society or alter major political futures. But here, he is angry. First he warns and then, when he sees his warning is not taken seriously, he follows through, perhaps just to prove that he is not to be trifled with. Through manipulation, the Tenth Doctor removes the Prime Minister from power and isn't sorry about it. Nor does he wonder how this will change the "golden age" future he knew previously existed for the UK with her in charge.

In the second season premiere "New Earth," he seemed to sum up the situation: "I'm the Doctor. And if you don't like it, if you want to take it to a higher authority, there isn't one. It stops with me."

DOCTOR-LITE

The first season of the modern show broke new ground with a companion's parent and ex-boyfriend as recurring characters. The second season took matters further. "Love and Monsters" included Rose's mother, Jackie Tyler, and delved into the stress a parent feels knowing that her only child is traveling through space and time, seeing incredible things but also facing terrible dangers for days or weeks at a time. Tennant's tenure as the Doctor also featured a kind of story never before done in the program's history, the "Doctor-Lite" episodes.

In order to spread the budget across not only another thirteen adventures but also another Christmas special, the *Doctor Who* production team decided to do one adventure during the season that wouldn't feature major special effects and would barely involve the Doctor and Rose, since reduced time meant less money spent on them. "Love and Monsters" instead showed ordinary people affected by the Doctor's adventures forming a group akin to some *Doctor Who* fan clubs. This same episode featured a creature called the Absorbaloff, a monster created by a young fan who'd won a contest on Blue Peter.

The Doctor-Lite episode successfully saved money and was repeated in the next season with the episode "Blink." This adventure was based on a story that Steven Moffat had included in *Doctor Who Annual 2006*, "What I Did on My Christmas Holidays by Sally Sparrow," featuring the Ninth Doctor sending messages to a twelve-year-old student twenty years in the future. Reworked to make Sally older and pitting her against a new menace known as the Weeping Angels, "Blink" quickly became a fan favorite despite barely including the Doctor at all. "Blink" also gave us the phrase "timey-wimey," the Doctor's pet name for paradoxes that don't disrupt the space-time vortex. Fans have adopted this phrase widely, sometimes using it to refer to instances when the show's internal logic gets a bit strange.

The fourth season had a "companion-lite" episode, as the Doctor had a strange adventure while separated from his friend. This episode,

"Midnight," received praise as one of the more frightening examples of *Doctor Who*, featuring a monster neither understood nor defeated.

JUST FRIENDS?

In his stories, the Tenth Doctor's connection to Rose seems much stronger than the Ninth's. More protective and playful, he also seems awkward and uncomfortable when she implies that she might want something closer to a relationship or when he senses her jealousy from her toward another woman. This personal envy comes to the fore in "School Reunion," which brought back Elisabeth Sladen as Sarah Jane Smith.

Starting in 2002, Elisabeth had been starring in the Big Finish audio drama series *Sarah Jane Smith*. The first audio adventure takes place years after Sarah Jane left the Doctor's side, just after her Aunt Lavinia has died. K-9 makes no appearance in her audio adventures (his absence later explained in "School Reunion"). The only reference made to the Doctor is when Sarah remarks that her ability to seem casually aloof while fighting evil is a habit she picked up from an old friend. Sladen starred in eight *Sarah Jane Smith* audio dramas in total, with her daughter Sadie Miller joining her.

In 2006, the audio adventures ended just in time for Sarah Jane to appear on television once again. Davies initially didn't want to bring a character back from classic *Doctor Who* just to please fans, but he knew that Sarah Jane's own close relationship with the Doctor would shock Rose into wondering whether she were truly special or just the latest in a long line of replaceable traveling companions. When Sladen was approached, she was initially cautious as well, not wanting to appear in a cameo role simply as a joke for older fans. After hearing the plans for the story, she was happy to return.

In "School Reunion," Sarah Jane doesn't realize that she already knows the thin science teacher with the familiar name of Dr. John Smith. When she does realize the truth, it's an emotional scene and older fans finally get to see Sarah Jane confront the Doctor about never returning for her after their forced departure. The story explored moving on with your life.

Tennant remarked that in the second season, the program developed into "a love story without the shagging" between the Doctor and Rose.

Some classic-series fans, as well as people involved in classic *Doctor Who,* debated the idea of unspoken romance between the Doctor and a companion. Along with this, there were other characters hitting on the Time Lord and he even had a more direct romantic interest when he telepathically connected with Madame de Pompadour, the two gaining a deep mutual understanding in moments.

Louise Jameson, who played Leela, remarked, "I'm not sure I can quite go with all the snogging! . . . I love the flirting, though. The almost-romance works better for me than an actual one."

Producer Philip Hinchcliffe reflected, "I loved Rose. She was just wonderful and brought such emotion and depth to the relationship of the companion. The idea that there's some chemistry beyond a mentor relationship is rather daring. I'm not sure I would have had the guts to go with that. There was an undertone with Sarah Jane, but it was such a rule at the time that you weren't to imply anything inappropriate. . . . Rose's feelings make sense when you consider that these people go off with this man who shows them impossible things. Who can they tell afterward who will truly understand? It's deeply personal, these travels they have with him. . . . I think it's important that you don't make it standard practice, though. Rose works as a special exception for a season or two, and I didn't mind at all Eccleston and Piper, but with Tennant it was becoming a bit uncomfortable that romance could actually happen. I prefer a balance where you imply feelings but then remind everyone that this is an alien who doesn't think like a human being, and a relationship can't really happen. The Doctor is always a little bit apart from humanity. How could he not be with the life he's led?"

Elisabeth Sladen saw the romantic elements as a natural progression for the program to stay relevant, telling *Doctor Who Magazine,* "I think the [modern *Doctor Who*] series is braver on relationships. Ours skirted around them, obviously, because of the times. . . . That's what 'School Reunion' is about, really. It's about having to accept growing older and letting go."

Writer Simon Guerrier perhaps said it best: "People are free not to like there being romantic implications between the Doctor and a companion, but it struck a chord with many people and was very much a part of what made the new show successful. It was a new area to explore and it worked."

The strange feelings between the Doctor and Rose came to a head in the season finale. There had been talks that Billie Piper would leave halfway through the second year, but instead she remained, allowing for a build-up to an explosive finale where Rose is literally torn away from the Doctor, exiled to a parallel world. The Doctor uses all his skill and resources to communicate with her one last time. Rose tearfully confesses that she loves the hero, who responds, "Quite right, too." Then tears welling in his eyes, the Doctor says "Rose Tyler—" only to be cut off.

Rather than have the Doctor move on to his next companion without mentioning the previous one, RTD had the hero deal with the forced separation. Whether one was a fan of the romantic implication or not, Rose Tyler was the first connection with a living being the Doctor had made since watching his entire race die. Unlike the abrupt departures of the past, the emotionally scarred Time Lord was so affected by the people who traveled with him that he needed some time to grieve each departure in different ways. Years later, it seems odd to many that it might have been handled otherwise.

SMITH AND JONES

"The Runaway Bride" featured well-known TV comedian Catherine Tate as Donna Noble, a direct contrast to Rose Tyler. Noble very much liked her life and didn't appreciate dangerous alien forces entering it. She also saw the Doctor more objectively as a man rather than a romantic hero, recognizing how dangerous he could be if he didn't have someone around to help him hold back his rage and judgment. When the Doctor invites Donna to join him, she respectfully declines.

The third season brought the official new companion Martha Jones, played by Freema Agyeman. The actor had appeared in season two as a different character, so Martha was quickly explained as that character's cousin. Like Donna, Martha didn't see the need to escape her life, but she did thrill at the chance to see incredible things across time and space. An older and more experienced character than Rose, she is more flirtatious with the Doctor, only to feel defeated when she sees time and again that he doesn't notice her advances.

In a BBC Audiobooks interview, Agyeman said, "I love playing Martha Jones. . . . I do relate to her as well. She's obviously embarking on this new journey in her life with the Doctor and I have started this massive journey in being involved in the world of *Doctor Who*. . . . I was thinking it was going to be this place where I would have to earn my stripes and go through the whole process of being the new girl . . . and it was just like walking into a room of friends."

Freema Agyeman (Martha Jones) at Gallifrey One 2013

Davies wanted to present Martha as a symbolic rebound relationship for the Doctor. When a person has lost a great love, the next relationship they attempt often involves a lot of comparison with the previous one. It's only at the completion of that new relationship that they might finally be ready to leave the past behind and move on—though not necessarily with the new person who's been spending time with them.

The Tenth Doctor was more introspective this season, more guarded. The first season had been very much about the Doctor being an enabler who helped others become heroes. The second explored this further, along with the Doctor realizing how he could still be surprised by the universe. The third season had the Doctor begin to face the consequences of his actions, something the Ninth Doctor had touched on in his final adventure. In one story, the Tenth Doctor hides in plain sight in a small village, only to have his enemies find him anyway, costing many lives that wouldn't have been targeted otherwise. He also learned that his decision to remove Harriet Jones from power, made in a moment of anger when he was still recovering from regeneration, wound up clearing the path for a much greater threat to become Prime Minister. The Master was back, played by actor John Simm and calling himself Harold Saxon. Some fans figured out "Mr. Saxon" was an anagram of "Master No. Six," referencing five actors who played the role before Simm, not counting Gordon Tipple who played him for one scene in the TV movie or Sir Derek Jacobi, who played him in *Scream of the Shalka* and for part of the modern day episode "Utopia" (before then regenerating into Simm).

The Doctor knew the Master couldn't be here, as he'd died before the Time War. But the villain gleefully revealed that the Time Lord had been so desperate to defeat the Daleks that they'd actually used their great technology to resurrect him, and in a new Time Lord body at that. He was truly back, with his old telepathic abilities and regeneration powers.

John Simm had become well known recently as the lead actor of *Life on Mars*, playing a time lost police inspector named Sam Tyler (named after Rose Tyler, in fact). Part of why he was cast was because his physical frame and energy made him a good visual counterpart to David Tennant. Having gone through the trauma of repeatedly dying and then being reborn, he was more unstable than ever, taking great joy in creating fear and chaos. To enhance the sense of a dark reflection, he armed himself with a "laser screwdriver" and, rather than acting somewhat asexual, married his "faithful companion" Lucy, a woman he'd traumatized with physical abuse and by showing her the worst the future had to offer.

RTD also added a new wrinkle, saying that the Master was haunted by the sound of war drums in the back of his mind, an unceasing four-part beat that resembled the opening notes of the *Doctor Who* theme. It is a flaw that makes the villain more human, a victim in his own way.

Learning that he and the Doctor were the only survivors of the war, he decides he will turn Earth into a new Gallifrey, with himself as its ruler. When the Doctor says he can't alter the course of human history, the Master echoes the hero's own declaration of power from "New Earth," saying simply, "I'm a Time Lord. I have that right."

Once again, the season explored the theme of the Doctor accepting responsibility. Rather than executing the Master, the hero decides he will become the man's jailer. The Doctor has forgiven the Master and will do what's necessary to bring back the man who had been his friend. But the villain is shot down and chooses not to regenerate, just because his death will leave the Doctor truly alone in the universe.

By the end of Rose's run, she'd regained a father, and her mother had regained the love of her life. Martha's divorced parents and younger sister wound up imprisoned and tortured by the Master. For this reason, and because she knows that a relationship with the Doctor is impossible, she chooses to leave the TARDIS. But Martha didn't remain gone for long. She later shows up in the fourth season as a member of UNIT, by which point the Doctor has found a new companion to keep him on his toes.

"YOU'RE NOT MATING WITH ME!"

"He saves planets, rescues civilizations, defeats terrible creatures, and runs a lot. Seriously, there is an outrageous amount of running involved."

—DONNA NOBLE, FROM "THE DOCTOR'S DAUGHTER" (2008)

Catherine Tate and David Tennant enjoyed working together, not only on *Doctor Who* but on other projects. Davies liked the idea of a character who had declined life aboard the TARDIS and then came to regret that decision. But while she was ready to travel with the Doctor, Donna had zero interest in romance, seeing the man as a very intelligent but flawed friend. In a way, Donna came from the mold of classic companions.

After Martha's departure, the 2007 Christmas special "Voyage of the Damned" had the Doctor aboard a space cruiser that suffered a tragic fate. He'd saved some passengers, as well as the Earth, but not a woman named Astrid (played by Kylie Minogue). The Doctor was now filled with guilt over the people he couldn't help. Donna helped him move past guilt and back to taking responsibility, leading him to confront the horrible truths behind the Ood, a race he had known was in servitude but had never investigated. Not long afterward, he's shaken when he encounters Jenny, a "daughter" cloned from his DNA and portrayed by Georgia Moffett, daughter of Peter Davison. Producer Phil Collinson explained that this was done to challenge how the Doctor saw his place in the universe. "To suddenly find himself with a member of family is kind of one of the biggest challenges you could give him, so I'm chuffed we did it."

In "The Doctor's Daughter," the hero is guarded about making a connection to this girl whom he considers an echo of what a Time Lord truly is. Donna confronts the Doctor about his insecurities, noting how ridiculous it is that they're friends yet he can't bring himself to share that he was once a father unless it directly comes up. Eventually, the Doctor admits he is being unfair and closed off, thinking he might find a way to change with Jenny at his side. But tragedy strikes and the young woman is seemingly killed.

In fact, RTD had intended Jenny to die, but writer Steven Moffat suggested she live so she could make another appearance later. "The Doctor's Daughter" ended with an energy effect similar to regeneration appearing around Jenny's body, healing her wounds. With a grin, Jenny grabs a space ship and flies off to find adventure.

Sadly, despite fan interest, Jenny has yet to return to *Doctor Who* since her appearance in 2008. Behind the scenes, Georgia Moffett and David Tennant began a relationship. The two had a child and later married, after which Tennant also adopted Georgia's older son Ty.

Concerning Tennant becoming his son-in-law, Peter Davison joked: "I'm apparently starting a *Doctor Who* dynasty! Their son could be the nineteenth Doctor one day."

CURTAIN CALL

As the fourth season was nearing its end, David Tennant was more interested in taking on new theatrical roles. Rather than do a full season in 2009, the actor agreed only to a few specials. But when Russell T. Davies, Julie Gardner, and producer Phil Collinson all decided to leave at the end of those specials, Tennant decided to follow suit. Four and a half years was longer than many of them had stayed on other shows. Davies had said before the new program had even begun airing that he imagined he should leave after four years because otherwise he'd be overstaying and possibly viewing it as work rather than fun.

With this in mind, the fourth season ended with a reunion. The walls of reality are breaking and the universe itself is now at risk. Jack Harkness, Martha Jones, Mickey Smith, Rose Tyler, and even her mom Jackie Tyler all return to help the Doctor in this epic battle. Rose's return was advertised before the season had even begun, which invited criticism from some who felt it would have been more effective to be surprised by her appearance. After the battle of the season finale "Journey's End," some thought that the Doctor and Rose would reunite. Instead, he sends her back to the parallel Earth, where her family lives and she has carved out a new life as a defender of that world. She also now has a new task.

During "Journey's End," a clone is created from a mix of the Doctor's and Donna's DNA (which technically made this the fourth episode of that season to involve cloning). This Meta-Crisis Doctor (known to some as Doctor 2.0) is partly human, with a single heart and a human's aging rate. His mind mixes Donna's and the Doctor's, resulting in a new persona, one that is violent and reckless as the Ninth Doctor had been before a shop girl taught him to cool his anger. The Tenth Doctor asks Rose to be a positive influence for this Meta-Crisis Doctor, just as she was before. Donna points out that 2.0 is also a gift to Rose, a version of the Doctor who can grow old with her and won't hesitate to express his love.

This particular story element caused controversy among fans. Davies wanted to give Rose a happy ending at last rather than leaving her heartbroken. A relationship with the real Doctor was impossible, so he saw this as the next best thing. Tennant understood the mixed reactions, remarking to *Doctor Who Magazine*, "It's the same character, but it's not. It's a tricky one because with Rose, at the end, you want to feel she's left with the person she loves, but also that she isn't. It's quite a subtle, ambiguous ending for Rose."

Donna's fate was less happy. Her brain had been enhanced to Time Lord levels by the same event that created the Meta-Crisis Doctor. But a human brain can't contain such power. The Doctor shut down the lethal energies, blocking her memories in the process, as had been done to Jamie and Zoe so long ago. Donna reverted to her younger self, before she'd ever met the Doctor. The hero she'd become was dead.

FULL CIRCLE

Tennant's next few adventures mixed tragedy and comedy, the Tenth Doctor now refusing to take on new companions. BBC Books followed the same themes, the Doctor's loneliness and regretful contemplation often emphasized. In the 2009 special "The Waters of Mars," the Doctor decides he is no longer bound by the Laws of Time and non-interference. But almost immediately, he realizes his folly, and this stumble from grace isn't mentioned again. For such an intense character moment, it seemed odd to drop it immediately. Some viewers were disappointed, hoping to see the Doctor follow a path similar to the Master, then realizing he'd gone too far and rededicating himself to the harder life of a hero.

The Tenth Doctor next appeared in two episodes of *The Sarah Jane Adventures*. Afterward, his final adventure was "The End of Time," the first part of which aired on Christmas Day 2009, the second part broadcast on New Year's Day 2010. It marked a new beginning in many ways.

Since the beginning of the new program, the Doctor had been haunted by the Last Great Time War and the knowledge that he had chosen to end it by wiping out not only the Daleks but his own people. "The End of Time" has him confront that fate again as he discovers that the Time Lords possibly found a way to prevent their own destruction. With the yet-again-resurrected Master at his side, the Doctor explains that the Time Lords had gone too far in the final days of the war, unleashing incredible horrors such as the Skaro Degradations, the Horde of Travesties, the Nightmare Child, the Couldhavebeen King with his army of Meanwhiles and Neverweres. The Time Lords had prepared to end time itself so that all other life would end, while they ascended to become creatures of pure thought. The Doctor had ended the war as much to stop them as to stop the Daleks. Neither side could win.

"The End of Time" reveals that during the last days of the war the Time Lords were again led by their founder, Rassilon. It wasn't said whether he had indeed achieved a form of immortality, as legends claimed, or if he'd been resurrected out of desperation as the Master had been. Timothy Dalton played Rassilon and certainly gave the part gravitas, portraying the character as an unforgiving force with technology his own people feared. With the Master and the Doctor standing against him, "The End of Time" comes down to a battle between the first Time Lord and the last Time Lords. Sadly, because Rassilon had never been mentioned in the modern day program before, the significance of the confrontation was lost on newer viewers unfamiliar with the classic series mythos.

Decades before, Roger Delgado was supposed to star in the Master's final story, the character dying while (intentionally or not) saving the Doctor's life. Davies at last delivered that ending, as the Master forces Rassilon and the Time Lords back into the last days of the war, apparently joining them in death. The Tenth Doctor's life then ends not in an epic battle but rather afterward, in a quiet moment, his body absorbing lethal amounts of radiation as he saves one ordinary man rather than a world. Tennant thought it a fitting ending.

Concerning his final story (though he actually filmed his appearance in *The Sarah Jane Adventures* later), Tennant told *Doctor Who Magazine* #417, "The Doctor's saying some things that you don't expect the Doctor to say. He's being quite selfish, in a way that we rarely see, and yet it seems very true, and right, that in the moment he should rage against the dying of the light." At the same time, there seems to be acceptance. RTD and Tennant both commented that the Tenth Doctor was holding back the final phase of his regeneration as long as he could. But after he says he doesn't want to go, the Tenth Doctor's body glows with energy, and he realizes it's now or never. He takes a few deep breaths and gives in to the change, ready to see what happens next.

David Tennant recalled, "I did my last bit on the TARDIS set, throwing back my head, then Matt came on, and we did a couple of photographs. As I walked off, I heard [director Euros Lyn] turn to Matt and go, 'Anyway, what we do now is . . .' I thought, *Wow, so that's how it works?* And of course, it does. One knows that's what will happen. Suddenly, what becomes important is getting the scene done, and I'm not in the next scene. That's it. Cheerio. . . . But then you go home, and you look at your lines for the next day. You get on with it because that's all you can do."

Some critics thought Tennant and Davies left at the proper time, that their vision of the Doctor would become predictable if they remained. Some were sad to see the team go and had hoped that Tennant would reconsider and stay longer under Steven Moffat's direction. During an interview with *Doctor Who Magazine* in July 2009, Tom Baker weighed in, appreciating the Tenth Doctor as "very brittle, at very high speed," and saying Tennant had made the biggest impact. "Of course, the real renaissance [of *Doctor Who*] is the young one . . . David. We all owe David Tennant a great debt because, with his style and brio, he has revitalized the whole thing!"

Unlike his predecessors, Tennant made sure to keep at least one of his costumes, just in case he was ever asked to come back for a multi-Doctor team-up.

The New Age of Spin-offs

The classic series had toyed with the idea of a spin-off a couple of times. The characters Henry Gordon Jago and Professor George Litefoot were introduced in the Fourth Doctor story "The Talons of Weng-Chiang" and were an instantly entertaining duo. But a TV spin-off featuring the two Victorian investigators never materialized. Then there was *K-9 and Company*, which at least got a pilot but still failed to produce a series.

Realtime Pictures, which filmed many *Doctor Who* documentaries, produced direct to video movie spin-offs starting in 1987. Some dealt with monsters from the show. Some featured familiar *Doctor Who* actors in new, though similar roles. *Wartime* starred Sgt. Benton of UNIT, while *Downtime* teamed-up the Brigadier, Sarah Jane Smith, and Victoria Waterfield.

After the classic program was canceled, Whovian Bill Baggs created the production company BBV. In 1991, he released the first of several direct to video adventures starring a nameless hero referred to as the Stranger. The lead role was played by Colin Baker and his character was evidently an alien who was living in self-imposed exile on Earth. He was assisted by a woman named "Miss Brown," played by Nicola Bryant. It was basically the Sixth Doctor and Peri, with adventures that could take place in between Baker's two seasons. Eventually, the Stranger developed into his own character with his own past. In 1993, BBV's *The Airzone Solution?* was a straightforward drama starring Jon Pertwee, Peter Davison, Colin Baker, Sylvester McCoy, Nicola Bryant, and Sophie Aldred as human characters. BBV also produced a series of videos called *P.R.O.B.E.*, written by Mark Gatiss, that featured Caroline John reprising her role as Dr. Liz Shaw, though like the Stranger this couldn't make direct reference to the show due to a lack of licensing. Other videos included some stand-alone adventures featuring *Doctor Who* characters and a trilogy of Auton stories written by Nicholas Briggs.

With the modern *Doctor Who* a huge success, RTD was asked to look towards a spin-off series that could exist independently. During the first season, he had arranged several film shoots using the alias "Torchwood," an anagram of the show's title, in order to keep fans and media from investigating. In the twelfth episode of the first season, he even inserted a reference to this alias in the dialogue, with a character mentioning the "Torchwood Institute."

Before heading *Doctor Who,* he had conceived a science fiction/crime drama called *Excalibur.* Now asked to produce a spin-off, RTD brushed off *Excalibur* and renamed it *Torchwood,* adding former Time Agent Jack Harkness as the leader. *Torchwood* premiered on BBC Three in the fall of 2006, following the end of *Doctor Who*'s second season and taking place just months afterward. Unlike *Doctor Who,* this wouldn't be a program for children and would involve a more cynical, pragmatic atmosphere. Violence, sex, death, and angst would each play a significant role in the story.

Critics had mixed reactions to the first season, but the program clearly had fans and would continue, though on BBC Two. The second season had a warmer reception with higher ratings and better reviews. After this, over a year passed before *Torchwood* returned to screens (not counting two crossover episodes in *Doctor Who*), this time in a five-part miniseries rather than a full season. *Torchwood: Children of Earth* aired a new episode every day for a week to high acclaim.

In between season two and *Children of Earth,* BBC radio transmitted Torchwood audio plays featuring the cast of the TV program. The first, *Lost Souls,* aired on September 10, 2008, just before the Large Hadron Collider was activated and featured a plot surrounding the famous machine. A trilogy of audio plays followed the next year, broadcast just before *Children of Earth,* effectively giving fans an extra mini-season of adventures.

The BBC also asked Davies to consider creating another spin-off geared toward young children, more simplistic and less scary than the Doctor's adventures. It was suggested that the show could feature the Doctor himself as a young boy living on Gallifrey, but RTD didn't think the premise worked properly with the character. Instead, he suggested a new program featuring Sarah Jane Smith with Elisabeth Sladen reprising the role, based on the success of her appearance in "School Reunion."

The Sarah Jane Adventures pilot aired on New Year's Day in 2007. The journalist briefly explains her previous life with the Doctor and that she now investigates alien occurrences on her own, helped by K-9 and a living alien computer that she lovingly calls Mr. Smith. Soon she finds herself the guardian of a genetically engineered child and has a young adolescent girl acting as her assistant.

After the pilot's success, *The Sarah Jane Adventures* began in full in September 2007. Along with Sarah Jane were her assistant, Maria Jackson (Yasmin Paige); her adopted son, Luke (Tommy Knight); and his friend from school Clyde Langer (Daniel Anthony). In the second season, Maria moves away, her character replaced by Rani Chandra (Anjli Mohindra). Unlike *Torchwood, The Sarah Jane Adventures* made many references to *Doctor Who* and its long history. Sarah Jane even made an archenemy of the Trickster, one of the Eternals, a race of powerful beings the Fifth Doctor encountered, able to control matter and read minds. The Trickster's agents appeared or were mentioned in *Doctor Who* and *Torchwood*.

The show's success led to a mini spin-off entitled *Sarah Jane's Alien Files*. The second season ended with Nicholas Courtney reprising his role of Sir Alistair Gordon Lethbridge-Stewart. The third season featured a crossover with David Tennant and was the last story he filmed in which he played the Tenth Doctor. In season four, Russell T. Davies wrote an adventure in which Matt Smith's Doctor reunited with Sarah Jane and Jo Grant. Sladen died months later on April 19, 2011, having lost her secret battle with cancer. The production team decided to air the episodes already in the can for the next season, ending on the note that Sarah Jane and her friends continued to defend the Earth for years to come.

Though K-9 was in Sarah Jane's care all along, he couldn't appear often in *The Sarah Jane Adventures* due to a rights issue. The character's co-creator Bob Baker had licensed the robot dog to an Australian science fiction series for children. The program, simply titled *K-9*, premiered on Halloween night 2009 on Disney XD in the UK and Ireland. Legal issues meant the program couldn't reference *Doctor Who* or *The Sarah Jane Adventures*.

The opening episode, "Regeneration," takes place in London in the late twenty-first century. Experiments in time manipulation wind up transporting dangerous creatures into a scientist's lab, followed by K-9.

The robot protects the humans from their attackers but is destroyed in the process. However, an internal "regeneration unit" quickly builds him a new, more advanced body. With no memory of its previous life, K-9 remains to act as a helper for the humans he's met.

Despite being unable to reference *Doctor Who* directly, the show still nodded to the dog's origins. The regeneration unit was decorated by "$\partial^3 \Sigma x^2$," referencing the name Terrance Dicks and Malcolm Hulke had proposed for the Doctor. Also, as K-9 is regenerating, his programming indicates that he is evolving from a Mark I mode to Mark II. Bob Baker later confirmed that this time-lost K-9 was the same Mark I model left in Leela's care.

K-9 has been nominated for and won several awards. Meanwhile, *Torchwood* made its way to America when the program moved to the premium cable Starz network, with Jane Tranter, Kelly A. Manners, Jane Espenson, and Vlad Wolynetz joining Davies and Gardner in producing the series. The year 2012 saw the release of *Torchwood: Miracle Day*, a ten-episode adventure featuring a worldwide event that brings the old team members out of retirement and unites them with a couple of American federal agents. The story ends on a cliffhanger of sorts, prompting many fans to hope that they will see more adventures with Jack Harkness and his team very soon.

The Woman Doctor

In the classic program, we met women Time Lords (which seemed to be the preferred term over the not as often spoken "Time Ladies"), so clearly Gallifrey had distinct genders. The differences between them have led to some speculation. As mentioned earlier, three different *Doctor Who* TV stories indicated that female Time Lords had greater natural control over regeneration than males, enough to determine the form of their next bodies. But many fans continue to ask: Can Time Lords regenerate into a different gender altogether?

Sydney Newman certainly thought so and suggested to the BBC that the Doctor become a woman as early as 1987. When Tom Baker's departure was approaching in 1981, he remarked during an interview that viewers shouldn't assume the Fifth Doctor had to be a man. Then producer John Nathan-Turner didn't mind the idea and encouraged such speculation. Since then, every subsequent announcement that the lead of *Doctor Who* would be recast has been quickly followed by news media asking if the next Doctor would be a she. When David Tennant was ending his tenure, there were even rumors that the next Doctor would be Catherine Tate or Billie Piper, despite both having played popular companions.

Steven Moffat played with the idea of a gender change when the newly regenerated Eleventh Doctor, on feeling his hair length, immediately wondered if he had become a woman. Like some Whovians, Neil Gaiman saw no reason that a Time Lord couldn't alter his or her gender (at least, under the right circumstances) and made it official in his 2011 episode "The Doctor's Wife" when the Doctor remarks how a Time Lord called the Corsair had been a woman on multiple occasions.

Of course, not everyone thinks that, even if a possibility, it should be done. Mark Campbell, author of *Dimensions in Time and Space,* says, "It's sort of like saying you can change James Bond or Sherlock Holmes into a woman. I don't think it's particularly necessary." In a Q&A feature on the BBC America website, Peter Davison said:

I've never quite liked the idea of a female Doctor. I think they've found a perfect situation now where they have the slightly faulted Doctor with all his mad genius, and you have the strong woman as the companion. I think that works very well. If you reversed it, it would be difficult because you'd have the woman as the mad genius, but is she vulnerable? And then you just have a strong man as the companion. And somehow that doesn't work well to me.

But not everyone agrees. When I asked actor Peter Purves, who had played Steven Taylor opposite William Hartnell, about it, he remarked, "What would be so wrong with having a woman in the role? It's already an alien who changes shape and has a brain we can't really understand. Just as long as she still acts like the Doctor."

Sylvester McCoy told me, "I wonder sometimes if *Doctor Who* would lose some fans with a woman in the role. But we need more equality among the sexes because it isn't there yet. We don't give women enough credit. Women can be heroic in science fiction and can be intelligent, complex characters, of course. If the Doctor can change from looking like Colin Baker to looking like me and change yet again so he looks like the not-as-handsome Paul McGann, then turning into a woman doesn't seem much stranger. It'd be interesting, and they should try it."

In an interview for this book, Big Finish director and actor Lisa Bowerman said, "I don't think there's a good reason the Doctor can't be a woman. I don't think we should fixate on it, either. We shouldn't cast someone just to have a woman Doctor or a black Doctor or an Asian Doctor. If it works well dramatically and it's the right person, then, yes, why not cast that person? If it's a woman that time, cast a woman. You'd probably lose half of fandom, as people can be very loyal to their ideas, but you have to have confidence in your conviction. If you have something appear on television, in the story, then that legitimizes it. The Doctor can be anything except—and I don't mean this to be offensive—anything other than British in character, atmosphere, and sensibility."

At the Armageddon Convention in New Zealand in 2010, Paul McGann was asked if the Doctor could be a woman and he said, "I'd watch it. . . . Tilda Swinton as *Doctor Who,* can you imagine that? Tell me you wouldn't watch that. You would; you know you would."

21

Something Borrowed,
Something New

"You are not of this world."

"No, but I've put a lot of work into it."

—AN ATRAXI AND THE ELEVENTH DOCTOR,

FROM "THE ELEVENTH HOUR" (2010)

It's an interesting experience, sitting across from a Time Lord.

Though I've interviewed others who've played the Doctor, speaking with Matt Smith is a different experience altogether. When we met, the Doctor was not a role he'd left behind but one he was still exploring—and loving every minute of it.

Smith grew up in Northampton, England, an avid sports fan who intended to play soccer professionally. After a back injury left him with spondylosis, a teacher suggested he try his hand at drama. He studied at the National Youth Theatre before taking up a stage career in London. During this time, he acted alongside Arthur Darvill, who later joined him on *Doctor Who*. He made his television debut in *The Ruby in the Smoke* in 2007, which also starred Billie Piper, and they shared the screen when he appeared on her series *Secret Diary of a Call Girl*.

In 2009, Steven Moffat and Mark Gatiss were putting together their new show *Sherlock,* modernizing Doyle's great detective. Moffat was also taking over *Doctor Who,* after having written (along with Gatiss) several episodes during Davies's tenure. To help move closer to some of the classic series notions of the show, Moffat wanted to cast a Doctor in his forties or even fifties: a Time Lord who was a bit aloof rather than wearing his heart on his sleeve.

During auditions for *Sherlock,* Matt Smith tried out for the part of Dr. John Watson. He didn't get a callback, but he did see Moffat again not long after when he auditioned for the role of the Eleventh Doctor. At just twenty-six, Smith certainly didn't fit the bill of the middle-aged actor whom Moffat wanted for the part. But during our interview in San Diego, Smith reflected, "You have to go into an audition thinking you deserve this part, that you're right for it. If you don't tell yourself that, they're certainly not going to believe it, either. What have you got to lose?"

Smith's performance surprised and impressed all involved. Moffat and the production team felt that the actor, despite his youth, delivered the sense of being an older Doctor that they were seeking. In *Doctor Who Confidential,* Moffat explained, "We got all these wonderful actors in deadly secrecy . . . to stand there and pretend to be the Doctor for a while. . . . He was just spot-on, right from the beginning. . . . The way he said the lines, the way he looked, his hair, you just thought, *Oh, oh, that's him.* Problem is, it's the first day. . . . We thought we had to keep going and keep looking. . . . In the end, it was Matt."

So, at age twenty-six, Smith became the youngest man cast in the role. The announcement went out on January 3, 2009, on *Doctor Who Confidential,* soon after the broadcast of David Tennant's special "The Next Doctor," which starred David Morrissey as a man who had suffered amnesia and now believed that he was the Doctor. The Tenth Doctor couldn't be sure at first if this was a confused man or his future incarnation. Smith's casting was kept secret for all the usual reasons but also in part so that viewers could won-

Matt Smith at Comic-Con 2011

der (at least, at first) whether David Morrissey's character was actually intended to be the Eleventh Doctor. By the end of the special, after it's clear this isn't the case, there was no reason to keep it quiet any longer.

"I spent days pacing around, sitting down, then standing up again, pace some more, smiling and thinking, *I'm the Doctor now!* I didn't watch *Doctor Who*—I was a bit too young to have really caught the classic stuff and with the new show I was in my twenties and often out or acting on Saturday nights—but you know it, of course, it's everywhere, and people are chatting about it on talk shows, and the Doctor seriously is an iconic part of our culture, like Holmes and Robin Hood. My father would talk about Tom Baker. Everyone in my family had their own Doctors and references. I had to tell my dad about the casting. I was going mad just sitting with my friends and not telling them I was the Doctor. He laughed and was very excited and proud of it all."

Following the announcement, there was expected criticism that Smith was too young to play such an ancient being with any sense of gravitas. In an interview for this book at Comic-Con 2011, Matt Smith said with a laugh, "When I first came, people said, 'Well, he's too young.' But actually, tell me someone who isn't too young to play a nine-hundred-plus-year-old Time Lord! I think that it's interesting to have someone young play someone old."

It's certainly interesting for us on the other side of the screen that an actor not deeply familiar with the program, modern or classic, created a version of the hero that very much recalled the classic series ideal: a strange, scatterbrained uncle or grandfather who wants to go on adventures your parents would think were too dangerous.

Hearing this appraisal, Smith smiles. "Yes! That's kind of what I want the Doctor to be, actually: your crazy, strange uncle. The Doctor should be funny, mad, brilliant, ridiculous. I think at the core what he reaches for is humanity. I think the one thing he can never be is human. He finds it peculiar that they fall in love and get married and have Christmas dinner. . . . He's a maverick, he's an alien, and his addiction is to time travel and running and saving the world. We all have our own opinion on the Doctor, and that's what's sort of wonderful. He's never one thing. Ever."

Smith did get around to catching up on the show, watching the classic series DVDs as well as the modern ones. He cites "Tomb of the Cybermen" as his favorite TV story of the classic era, and his Doctor's outfit even resembles Troughton's with bow tie and suspenders. As Tennant evoked the idea of being a professional student, Smith in his turn looked more like a professor, wearing a tweed sport coat with patches on the elbows. The

Doctor went from geek chic to nerdy and proud. The bow tie made sense after his first adventure, when a traditional necktie left him vulnerable to being trapped in a car door by companion Amy Pond.

Smith finally appeared as the Eleventh Doctor in the last scene of "The End of Time" on New Year's Day in 2010 (by which point he was twenty-seven years old). After checking out his new body, the Doctor realizes that his ship is crashing and greets the event with gleeful anticipation, hurtling happily toward the next stage of his life and shouting "Geronimo!"

As time went on, much of the criticism toward Smith faded away, replaced by praise that the young actor actually seemed older than several previous incarnations. At WonderCon 2011 in San Francisco, a *Doctor Who* panel included writer Neil Gaiman, comedian/host Chris Hardwick, and actor Mark Shepard, who all discussed Smith's portrayal of the Doctor.

Shepard grew up watching the adventures of Pertwee and Tom Baker, the latter being his favorite incarnation. But after seeing Smith in action and filming episodes alongside him, he admitted that he now feels differently. "I gotta tell you: Matt Smith is my Doctor. . . . He carries that weight [of the character] so superbly. . . . He took me around the TARDIS and showed me how *every* button and wheel works."

Chris Hardwick: "He manages to strike this insane counterbalance between incredible boyish curiosity but then also you sense that he's nine hundred years old inside."

Neil Gaiman: "That's the most interesting thing about writing for Matt in some ways. He's the first of the [new series] Doctors who actually feels vastly ancient. They all had these glorious different qualities. . . . But with Matt, you actually feel his age all the way through, going all the way back. Almost for the first time since Tom Baker, the idea that the central entity and the body are two slightly different things. You *know* this is an alien. This is not someone that you know, and it's amazing."

Former Doctor actors agreed. During an interview at Memorabilia Expo in 2012, Colin Baker remarked that Smith now rivaled Patrick Troughton as his favorite Doctor. "I think he's brilliant. He's almost my all-time favorite Doctor. . . . He's just so engaging and so real. . . . When you're playing a character that is inherently unreal, you've got to be as real as you can. He is, and I just believe every word he says."

At Gallifrey One 2013, Sylvester McCoy lit up with excitement when asked about the Eleventh Doctor. "How about Smith? Incredible! This twelve-year-old shows up, and yet he's older than *all* of us. He's an ancient Doctor, an ancient alien, not someone raised on Earth. When I heard they were casting such a young person, I thought, *Oh, they're going into that world still, where the hero has to be young and handsome,* and I miss the fact that the Doctor is an older man, a wise man who's led an ancient life.

"But David Tennant was lovely in the role, and Matt Smith—he is astonishing! His face has so much experience in it, and his performance is just excellent in how you feel how ancient he is. Somehow he's got bits of Patrick Troughton in him and bits of Tom Baker. You can believe that his Doctor remembers all that, that he doesn't just remember his life as David Tennant, he remembers and feels the weight of being Patrick and Tom and Colin and *me*! I'm such a fan."

A FAMILY AFFAIR

In the second season episode "The Girl in the Fireplace," the Tenth Doctor meets a girl and then visits her again as an adult, with her recalling him as an imaginary friend. The fifth season premiere "The Eleventh Hour" uses the same idea, setting up the year to have a fairy tale atmosphere. The young Amelia Pond meets the strange Doctor who wears raggedy clothes and lives in a time machine that has a swimming pool and a library. No one believes her, of course, and she grows up to become Amy Pond (played by Karen Gillan), a girl with no patience for fairy tales. But then the Doctor returns, and she realizes, at first with fear, that the universe is indeed as large, dangerous, and exciting as she believed as a child.

Amy's character herself was a message to the audience. Many parents and older viewers enjoyed the classic series but also took it with a grain of salt and didn't necessarily wish to engage in a similar way with the modern program.

Amy's story is a response to people who say this, either seriously or with tongue in cheek, arguing that adults can enjoy silly, children's stories, and that one shouldn't forget to dream because you're never too old to see something impossible and venture off into strange new worlds. Just as Rose had been introduced alongside her on-again, off-again boyfriend, Mickey, Amy was introduced with Rory Williams (played by Arthur Darvill). But Rory was established as a much more serious love interest—even if Amy was reluctant to admit it at first—and by the end of their debut episode, the two were engaged.

Karen Gillan earned her acting degree at the Italia Conti Academy of Theatre Arts in London. Working as a model first, she appeared at London Fashion Week 2007, later returning to acting, making several television appearances and becoming known for comedic roles. Gillan appeared as a soothsayer in the 2008 David Tennant episode "The Fires of Pompeii," and by sheer coincidence Gillan's cousin Caitlin Blackwood landed the role of seven-year-old Amy Pond in "The Eleventh Hour." (Gillan and Blackwood didn't know they were related until they met through the program.)

Arthur Darvill (Rory Williams) and Lisa Bowerman
(Bernice Summerfield)
Photograph courtesy of Big Finish Productions

Arthur Darvill trained at the Royal Academy of Dramatic Art and in 2007 received high praise for his performance in the Vaudeville Theatre production of *Swimming with Sharks,* starring alongside Matt Smith, Helen Baxendale, and Christian Slater. His *Doctor Who* character, Rory Williams, a nurse, was quite content to spend the rest of his life in the fictional town of Leadworth rather than run away in a time traveling police box. (The *Doctor Who* reference guides indicate that Rory chose medicine as his profession because of Amy's strange interest in the "Raggedy Doctor" who she claimed had visited her as a child.)

But there was a third companion of sorts. In Tennant's final season, Steven Moffat had written a two-part story introducing Professor River Song. In the first episode, "Silence in the Library," the Tenth Doctor and Donna are in a sealed library when a team of archaeologists appears. Originally, the Doctor was going to recognize one of the archaeologists as an old friend, but Moffat decided that plot device was too easy and dull. Instead, he had one of the archaeologists recognize the Doctor and reveal herself as a paradox. From her perspective, the two are extremely close: She knows his real name; he has given her a sonic screwdriver; and, another character implies that she is possibly his wife (or will be). But as far as the Doctor is concerned, they've never met.

Davies took partial inspiration for the character of River from Audrey Niffenegger's science fiction romance *The Time Traveler's Wife,* which depicted the relationship between a woman and a man repeatedly sent backward and forward through time, leading to a decidedly non-linear relationship. After creating River, Moffat decided to bring her back as a recurring character once he took over production duties on the program. He had hoped to secure Kate Winslet for the role, having worked with her before. When that didn't happen, the part went to Alex Kingston, a former member of the Royal Shakespeare Company best known to American viewers for her turn as Elizabeth Corday in the medical drama *ER.*

River's debut also depicts her death, which adds a weight and tragedy to all her later adventures. We and the Doctor know that River is never truly in danger of dying during later adventures because we've already seen how her story will end. This paradoxical relationship also means that every time the Doctor and River meet they must first figure out what the other knows so as not to give away spoilers concerning their personal futures. Moffat later said that he had told Kingston that River has encountered all of the Doctor's previous incarnations at different points (a plot point that Moffat would later repeat for a different character and which is used in the BBC Worldwide Digital Entertainment video game *The Eternity Clock,* in which each previous Doctor has his memory of the encounter erased).

Moffat explained River's true origins to Kingston but kept them secret from the rest of the cast. Viewers responded positively to River Song, and many polls showed that she was one of the most popular characters of the modern-day program. Still, others criticized that she began to appear too often, seeming more and more a supporting player to the Doctor rather than someone strong and independent enough to have her own adventures.

Gary Russell commented, "I think the problem with River is that, while it's fun and funny to have her sometimes frustrate the Doctor, you also don't want her to outshine him too much. River Song is more like the Doctor than the Doctor is at times, and I think you need to be careful that, while you poke fun at your title character, you don't want to undermine him and completely ridicule him, too. It starts to make him weak."

Certain fans also saw Professor River Song as a strange echo of Professor Bernice Summerfield and wondered why a novel-born companion couldn't have been brought into the TV program. Having played Benny for years, Lisa Bowerman had her own thoughts on the matter. "When River Song first turned up, I was quite pissed off actually. I thought, *Wait, she's an archaeologist, she has a diary, she's tough, she knows the Doctor. What's this?* But obviously Steven had turned her into a very different character and took her down such a different path, a completely different direction. She means something else entirely to the Doctor than Benny did, and she's really in the Doctor's world, while Benny goes down her own path and her own life for years afterward."

TIME CAN BE REWRITTEN

The fifth season of *Doctor Who* presented a long fairy tale adventure that begins with a girl praying to Santa and ends with that same girl getting married to her true love. Unlike other fairy tales, though, marriage was the beginning of new adventures rather than the end of the story.

In the fifth season, Moffat wanted to truly explore what it meant to be a Lord of Time. While the Ninth Doctor had warned that it was dangerous to create one too many paradoxes, the Eleventh Doctor encountered them frequently, hunting down "cracks" in the universe that seemed to be connected to his new companion. Ironically, he used paradoxes in his own timeline to eventually heal these cracks and rifts across space and time.

In the 2010 Christmas special, "A Christmas Carol," the Doctor employs a strategy that may have been unthinkable to some of his previous incarnations. Realizing a villain he's encountered still has some good in him, the Doctor goes back in time to visit the man throughout his childhood (again, echoing Amy Pond and Madame de Pompadour), slowly changing his past and his temperament. "Time can be rewritten" practically became the show's motto, an interesting contrast to the original creators' thoughts on the matter. For the Eleventh Doctor, time travel was no longer just a plot device allowing entry to a new story; it was a churning force that needed to be reined in, manipulated, and commanded.

The fifth season was a hit with many and the Eleventh Doctor had cemented his place in the hearts of many fans. As the sixth season approached, BBC America made a bigger push in marketing *Doctor Who*. A new wave of fans emerged in the US, aided by the show actually filming episodes in America and visiting various cities and conventions there, which the previous production team hadn't really focused on.

SILENCE WILL FALL

The premiere episode of the sixth season features the companions watching the Doctor's death, now knowing his future but unable to share it. While RTD had treated episodes fairly separately while peppering hints of what was coming in the finale each year, Moffat turned most of the season into a plot-driven story arc.

With the Doctor's death hanging in the balance, the sixth season contained more complexity, full of time paradoxes and layered manipulations. We also see the Doctor confronted by how dangerous and deadly he had become over the years, evolving from a strange old man exploring the universe with his granddaughter to a destroyer of worlds. Many races now feared him, the man who had led empires to their destruction, who'd held the Key to Time, and had committed genocide more than once (even if he'd had good reasons). Had he lost his path?

During RTD's run humans became more aware of aliens and the Doctor began frequently encountering fans and people who saw him as a fearsome protector of Earth. Moffat, however, wanted to go back a few steps. The cracks in time seen during the fifth season wound up rewriting parts of history, making this fictional version of Earth closer to our reality, in which the public often dismisses the possibility of alien life. Still, planets beyond Earth, particularly in the future, know full well about the Doctor. The Time Lord considers the fame he's acquired in the modern day series and wonders whether it might be time to revert to the unknown and largely unnoticed wanderer he'd been during his first several incarnations.

The seventh season also recalls McCoy's era, revealing an organization determined to prevent a secret from being shared, a secret that would answer "the first question" to haunt the universe: Doctor who? As Moffat's episode "The Girl in the Fireplace" pointed out, the Doctor's name was "more than just a secret."

The season was about life and birth. While the Doctor seemed to be heading toward his final hour, Amy discovered she was pregnant (though, it being the Whoniverse, it turned out to be more complicated than that). Amy's child Melody Pond was conceived in the TARDIS and affected by "artron" energy, temporal radiation that exists in Time Lords and the space time vortex. This made the child valuable, and neither Amy, Rory, nor the Doctor could stop others from stealing her. But then, they learned that, all things considered, it would be OK. Melody Pond would one day grow up to be the hero River Song.

Fans were very much divided on this revelation, as a fair number had predicted this scenario (or something similar) based on the fact that River Song and Amy Pond both had aquatic themed names. Steven Moffat even admitted that his own child had accurately guessed River's true identity at the top of the sixth season. But for her fans, it didn't matter if the truth was obvious; they still loved her all the same.

In a stand-out episode of the season, "The Doctor's Wife," written by Neil Gaiman, the Doctor finally gets the chance to speak with his ship directly when she takes on human form. It's a touching meeting, giving voice to a few fan theories and confirming the living ship as the Doctor's truest and most faithful companion. Her first word to him is "goodbye" and her last "hello." The episode won the 2011 Ray Bradbury Award for Outstanding Dramatic Presentation and the 2012 Hugo Award for Best Dramatic Presentation, Short Form.

The sixth season is also significant for introducing a trio of new characters to the Whoniverse. Having played two reptilian Silurians who fought the Doctor before, actor Neve McIntosh was reintroduced as a different Silurian character named Madame Vastra. Like the rest of her people, Vastra had gone into hibernation before the ice age, though she woke up in Victorian England. After befriending the Doctor, she established a secret life for herself in London, gaining a reputation as a detective and evidently inspiring some of the Sherlock Holmes stories. At her side was her housekeeper and then wife Jenny Flint, played by Catrin Stewart.

Rounding out the trio was Strax, a Sontaran who owed the Doctor a debt and fought at his side. Played by Dan Starkey, Strax quickly became a great source of rough-edged comedy. He was an over-the-top character who cherished proving himself in battle yet couldn't tell the difference between boys and girls. Strax was killed during his first appearance, but Moffat decided later to resurrect him off-screen, reintroducing him as a constant ally to Vastra and Jenny. By the time Strax was resurrected, Amy, Rory, and the Doctor had all seemingly died and come back in one story or another, so it seemed to just be one of the tropes of the new *Doctor Who* era.

While the fifth season showed the Doctor using some paradoxes to save the day, the sixth season finale showed how much chaos erupted if you let them run amok. Skipping between alternate timelines, the Doctor marries River Song (though why this is part of his victory plan exactly is not made clear) and then uses more straightforward time travel and basic trickery to avoid his own death. But he doesn't mind people thinking he's dead and, again, wonders if perhaps it's best that he travels alone.

EVERYTHING CHANGES

Rather than do a full season in 2012 and 2013, it was decided to split the season in half. The first several episodes aired in the summer of 2012, followed by a Christmas special. The first half was set up to be stand-alone episodes, to contrast against the heavy story arc of the previous year. Responses were mixed. There was also a sense of approaching loss behind the stories, as it was known that Amy Pond and Rory were leaving. The season actually begins with them already separated, later realizing that they still love each other and had somehow stopped really listening to each other.

Family is a major theme in these episodes. Rory and Amy are concerned about the possibility of trying to start a family again. We meet Rory's father Brian Williams in the episode "Dinosaurs on a Space Ship," played by Mark Williams. And in the episode "The Power of Three," the Doctor meets UNIT's new top scientist Kate Stewart—daughter of Alistair Gordon Lethbridge-Stewart (though this was lost on some viewers, as Alistair was only briefly mentioned in two episodes of the modern program and his relationship with the Doctor was never explained).

The first half of the season ends with "The Angels Take Manhattan," where once again paradoxes are a thing to avoid rather than use. Despite the Doctor's best efforts, he is separated from Amy and Rory, seemingly unable to reunite with them. Again, viewers were divided. Some appreciated the story and considered it an excellent farewell, while others said there were too many contradictions to established continuity of the past few years, making the ending convenient rather than heartfelt.

In any event, Amy Pond and Rory Williams were gone now, having enjoyed every minute of their impossible lives with the Doctor. But the hero does not take the forced separation well. When we see him again in the 2012 Christmas special "The Snowmen," he has decided to retire, leading a hermit life with the TARDIS parked on a cloud over Victorian London. Based on revelations in the 2013 episode "The Name of the Doctor," it seems that in between "The Angels Take Manhattan" and "The Snowmen," the Eleventh Doctor and River Song had their last date before she was fated to meet his Tenth incarnation and face her death. So the Doctor's retirement was not just spurred by the loss of two friends, but by the loss of his wife.

THE IMPOSSIBLE GIRL

Before the seventh season began, it was announced that the Doctor would be meeting a new companion in the 2012 Christmas special, a girl named Clara, played by Jenna-Louise Coleman. So it was quite a surprise to see the actor playing a different character named Oswin in the season opener. Oswin was a brilliant girl who sacrificed herself to save the Doctor, smiling as she asked him to remember her.

In the 2012 Christmas special "The Snowmen," the Doctor meets another version of Oswin, this one named Clara. The two join forces against a new villain played by Richard E. Grant, making it the third time the actor had participated in some kind of *Doctor Who* broadcast. Clara dies at the end, saving the Doctor's life. The hero wonders how it was possible for this person to be the same girl as Oswin and yet not.

Clara quickly gained fans for her clever wit, playful nature, assertiveness, and intelligence. But some criticized that she was too obviously attracted to the Doctor. Rose had been one thing, but the hero was married now and it seemed even worse that he seemed to share the attraction. Moffat freely admitted that the Doctor was indeed smitten with the different versions of Clara, not explaining at the time that the hero apparently now considered himself a widower, as revealed in "The Name of the Doctor."

The second half of the seventh season opened with "The Bells of St. John." Now the Doctor meets the modern day Clara Oswald, a girl whose existence in multiple points of space and time seemed simply impossible. Clara helps the Doctor feel like his old self again, though he still wears a noticeably darker and more somber outfit than his early days. Unlike other companions, she expects the Doctor to work on her schedule. He has a time machine, so he is able to visit her on certain days when she is free, at which point they'll enjoy an adventure but then she must get back home and take care of her responsibilities.

After several adventures, including a journey through various parts of the TARDIS, the Doctor and Clara wind up on Trenzalore, a graveyard world that he knows holds his own remains. He is not supposed to be here, as a person should not encounter his own death or dead body (although, two previous Steven Moffat episodes seemed to have the hero do just that).

Entering his own tomb, the Doctor sees dust on the floor and energy erupting from it, a manifestation of his own timeline. An old enemy enters the energy field, scattering himself across reality in an attempt to corrupt the Doctor's history. To save him, Clara follows, knowing she will likely die.

Copies of Clara fly across space and time, each not knowing their true origin, each driven to help and save the Doctor in some way. With clever camera tricks and editing, this episode, "The Name of the Doctor," was able to provide appearances by all of the previous incarnations (although McGann's cameo is so quick that some viewers missed it, while others wondered why they didn't have him simply come in to film a short scene as Peter Davison had done for Children in Need).

The Doctor follows Clara, breaking several laws of time and finding her impossibly still alive in a strange limbo inhabited by all his different selves. Clara is startled to see one Doctor she doesn't recognize. The hero explains that his name is not important; calling himself the Doctor is a promise. This man before them is a version who broke the promise.

The figure turns, revealing actor John Hurt. And so ends the seventh season. Fans would have to wait months before seeing what mysteries await in the fiftieth anniversary special, which teams up Matt Smith with David Tennant and Billie Piper.

Along with this, Big Finish is releasing its own fiftieth anniversary audio drama special, *The Light at the End,* staring Tom Baker, Peter Davison, Colin Baker, Sylvester McCoy, and Paul McGann. Joining them in the story are Louise Jameson as Leela, Sarah Sutton as Nyssa, Nicola Bryant as Peri, Sophie Aldred as Ace, India Fisher as Charley Pollard, and Geoffrey Beevers as the Master.

TIMES TO COME

Soon after "The Name of the Doctor" was broadcast, Matt Smith confirmed rumors that he would be leaving the show. The Eleventh Doctor's last adventure would be the 2013 Christmas special. Steven Moffat confirmed earlier in the year that he was set to produce another season of *Doctor Who*. So once again, the question is: who will be the next Doctor?

Many names have been suggested, with some fans hoping for famous stars and others hoping for unknowns, some hoping for older actors, some for a woman Doctor at last. Online, there has been speculation and support for the role to be filled by Idris Elba, Sheridan Smith, Benedict Cumberbatch, Chiwetel Ejiofor, David Mitchell, Rory Kinnear, Sue Perkins, Eddie Izzard, Stephen Fry, Hugh Laurie, Rowan Atkinson, Richard Ayoade, Simon Pegg, Miranda Hart, and Bill Nighy. Arthur Darvill suggested Helen Mirren. While she didn't think she had much chance of being cast, she told reporters, "I think it's absolutely time for a female Doctor Who. I'm so sick of that man with his girl sidekick. I could name at least ten wonderful British actresses who would absolutely kill in that role."

Some critics have suggested that the program should rest again for a few years. Some worry that, if the old thirteenth-life rule still applies, the Doctor is running out of lives. But many Whovians argue that the show, which consistently reinvents itself, has no reason to stop.

According to Gary Russell, "No one should seriously worry about what happens at the end. Any decent writer can have the Doctor encounter something that suddenly gives him extra lives. You can say something happened during the Time War to change this already. And even if two, three years from now, the BBC decides 'All right, it's nice, but it's getting tired, so let's give it a rest,' that's not something to panic about. You'll have some people shouting that this is it, it's all over, and the rest of us will say, 'No, we've been here before; relax.' It's too good an idea and has too strong a fan base to go away entirely. Give it a few years, and someone will do what Russell T. Davies did, and we'll get to start fresh again."

As Paul McGann said: "There's no reason for this show ever to stop. It's bigger than all of us, and it's just too much fun. You can do anything with it. Isn't that fantastic?"

ACKNOWLEDGMENTS

It is impossible to write a book like this on your own. Brandi Bowles is a ninja agent and invaluable help. James Jayo and Lynn Zelem are great professionals whose care and patience made this better. Bryan Q. Miller, Travis Langley, Lisa McMullan, Sterling Gates, Hilary Thomas, Kiri Callaghan, Jessica Mills, Jennifer Ewing, Bonnie Burton, Jenna Busch, Chase Masterson, Paul Simpson, and Jill Pantozzi all lent good aid, advice, and insight.

I cannot express enough how helpful Paul Spragg was in helping this book come into existence and connecting me to the wonderful people at Big Finish who have expanded the Whoniverse in fantastic ways.

I am grateful to Philip Hinchcliffe, Louise Jameson, Neve McIntosh, Dan Abnett, Simon Guerrier, Lisa Bowerman, Paul Cornell, Gary Russell, Peter Purves, Frazer Hines, Karen Gillan, Arthur Darvill, Nicholas Briggs, Daphne Ashbrook, India Fisher, Grant Imahara, and Jane Espenson for taking the time to chat with me.

Peter Davison, Colin Baker, Sylvester McCoy, Paul McGann, and Matt Smith are all just as wonderful as you hope they would be. Over the years, they've all been kind enough to chat with me. Sometimes it was only for a few minutes, always it was interesting and I am thankful. They are all the Doctor and always will be.

INDEX

An italic page number indicates that only an epigraph or photo caption is referenced.